THE
BANTAMS

THE
BANTAMS

by

SIDNEY ALLINSON

Pen & Sword
MILITARY

First published in Great Britain in 1981
by Howard Baker Ltd

Published in this format in 2009 by
Pen & Sword Military
An imprint of
Pen & Sword Books Ltd
47 Church Street
Barnsley
South Yorkshire
S70 2AS

ISBN 978 184884 030 0

Printed and bound in England
By CPI Antony Rowe

Pen & Sword Books Ltd incorporates the Imprints of Pen & Sword Aviation,
Pen & Sword Family History, Pen & Sword Maritime, Pen & Sword Military,
Wharncliffe Local History,
Pen & Sword Select, Pen & Sword Military Classics, Leo Cooper, Remember
When, Seaforth Publishing and Frontline Publishing

For a complete list of Pen & Sword titles please contact
PEN & SWORD BOOKS LIMITED
47 Church Street, Barnsley, South Yorkshire, S70 2AS, England
E-mail: enquiries@pen-and-sword.co.uk
Website: www.pen-and-sword.co.uk

CONTENTS

In memory of my father,
Pte. Thomas William Allinson
1898-1976
who fought in the Great War
10th. Battalion, The Green Howards.

Ban'tam, n. Small kind of domestic fowl, of which the cockerel is very pugnacious; or small but spirited person.

—Oxford Dictionary

INTRODUCTION

The little men in khaki seemed unbelievably small to be British soldiers. Barely over five feet in height, they swarmed over the decks of the Channel steamer *Caesarea*, moving briskly to shouted orders of sergeants, to sling rifles, packs, and kitbags, then file quickly down the ribbed gangplank to the Le Havre quay. Short legs bowed under their heavy loads of equipment, they tramped ashore—loudly and cheerfully baahing.

The tiny soldiers of the Cheshire Regiment amazed the French onlookers. After two years of war, the local civilians thought themselves blasé to the variety of types of soldiers the British Empire brought through the port. They had seen black Nigerians, giant Australians, bronzed New Zealanders and Maoris, colourful Rajputs and Sikhs, confident Canadians, splendid Grenadiers, and even blue-uniformed Chinese labourers, but never anything like these almost Lilliputian newcomers. Certainly, no unit ever arrived with such an irreverent display.

Boots polished to a black sheen, buttons and brasses glinting in the grey early morning, trousers pressed and puttees tight, soft peaked caps set square on heads, the men were like miniature Guardsmen in their smart military turnout, but the noises they made were like nothing ever heard at Caterham Barracks. "Baaaah! Baaaah! Baaaah !"

After being shunted across southern England in crowded trains for over twenty-four hours, packed into a wallowing tub of a ship through a night of miserable Channel weather, denied breakfast, and kept standing on deck in full marching order for two more weary hours, the short sturdy men saluted their orders to be finally herded ashore by giving tongue to a chorus of prolonged sheep-like noises.

"Baaaah !"

They swung down the gangway onto the docks. Seeing these uniformly small soldiers loaded with the kit of war, struggling gamely under the weight, yet cheerfully voicing their opinion of all set in authority over them, convulsed many French onlookers. The laughter grew as furious sergeants and Provost Corpsmen barked orders for silence and chivvied the troops into more orderly groups. The mirth spread infectiously to the soldiers themselves, until the docks were a chaos of hilarity.

A red-faced Rail Transport Officer clattered up on a horse, to take a horrified look at the scene of hundreds of British soldiers laughing amidst civilians. Apparently singling out one particularly offensive individual, he was heard to roar, "Take that man's name !" The result was to only further entertain the crowd. The RTO rode up to an amused young lieutenant of the Cheshire Regiment, hauled back on his reins and shouted, "You! Take charge of this damned rabble!"

At which point, the mishandled horse shied, slipped on the wet cobblestones, and sent the officer into a frenzy of desperate horsemanship to retain his seat. When the RTO recovered himself, he was the centre of more laughter, and shrieked at the young officer, "Dammit, straighten out the little bastards!" He cantered away to find more respectful units.

The troops quickly settled down at a colour-sergeant's bellow of "Attention!" Further orders and a good deal of hissed threatening by corporals helped shake them out of their laughter and succumb again to accustomed discipline. "Riiii-ght dress!" brought short muscular forearms snapping out to punch the shoulder of each man next along the ranks. Polished boots shuffled into straight lines. "Ey-ees front ! " . . ." Le-heft turn! " . . ."Qui-hick march!" The Cheshires moved off in column of fours, quick-timing through the streets of Le Havre towards Top-of-The-Hill Camp.

After this less-than-dignified arrival, the troops began to be taunted by French townspeople, who cried out, *"Hey, piccininy! Petit piccininy soldats!"* The jeer began to be taken up more and more while the men marched along, drawing crowds as they moved into residential streets of the town itself.

More thoughtful observers on that cold January morning in 1916 must have wondered at the new arrivals for other reasons than their novelty. Here were perhaps living symbols of the extreme poverty of British manpower reserves, that such undersized men had now to be flung into battle against the Germans.

The small troops themselves took the name-calling with a resigned silence born of similar gibes in a succession of training camps from North Wales to Yorkshire to Salisbury Plain. They strode along the grimy streets, staring at the prosaic reality of surroundings which were disappointingly less exotic than what they had somehow expected to see in France. For they, like most of their generation, had never previously been abroad beyond the industrial towns or isolated farms of their childhood. The taunts of the French left them unmoved as being those of inferiors to their mind, mere foreigners, whom they casually despised, as befitted the outlook of typical Englishmen of that time.

There was less acceptance of the jeering after the Cheshires were halted at a railway crossing for one of those inexplicable delays inflicted on all soldiers in transit. Standing in rows, with kitbags down and rifles at "Stand easy," the objects of ridicule looked reassuringly short, and were under strict military order again. The taunting reached an ugly pitch, though, when some young male munitions workers came out of an *estaminet* after a few breakfast brandies.

These Frenchmen, all exempt from military service because of their wartime reserved occupation, took exception to the flirtations which quickly began between the soldiers and some girls from a nearby shell factory, whose prettiness was not marred even by the yellowish tinge lent to their skin as a result of handling explosives. The girls were giggling at the advances and roguish jokes of the Englishmen, delivered with twinkling good humour and obvious meaning that needed no translation. The overtures were made in such a comical manner, with much eye-rolling, twirling of waxed moustaches, and dances of eagerness by the miniature soldiers that the girls were soon crowding around, enjoying the entertainment of such gallant little suitors.

The young men from the factory were irritated, and began to chant *"Pic-in-ni-ni"* even louder, and to hoot their disdain of such apparently puny soldiery. Some accounts say the troops were physically jostled by the munitions workers, others believe the troops were simply tired of standing fast under such gibes, especially with girls looking on.

One eye-witness, Corporal Joseph Mainwaring of the Service Corps, recalled, "It was bad enough for them to put up with all that slanging, but when some of those tipsy civvies started pushing the little fellers about, that put the top hat on it!" Whatever the trigger, several of the soldiers suddenly erupted in rage and proceeded to attack their tormentors. Fists toughened by a lifetime at the coalface, in warehouses, or on farm fields, now began to thump satisfyingly into sneering civilian faces, to the accompaniment of strange Northern curses, the shrill of officers' whistles, and bellows of "Steady on, lads !" from harrassed sergeants.

The flurry was over in moments, halted mainly by the prompt flight of the French opponents, and sealed by six or eight infantrymen being placed under open arrest. Refreshed by their first scuffle in foreign parts, the little men swaggered off towards the war, bellowing a bawdy chorus of "Madam'me'sel from Armenteers, Parly-Voo!" The first of the Bantams had arrived— volunteers all—and keen to be getting their chance to fight at last. Less than half of them would live to see England again.

Twenty more battalions like theirs would follow, to fight, and many to die, and then be almost forgotten. Slaughtered, ignored, their survivors even dismissed as failures, the Bantams formed one of the most unusual and unknown chapters in the annals of the British Army.

The idea for this book began with a single photograph I noticed in a yellowed old newspaper of 1916. It showed a Grenadier Guardsman towering over a boyish soldier almost half his size. Each was in shirtsleeves, suspenders dangling, thrusting bayonetted rifles at each other with looks of mutual exasperation. The caption read, "Burly Guardsman trains one of Bantams how to skewer the Hun!"

Bantams? Though a lifelong student of military history, I had never heard of such troops. Who were they? Were they ever used in combat? Over the next couple of years of reading, I kept an eye open for further references to them. Finding none, I made a few enquiries, which drew blank stares, except for a few almost embarrassed hints of a topic vaguely "infra dig."

Intrigued by this apparent mystery, I decided to solve it for my own interest. What I learned was that here was a neglected story which involved over fifty thousand British and Canadian soldiers who never quite made it into the military history books. They had volunteered to serve when they could have stayed safely at home, suffered physical hardship and hand-to-hand combat that challenged their capacities, and often endured the prejudice and ridicule of less courageous men, all for the privilege of fighting for their country in some of the fiercest battles of the Great War. Their reward was now total obscurity, or from the few who had heard of them, a condescending shrug, "Nice try, of course, but . . ."

The Bantams seemed to deserve more than that, and I set out to put together their saga. It was to send me off on journeys that ranged over Britain, France, and Belgium, and from coast to coast across North America. Personal interviews and correspondence with 340 survivors, plus hundreds of other letters from all over the world, and information from relatives and military records, provided me with first-hand documented details. This research took place during the late 1970s, so I was just in time to personally contact many elderly Bantam veterans, sadly very soon before they each passed away.

My resulting book about them was originally published in 1981, and maintained an interested readership long after it went out of print. However, at the time I wrote it, some important additional information related to them was not available because of official confidentiality laws. Then, in November, 1996, the UK Public Records Office began to release batches of individual soldiers' papers and court martial documents that had been previously kept confidential. The documents revealed disturbing new facts about military executions, some of which involved Bantams, that clearly needed to be told to complete the record. Other related details of personal achievements and commemorative events have also been gathered by me since, and are now included in this revised new edition. They further confirm that the Bantams warrant a place of recognition among the gallant 5,000,000 men who served Britain's cause in the Great War. All the Bantams are long gone now; we shall not see their like again. This is their story.

"Diehard" Henry Thridgould [left] paid his own way from
New York back to England to join the Middlesex Bantams.
At 4ft. 9 ins., Thridgould claimed to be the shortest corporal
in the British Army.

CHAPTER ONE

Blood of the Breed

Later, the world might wonder at it. Yet, at the time—August, 1914—few people thought it strange that millions of men and boys were rushing to join the British army. Hordes of them converged on recruiting offices all over the country, to stand for hours in the heat or rain, struggling to push their way ahead of each other to the enlistment tables, there if necessary to lie about their ages, health, and family responsibilities in their frenzied desire to be accepted as soldiers. Within the first month, over five hundred thousand managed to enlist for the chance to throw themselves into the worst, the bloodiest, war that mankind ever endured.

What was referred to as a "boom in volunteering" started in London when the Central Recruiting Office in Great Scotland Yard opened on August 5th. The building and the courtyard were filled with so many men eagerly trying to sign up that extra doctors had to be brought from nearby hospitals to handle the medical examinations.

One would-be volunteer that day—rejected as being too short at 5 ft. 2 ins.—was Cyril Wright, who explained how most people then felt about enlisting. "You have to remember that nobody expected the war to last very long. We all thought it would be over by Christmas, or the spring of 1915 at the latest; so every man Jack of us wanted to have a crack at the fighting before it was too late."

Billboards blossomed with recruiting posters, and newspaper advertisements appeared overnight, urging, "Your King & Country Need You! Single men between 19 and 30 in good health, above height of 5 ft. 3 ins., chest 34 inches minimum, are urgently required now. Terms of service: for a period of 3 years or until the war is concluded. Join the Army!" The provision for three years' service was a hint that Field Marshal Lord Kitchener, who led the recruiting drive, did not share the popular delusion that hostilities with Germany would last only a matter of weeks. As there was no compulsory military conscription in Britain then, volunteers could be the only source of new manpower.

The recruiting campaign was part of the Kitchener Plan to raise a massive army of civilian volunteers to augment the 100,000 Regular Army soldiers who were already on their fateful way to annihilation in Flanders. That first contingent of the British Expeditionary Force would suffer an appalling total of 96,000 casualties before the end of 1914. Unaware that such sacrifices lay ahead, the early appeal for citizens to join up seems to have tapped some deep chord of response among British males of the day, if we can judge by the overwhelming number of applicants who besieged recruiting offices. Upbringing, schooling, the bellicose press, or a combination of all the factors which made up British national pride, created a driving national desire to enlist.

One surviving officer of the Green Howards regiment recalled the simple morality of the time, "People in England then were far more influenced by the traditional ideas of right, wrong, and duty. While few amongst the officers had a clear idea of the history and politics of the Balkans, which had brought on the war, every private knew that Belgium had been brutally attacked, and that unless Belgium was rescued, it might be Britain's turn. It was that point, and no other, that brought the crowds to the recruiting offices, and it was that point which maintained morale until 1918, in spite of colossal casualties."

What became known as the Great War cost the lives of over 8,500,000 combatants on all sides, plus countless millions' more civilian casualties. After Archduke Ferdinand of Austria was shot by a Bosnian Serb fanatic at Sarajevo on June 28, 1914, all the Continental nations began to stumble towards war, falling one after the other like deadly dominos. Russia mobilized to protect

Serbia from the vengeful Austro-Hungarian Empire. Germany rushed to support Austria, demanding that Moscow cease all military preparations, but secretly hoping for an easy victory over Russia, so as to have a free hand to conquor France. At the same time, Berlin insisted that France promise to not support its treaty ally, Russia. Instead, Paris mobilized for war and called up the French reserve army of three million men. Public support was overwhelmingly enthusiastic at the possibility of avenging France's humiliating defeat by Germany in 1870, and gaining restoration of the annexed provinces of Alsace-Lorraine.

Alone among the squabbling European nations, Great Britain remained aloof at first; hoping to avoid the rifts that could lead to Armageddon. England had no treaties with France for mutual military support, and might have stood aside from the continental conflict. But Britain did have a long-standing obligation to guarantee Belgian neutrality, under a century-old treaty signed in 1839. The same guarantee had been signed also by Prussia at that time, but it was now sneeringly rejected by German Chancellor Theobald von Bethmann Hollweg as "a mere scrap of paper."

He suggested to Foreign Minister Sir Edward Grey that a separate new general neutrality agreement be arranged between Germany and Great Britain. But Prime Minister Herbert Asquith was adamant that the United Kingdom would honour its long-standing pledged obligation to defend Belgium. With the near-unanimous approval of Parliament, he sent Berlin an ultimatum that the Kaiser's army must refrain from violating Belgium, or Britain would have to declare war. Despite this rebuff, the German Foreign Office experts still believed, as did most people in Germany, that the British were so pre-occupied with troubles in Ireland they would not really bother to protect Belgium by force of arms.

Britain's King George V, a cousin of both the Russian Tsar Nicholas and Germany's Kaiser Wilhelm II, telegraphed to each of them: "I cannot help thinking that some misunderstanding has produced this deadlock," he wired. "I am most anxious not to miss any possibility of avoiding the terrible calamity which threatens the whole world." He was too late. Within 24 hours, Germany had declared war on Russia and France. Next day, one German army attacked the Russian-Polish frontier, while another prepared to invade neutral Belgium, en route to attacking France on its vulnerable northern flank.

All Germany demonstrated its approval when the order to mobilize came on July 31. Berlin's Unter den Linden filled with cheering crowds, some throwing flowers to army officers standing erect and saluting in their cars. The crowds sang "Now Thank We All Our God" in the Palace Square, and roared for their Emperor. From the balcony he declared to them, "The sword has been forced into our hand!"

Though itching for war and publicly confident, Kaiser Wilhelm was privately surprised and depressed by Britain's stand. He saw Britain as having ganged up with France and Russia against Germany. He spoke of his dear grandmother, Queen Victoria, and wished she were still alive. "She would not have allowed it," he said. He reconsidered the outcome now, and warned his War Cabinet that the conflict would be long because England was an obstinate nation. Fleet Admiral Alfred von Tirpitz was more sanguine about the consequences, and grimly predicted, "If Britain is against us, all is lost!"

James Gerard, the American Ambassador in Berlin, noted the excitement of tens of thousands of flag-waving people "parading the streets singing *Deutschland uber Alles*, and demanding war." Near demented with mass fervour, they chanted "Down with Russia!" and "*Nach Paris!*" and cheered patriotic speeches that described neighboring countries as being so jealous of Germany's progress they conspired against it. Crowds felt particular rage towards England for opposing them, and shouted angrily about *Rassen verat* (race treason.) Gerard observed, "When news came that Britain had declared war, the rage of the population of Berlin was indescribable."

An infuriated mob of Berlin civilians tore up pavement asphalt along Wilhelm Platz for missiles, then smashed every window of the British Embassy without police intervention. Roving gangs of previously placid civilians savagely beat any man on the streets they suspected of being English. Gerard described how, "Many British subjects, without distinction as to age or sex, were seized, wherever found, and sent to the fortress of Spandau." Suddenly, every foreigner was in a dangerous situation, and even neutral Americans became targets of mob resentment. The fearless Ambassador Gerard had to personally rescue some fellow-countrymen who were attacked when mistaken for being English.

In Munich, a 25-year-old Austrian named Adolf Hitler joined the cheering crowd that gathered in the Odeon Platz on August 2. He found the Teutonic patriotism overwhelmingly satisfying, and yearned to get into combat. Hitler wrote later, "I sank down upon my knees and thanked Heaven for the favour of having been permitted to live in such a time."

Patriotic fever was equally strong in London on August 4th, 1914, where crowds sang *God Save the King*, and *Rule Britannia*, and cheered the sight of any man in military uniform. Soon, one of Britain's famous young poets, Rupert Brooke, would capture the feeling common in Britain at the start of the conflict. He thanked God for "matching us with His hour," and described Britishers going to war "as swimmers into cleanness leaping."

Before dusk fell on August 4th, the whole of London was wound up tight as the mainspring of the House of Parliament's "Big Ben" clock, waiting to see what the stroke of eleven would signal. People poured into the centre of the metropolis, forming huge, strangely excited crowds in Trafalgar Square, Piccadilly, and the Strand. The lions of Nelson's Column, statues in Whitehall, ornamental railings, and the window sills of government offices all became grandstands for the demonstrators. Union Jacks were waving everywhere, as opportunistic flag hawkers did a lively trade.

As the 11:00 p.m. deadline hour approached, thousands tried to press their way into Downing Street, peering through a cordon of police at the bustling diplomats and generals visiting Number 10, while urgently anticipating news of Germany's respose. Shortly after Big Ben struck eleven times, confirmation reached the streets that as no reply from Berlin had been received, Britain was now at war with Germany. Immediately, the massed people burst into loud cheering which lasted for twenty minutes.

The party atmosphere grew more intense as the night went on, with every main street jammed tight with cheering masses, among which scores of motor cars moved slowly carrying champagne-drinking men and women in formal evening dress. Crowds rippled and moved from Parliament Square, hurrying towards the War Office, and surging down the Mall to Buckingham Palace—the traditional place where Londoners gather in times of stress or of joy. Hundreds of thousands of people assembled there, singing the National Anthem over and over again. The area in front of the Palace became so congested, "not an inch of ground was to be seen and the Victoria Memorial was black with people".

For more than four hours, the crowd kept up its singing and cheering, pausing only when King George and Queen Mary finally showed themselves briefly on the balcony. This brought tumultuous applause and the mass singing of "For he's a jolly good fellow!" Drunk with patriotism—and some with a good deal of brown ale—the people kept up their loud enthusiasm until the King and Queen returned to the balcony, this time with the popular young Prince of Wales.

Queen Mary might have been a trifle disconcerted when her loyal subjects began a laughing chant of "We'll hang the bloody Kaiser!" considering her father was an aristocratic German. Likely, King George also had mixed emotions; after all, he was close kin of the German monarch.

Clyde Davis was among the 20,000 American tourists caught in London at the outbreak of war. He clearly remembered that night. "After the King went inside for the third time, the people fell quiet. Everybody moved off to go home, and the crowds were thick it took me hours just to get to the Underground station. A lot of the women were close to tears, and I guess it was dawning on them that war was not a picnic to be looked forward to. I overheard one very small man carrying a sleeping child say to his wife who held a baby, 'Well, Mary, I'll have to join up in the morning.' She stopped short, looking stricken and said, 'If you go, what'll happen to the babby?'"

Such family responsibilities did not hold back volunteers. So many began to enlist next day that mounted police were needed to patrol Great Scotland Yard to keep the way clear for the streams of men anxious to serve their country.

Even the heavy rain which fell during the afternoon of August 5th had no affect on the crowds which gathered to watch the early arrivals. Often, curious onlookers who'd originally just come for a look, ended up going inside the recruiting office themselves, caught by the fever to get into uniform. When the doors were shut at 4.30 p.m., hundreds of men still waiting were told to come back next day.

Among the millions trying to join up, there was a particular group of repeatedly frustrated volunteers. They were men considered physically unacceptable, being below the army's regulation minimum height of 5 ft. 3 ins. Strong or weak, no undersized recruit was accepted for even a preliminary medical examination. The authorities saw no need for reducing height standards for soldiers, however spirited or patriotic, while they could have the pick of Britain's tallest manhood.

Even as a more realistic policy began to relax general standards of physique and the authorities began to take virtually any healthy recruit who stepped forward, there was no wavering from the rules of height requirements. With either kindness or ridicule, extra-short men were turned away in their tens of thousands, no matter that the bugle call found a response among tiny patriots who were themselves barely taller than a rifle.

From all accounts, there was then a fairly large number of under-height Britons—their lack of stature either a result of the hideous living conditions and poor nutrition of industrialized cities or, particularly in Wales and Northern England, merely the adaptive evolution of populations employed as coal miners for many generations. Vigorous but too-short Welshmen were turned away in droves. Among them was 17-year-old William Parkes, a merchant seaman from Newport, Monmouthshire. Preferring to fight aboard ship, he tried several times to join the Royal Navy, but was rejected each time because of his lack of inches. When he approached several army regiments, he found they were not interested in him, either, because of currently acceptable standards.

However, the situation did begin to be noticed. Central London recruiting station reported: "It is unfortunate that so many otherwise fit men must be turned down for lack of the regulation height." In late August, the Rugby town recruiting committee was mildly reprimanded for "attempting to pass very small men into the army," as zeal to create volume numbers of troops overlooked the rules. But usually there were no exceptions made to accommodate the indignant bands of short men who pestered the staff at every recruiting office in the country.

At the headquarters of the London Scottish Regiment in Buckingham Gate, an officer told a reporter, "We needed only sixty men, and today we have completed our establishment." One of them turned down there was James Robertson, a coal-heaver from North Lambeth. "They didn't even let me inside," he recalled. "They said, 'Get away home, Titch!' I told them 'I'm all Scottish', but they just laughed and said, 'To get in, there'd have to be two of you!" Robertson was 5 ft. 2 ins., and he was to wait another two years before being allowed to wear the tartan of a Highland regiment.

Patriotism reached out in many ways. A police constable in Whitehall was approached by a young man who said, "I am a deserter from the Marines. I cannot stand by now. I want to go back and do my share in the war." Charged at Bow Street, he was whisked back to his unit by a sympathetic magistrate. Another repentant young man, Able Seaman Tom Linns, gave himself up to police at the Guildhall. He was a stoker who had deserted his ship months before, but now his pleas to go back aboard were also quickly answered. He was one of many cases of surrendered absent-without-leave servicemen reporting back for duty. So many turned up that a War Office telegram was sent to Marylebone Police Court asking that all deserters should be given a railway pass for return to their depots without bothering with prosecutions.

Within hours of the declaration of war, over 4,000 applications arrived at the War Office from retired commissioned officers in all parts of the Empire. That same day, another 4,500 ex-officers came forward in person to seek re-appointment, and hundreds more applied every hour. Their burning enthusiasm to serve can be measured in one personal tragedy briefly reported in The Times of August 9th, 1914:

"At an inquest on the body of Arthur Sydney Evelyn Annesley, aged 49, formerly a captain in the Rifle Brigade, who committed suicide by flinging himself under a heavy van at Pimlico, the Coroner stated that worry caused by the feeling that he was not going to be accepted for service led him to take his life."

If the rest of Britain reacted to news of war less demonstrably than London, it was not because of any lack of patriotism. Outside the capital, people were simply further removed from the immediacy of events, and the provincial populations were inclined to be more restrained by temperament, particularly in the North.

Alice Turner says they long told the tale of how the news arrived at the public house of a small village near Bradford, Yorkshire. "A very red-faced sporting gentleman dashed in, waving the newspaper, shouting 'It's war, and every man must do his duty!' He raved on in this way for quite five minutes while the locals peered silently over their beer mugs. Then the publican behind his bar responded solemnly, 'Oh, aye?' The excited fox-hunter said angrily, 'Every man must join up! Don't you understand?' 'I do an' all', the publican said," 'Appen you'll be leavin' us t'join oop in t'mornin', then?"

Outside London, populous cities such as Manchester and Birmingham, Liverpool and Bradford, Leeds, Newcastle, Glasgow, Cardiff, and Belfast took the fact of war in their stride. For many people there, it may have been almost casual interest at first, another event incidental to their more immediate concerns of earning a living or of finding their next meal.

Life was never easy in the industrial cities, mill towns, and colliery villages where many people still existed in Dickensian conditions that shared none of the splendours of Empire. Though conditions had improved greatly since the turn of the century, the threat of want and even starvation was still real to Britain's working class in 1914. Nowhere was it more bitterly obvious than in the Midlands, South Wales, Northern England, and Lowland Scotland. In those regions, the closing of a mill, a coal mine, or shipbuilding yard had often brought misery overnight to the endless rows of terraced houses that undulated across a polluted landscape under smoke-filled and often rainy skies.

At first, the outbreak of hostilities brought more problems to industrial Britain—mills closed, railways snarled, coal deliveries halted, seaports awaiting instructions. Only Birmingham prospered immediately, as its giant weapons factories began to turn out the cannon and small arms hastily ordered in the nervous days of late July. It would be weeks before the urgent need for munitions and equipment would infuse massive funds and widespread job opportunities in Britain's new war economy.

The grimy streets of Manchester were virtually deserted the morning after war was declared. Only the polished brass knockers and freshly yellow-stoned doorsteps, the housewives' morning ritual of defiance against poverty, showed any sign of people being abroad. "We little ones had to stay in that day," recalled Winnie Parker. "As soon as he heard about the Germans, my Dad said, 'This'll be bad on the docks. I'd best go and see.' We were kept in because my Mam was worried about him losing the two days' work a week he had, I suppose."

"He came back in a while to tell us that the Manchester Ship Canal was completely at a standstill and there'd be no more work for who-knows how long. My oldest brother Tom was seventeen, and he told Mam not to worry, as he'd join the army and give her his pay. 'I'll be a general in no time,' he said. The dear lad was always cheering us up. 'They'll never take you', my Dad said, 'You're not the height of two-penny-worth of coppers!' But he was big enough for the Bantams, and lay dead in France less than two years later."

With textile machines silent and canal traffic halted, Lancashire could have been expected to raise an outcry in favour of peace. Yet, as it happened, no-one spoke against a war's likely harmful effects on the local population, even though Lancashire held grim memories of privation caused by foreign conflicts. Widespread deprivations had been suffered locally during the American Civil War. Back then, Lancastrian workers stoutly supported the anti-slavery Union, even though blockades prevented Confederate cotton crossing the Atlantic and ended jobs in English mills.

There were no flags waving, no cheering mobs anywhere, as Northcountry folk went about their business, stolidly prepared to shoulder the inevitable load of patriotic duties they would no doubt hear about in due time. For the young men, of course, there were the recruiting halls to be visited, with matter-off fact readiness to fight 'yon Germans.'

The same urgency to get into the war swept across the world to distant cities of the British Empire. Crowds filled the streets of Sydney and Perth, Auckland and Wellington, Durban and Cape Town, chanting their ardour to enlist and battle the suddenly hated Hun.

In South Africa, the bantam-sized emerging poet Isaac Rosenberg wrote to a literary friend in London: "By the time this [poem] reaches you, I expect the world will be in convulsions and you'll be in the thick of it. I know my poor innocent essay stands no chance by the side of the bristling legions of war-scented documents on your desk; but know that I despise war and hate war, and hope that the Kaiser William will have his bottom smacked, a naughty aggressive schoolboy who will have all the plum pudding. Are we going to have Tennyson's 'Battle in the air', and the nations deluging the nations with blood from the air? Now is the time to go on an exploring expedition to the North Pole; to come back and find settled order again."

Nowhere was the enthusiasm to fight greater than in Toronto, Canada. Then a city of 470,000, it was ultra-patriotic, with most of its population either of direct British descent or recent immigrants from the United Kingdom. Though the most Americanized of Empire cities—the open U.S. border being close by—Toronto showed where its heart lay in a surge of emotion towards the "Old Country" during the final days before the declaration of war.

Dependent for international news via the pages of the Toronto Daily Star, the Telegram, and The Globe, people in Ontario had no forewarning of war until a week before it began. Though the shooting of an obscure Austrian duke in Sarajevo had been reported in Canada, and the sabre-rattling speeches of the German Kaiser were quoted, there was no hint of a coming major European conflict until the last days of July.

Then, daily dispatches of armies on the march and threats from Berlin, Paris, and London began to dominate the front pages of newspapers, forcing aside all other news. In Toronto, a Daily Star headline screamed "Blood Of The Breed Quickens!"—echoing the bellicose mood of most Canadians during those hot August days.

Civic holidays freed most people from their normal activities on August 3rd, allowing many to relax and escape the heat by boating at Centre Island, picnicking in High Park, or taking the train for a day up at Lake Simcoe. But thousands more did not take part in these usual summertime diversions. Instead, huge crowds began to flood into the downtown area during the afternoon, restless for the latest word on the ultimatum then running out. The crowds began to pack the humid streets in the newspaper region—Richmond, Bay, King, and Melinda Streets. Shouting enthusiastic "slogans of Britishism," crowds circled the newspaper offices, snatching each papers' edition from the hands of newsboys as they stepped out the doors.

The next day, August 4, 1914, before Canadians officially knew Britain had declared war, Toronto was in the grip of patriotic fever, with hundreds of volunteers outside the Armouries on University Avenue and every other regimental depot in the city. There was a continual lineup of men moving into the Military Headquarters on Simcoe Street, jostling each other in their keenness to be signed up for service. Uniforms were to be seen everywhere, as Reserve men in thick khaki serge or bell-bottomed blues marched proudly about, despite the punishing heat. The Queen's Own Rifles had to close its doors at noon because of the crush of volunteers, and the 48th Highlanders appealed for "a more orderly progression of applications."

"Schoolboys went running through the streets next day, waving newspapers and shouting, 'Hurray, it's war!'" said Adelaide Kemmel, a schoolgirl herself at the time. "Everybody was so excited, laughing and talking of nothing else. All the boys I knew wanted to get into uniform of any description. As they were too young for the army, they even started going to the Boy Scouts or joining the Young Soldiers' Clubs that sprang up everywhere."

The stark headline "WAR" was the headline that sold three extra editions of the Toronto Star that August 5th. Boldly displayed amongst the breathless prose on the front page, was mention of the British War Office advertisement that "King and Country Needs YOU!" A lead story explained to eager readers that the Empire was on the brink of the greatest war in history, and that there was an appeal out for all unmarried men between eighteen and thirty to volunteer immediately.

Relative to population, the response in Toronto was as overwhelming as it had been in the United Kingdom. For instance, on August 6th, over two hundred and fifty men signed up with the Queen's Own, 300 joined the 48th Highlanders, and similar numbers were taken on strength by a dozen other city regiments. Thousands more got their names taken as being ready to enlist. Confident of their attraction, the exclusive Royal Grenadiers opened recruit classes. At that stage, the regiment insisted that would-be soldiers were first groomed in military deportment before being accepted.

A new spectator sport began, as people began to jam the public galleries of the Armouries and stand five deep around army parade grounds, enjoying the sight of local men being put through the earnest movements of military footdrill. A great number of men were barred by the rigorous standards of medical fitness and, in some units, lack of the proven ability to shoot straight.

Soon, volunteers were being signed up at the rate of seven hundred a day, and competition grew keen. "One boy I knew was a six-footer, though only seventeen, and a fine athlete as well," said Adelaide Kemmell. "He had three regiments after him, yet was rejected after all because of poor eyesight."

Military men became the social lions of the moment, and were lavishly quoted in the press. "I have just come from the Armouries," General F.L. Lessard told The Globe. "I counted twenty-five men in one group who came to volunteer; all fine, well set up, likely-looking fellows."

Not only were physical standards high in those early days, there was to be no nonsense with deportment, either, as Major General Davies made clear while addressing a training corps meeting. "Long hair may be all right for the knuts and dudes, but it has nothing to do with soldiers," he pronounced. "There is a great deal too much hair about. It gives soldiers the appearance of something between a civilian and a foreigner. It is unsoldierly and distinctly un-English!" Barbers did a sudden brisk trade in cropping hopeful recruits.

Within days, large drafts of British Army reservists were leaving from Union Station, bound for ships to take them to their parent regiments in the United Kingdom. The Globe reported, "Carriages filled with brave Tommies were cheered to the echo, amid choruses of 'God Save The King.'" They were universally envied by Toronto men still trying to join up. Even volunteers headed for training at nearby Camp Borden were seen off by such large, enthusiastic, crowds that a special squad of police constables was detailed to manage the daily departures.

"We used to go and see leave-taking events every day," said Miss Kemmell. "It was quite the thing to see; men shouting, singing, quite a few of them pretty drunk, and roaring threats about what they would do to the Kaiser. The soldiers would come down to the station, with a big banner at the front to say which regiment they belonged to. We children would each have a Union Jack to wave back at them. Toronto was a small place then, so there was usually somebody we knew personally among the men going away."

"I still remember that the wives would hold up their little ones so they could see over the crowd for a last sight of Daddy. The only women I recall to do any cheering were the flirty young girls who were caught up in the excitement. Even then, I used to feel sad when I'd notice how some of the married women would be crying loudly, while many more had tears swimming in their eyes as the trains pulled away with their men singing in them until you couldn't hear them anymore."

One of the hopefuls to arrive at the University Avenue Armouries in late August got no further than the front steps. Alexander Batchelor [name changed at request of his widow] was a nineteen-year-old ex-miner from Staffordshire who had become a familiar sight at recruiting offices all across Toronto during the past few days. Though sturdily built, he was only five feet high, and for that reason had already been turned down by the Mississauga Horse, the Signals, the Engineers and the Queen's Own Rifles.

Like many young men of his age, he was desperately keen to get into the army, well-prepared to give up a good job with the Street Railway for the privilege of going overseas. Now, as he elbowed his way through the queue, he was halted by the powerful voice of the Imperial recruiting sergeant. "You again, shorty! Don't bother going inside. There isn't a place for you here either."

Batchelor remembered the sympathetic glances of the other volunteers pressing forward around him. Squaring up, the immigrant youth who had been in the country less than a year said, "Come on, Sergeant, give us a break. I hear that they need men to be cooks. You don't have to be big for that, do you?"

Scoffed the sergeant, "Last time, you said you was a miner. Don't tell me you can cook, too!"

"Been doing it all my life," said Batchelor, desperately.

Resplendent in red sash, campaign medals, and a luxuriant moustache, the recruiting sergeant exulted in over six feet of muscular height as he pronounced sentence. "Just you hop it, lad. You're far too small to ever wear the King's uniform, so quit pestering us."

"But, I can march as well as any man, and I can shoot right well," said Batchelor. "Somebody must want to take me."

"Well, not on this side of the water, sonny," the sergeant turned away, then as an afterthought threw over his shoulder, "You might make it in the Old Country though. I hear they're taking just about anyone in Kitchener's mob over there."

The new force in England—more respectfully known as Kitchener's Army—was planned to consist of five hundred battalions, organized in thirty divisions. Each newly-raised battalion was absorbed into its parent regiment.

Army Order 324, dated August 21, 1914, detailed how the new battalions were given numbers consecutive to the existing battalions of their regiments, and were to be identified by the word "Service" after the unit number. Groups of six service battalions were organized to form divisions of the four new armies: First Army, 9th to 14th Divisions; Second Army, 15th to 20th Divisions; Third Army, 21st to 26th Divisions; and Fourth Army, 30th to 35th Divisions. Soon after, the Fifth Army was raised, which included the 36th (Ulster) and the 38th (Welsh) Divisions respectively recruited in Northern Ireland and Wales.

Among these new formations were the 35th and 40th Divisions which would be further distinguished for a while by the parenthetical word "(Bantam)" in their title. The uniqueness of their origin and their great popularity at the time makes their later demise all the more poignant.

Recruiting trams toured streets of Birkenhead in late 1914 to sign up volunteers for the two original Bantam battalions raised by the Cheshire Regiment. Note rooster symbol at top front.

Bantams' founder, six-foot-six Alfred Bigland, MP, inspects troops of the 15th. Bttn. Cheshire Regiment on their first public parade outside St. George's Hall, Liverpool.

CHAPTER TWO

"B.B.B." Battalions

Today, nobody knows his name. The first Bantam was a short, wide-shouldered coalminer who had walked the entire one hundred and fifty road-miles from Durham to Birkenhead—crossing the Pennine Mountains and the Lancashire plain, visiting Preston, Manchester and Liverpool on the way, doggedly trying to enlist in the army. Each time he was turned down because of his lack of height, he set out again on foot to find a regiment that would accept him. By mid-November, 1914, his journey finally took him across the Mersey River to Cheshire, where he met the one man in England able to organize a fresh new source of manpower.

Alfred Bigland was the Member of Parliament for Birkenhead, a large vigorous man 6ft. 6ins. tall, who had thrown his powerful personality into enlisting local men to answer Lord Kitchener's call for volunteers. He headed the City Recruiting Committee, working tirelessly to stage public rallies.

He was particularly effective in cutting through any red tape that threatened to hamper every advance of his Committee. Stores, accommodation, and food were in desperate need as tens of thousands of men poured into Birkenhead, eager to enlist. Time and again, Bigland would slash through the delays and bureaucratic procedures set up by civil servants and officials which might otherwise have delayed the effectiveness of his recruiting drive. He was not only interested in signing up a satisfactory volume of bodies; his attention never wavered from the human side of war.

Bigland later wrote, "It was painful and discouraging to find how many cases of severe hardship existed owing to the men who had joined up having failed to fill in the forms correctly as to wives, children, parents, or others absolutely dependent on them. It was our first duty to get all the papers in working order."

"It was brought to the notice of my Committee that totally inadequate accommodation was furnished for the thousands of men being sent to Chester to create Kitchener's Army. A deputation of the Committee waited on the G.O.C. of the Western Command and insisted on an immediate improvement in the whole system of billeting the new recruits, which the authorities in Chester quickly adopted."

How the Durham miner's arrival caused the Bantams idea to be born is best told in Mr. Alfred Bigland's own words:—

"One morning, Mr. Alfred Mansfield, who was an active member of the Committee, came to me and said that they had had a lively scene in the recruiting office the night before, caused by a young man who presented himself for enlistment. The sergeant said: "Take off your hat and stand under that measuring machine." He did so, and the sergeant said: "Nothing doing, you must get out.' The young fellow demanded an explanation, and the reply was, 'Army height is above five feet three inches, you are only five feet two.' Then ensued the scene. The aspirant for fighting the Boche threw down his coat and offered to fight any man in the room. He scoffed at the idea that an inch in height precluded him from joining the Army. Though he raged and swore, the sergeant was obdurate and refused to give him the usual papers and with great difficulty, got him out of the office."

"Mansfield said: 'This is a serious matter. When we only wanted a small army a regulation height of five feet three inches might be good, but now every available man is wanted, and the subject should be reconsidered.'"

"After discussion, it was decided that I should write direct to Lord Kitchener and inform him of our view that a very valuable contingent of his army could be raised of "Bantams" five feet to five feet three inches, provided they were strong, sturdy fellows and suggesting that by stipulating for an extra inch in the chest measurement over the regulation 33 inches, sickly weedy men with insufficient stamina would be excluded. Although we could not raise a battalion of such men in Birkenhead alone, we expressed the opinion that if he saw his way to give us authority to enlist over the whole of the country, we could do it."

"I wrote accordingly, but did not get a reply direct from Lord Kitchener. However, in a few days there came an intimation that Sir Henry McKinnon, the G.O.C. of the Western Division, desired to see me. I waited on Sir Henry, and he informed me that the War Office was interested in the idea of Bantam battalions but were too much pressed to undertake the formation of a new type of regiment."

"However, he had authority to say that if the Birkenhead Recruiting Committee would undertake the whole service we should have every assistance from the War Office. For specially raised battalions, regulations had already been drafted fixing a definite amount of so much for housing, a ration allowance, and payment for uniforms and equipment. The War Office would provide rifles, baggage wagons, etc., but all other matters must be undertaken by the parties raising the battalion."

"I summoned my Committee and put before them Sir Henry McKinnon's message. They suggested that the Town should become responsible, as it was quite possible the sums named might prove quite inadequate to house, feed, and equip the men and someone must be responsible for such a deficit if it occurred."

"I saw the Mayor, but after consulting the Town City Clerk, he said it would be quite impossible, as the members of the Town Council would be personally charged if they voted to undertake the work and there was a deficit. No charge, even if voted by the Council, could be met by the ratepayers. My Committee, too, declined to take responsibility for an unknown liability and it looked as though the bright idea would fall through."

"So keen was I, however, to form a Bantam battalion, that I studied the financial risk very carefully and came to the conclusion that the appropriations in aid fixed by the War Office might, with good management, be made to fit the bill. I saw Sir Henry McKinnon again, told him I would take the risk myself, and so it was agreed."

Bigland estimated that he would likely be able to raise the whole battalion of one thousand men in a Bantam unit. He began reserving dining rooms, stables for officers' horses, drilling grounds, and housing for the men. He looked around and found all these facilities under the roof of the local Agricultural Show Ground. He briskly set about taking over the buildings for his new project.

He somehow managed to pass along specifying information about the Bantams to every recruiting office in the United Kingdom within a matter of days. His announcement informed each local medical officer about the requirements for men with chest measurements of 34 inches, minimum height of 5 ft., and a maximum height of 5 ft. 3 inches. These men would be provided with railway warrants to Birkenhead where they could join the newly designated 15th (Service) Battalion, 1st. Birkenhead, The Cheshire Regiment.

"On the morning of November 30th, 1914, we had everything in readiness to receive one thousand one hundred men," wrote Bigland. "As each man coming from a distance would already have passed a medical board before he received his railway warrant, we provided half a dozen doctors to examine all recruits coming from our own neighbourhood. As I passed along these volunteers, I was depressed to find large numbers of them being turned down as ineligible. A very considerable number were satisfactory, but they could not expand their chest measurement to the required 34 inches and I began to fear for my promised thousand."

"But throughout the day telegrams were received from many distant towns stating the number of recruits who had passed their examination and were coming. The next morning more telegrams were received from Ireland, Scotland, South Wales, London, and so on, saying more and more sturdy physically suitable men were coming. By noon that day, we added the total and found to our consternation that instead of the eleven hundred men we had provided for, two thousand had arrived or were on their way !"

"I telephoned to Chester to wire the principal recruiting centres that the Bantam Battalion was full, and to stop enlistment. We were up against a real difficulty—only housing and sleeping accommodation for one thousand one hundred men, and what were we to do with the thousand more. All needing food and sleeping places to be found within a few hours! The Mayor opened the Town Hall to house them for the night, and fortunately I was able to get the promise of two thousand blankets which the Army Stores Department at Burscough said would be delivered in Liverpool by eight p.m. if I would have carts in attendance to bring them over the Mersey.

"We ransacked the town for bread, ham, and other comestibles, and as each party arrived we were able to feed them. To keep them cheerful and merry, we organized a concert and found that many of our Bantams were ready with songs to while away the time until the blankets arrived. To our dismay, nine and ten o'clock came and still no blankets. However, just before eleven the welcome news came that the carts were at the door. By twelve-thirty, we had them settled in for the night—sleeping on the floor of the concert hall, in the passages, and the committee room, two blankets for every man."

"It spoke well for the way they would face greater hardships at the front to see the cheerful adaptability of these good fellows in taking the situation with the merriment of boys out for a picnic. The next day, we commandeered the most modern school in the town, secured mattresses from shipping companies' stores, and had the second thousand comfortably settled in by nightfall. I came to know many of these men individually and their stories of self-sacrifice, their belief that they would be looked after, their keenness to learn and to serve touched me to the quick."

"Most of them brought a small bundle of spare clothes and a little money, but one attracted my attention and I asked him where his kit was. He naively replied he had it all on his back. Think of it, leaving home, with no money, no spare clothes, no food; trusting himself absolutely without a thought to the care of those who called for his service. These things became known. The townspeople soon made them welcome, arranging clothing centres and amusements of all kinds, and were never tired of planning pleasant surprises to meet the exigencies of the day."

A new wrinkle was added to speed up the process of attestation. Several trams were bedecked with the Bantams' rooster symbol and posters exhorting short men to join up on the spot. These mobile recruiting stations were sent touring city streets in Birkenhead and Liverpool, enabling volunteers to step aboard and be signed into the battalion while en route to the depot. It was an innovation so successful that "recruiting trams" became a familiar sight on city streets all over Britain throughout the war years.

Arnold Weymouth was a schoolboy at the time. He recalls the impact of these recruits when they arrived in town. "Me and some of my pals walked by the main railway station every morning on our way to school. We were already used to seeing hundreds of men come crowding off the trains, clutching their brown paper parcels on their way to recruiting stations. However, on that particular morning, we were amazed to see what seemed like thousands of very small men, swarming off the trains, laughing, and singing and fairly skipping in their eagerness to get down to the town hall. They had a holiday air about them; chattering and shouting excitedly, and often formed into groups with arms linked to sing the popular songs of the day. Many of them were Welshmen, and I can still remember their beautiful voices raised in song, booming against the high glass roof of the railway station.

"Though a good many of the Bantam volunteers were obviously from poor homes, most of them were dressed up in their best Sunday blue suits, though many of them did not have collars and ties. I particularly remember a large group of Lancashire men dressed in their best clothes, yet wearing heavy clogs, doing an impromptu tap dance in a crowd, then making their way towards the station exit by the expedient of leap-frogging over each other in turn as a sign of their exuberance."

After a decade of peace since end of the Anglo-Boer War, during which Parliament had refused to allocate funds for more than basic military needs, the War Department was unprepared in August, 1914, to equip a suddenly burgeoning army. Massive orders were placed for stores; injecting millions of pounds into the economy and creating hundreds of thousands of jobs in Britain's industrial towns. Rifles from Birmingham; uniforms from Manchester and Leeds; machinery, food, transport, ammunition, boots, tents, from London, Glasgow, and hundreds of other manufacturing centres.

Suddenly, businesses that had become stagnant had un-dreamed-of demands placed on them by their biggest customer ever. The remarkable genius and power that was the industrial base of post-Edwardian Britain was unleashed to produce stores in record time. But in the meanwhile, the army found itself unable to equip the hundreds of thousands of men who had already flocked to join up.

From the start, the Birkenhead Bantams enjoyed the support of local citizens who saw to it that the men did not lack what the government was yet unable to supply. It was a very personal solicitude that was later to show itself where-ever else a Bantam unit was raised.

Uniforms would have been a problem for these "big men on short legs" at the best of times. With arms, thighs, and chests thickened by hard work at the coalface and on the docks, yet being disproportionately short in the leg, Bantams were not easy to properly clothe from normal stocks. Those chaotic early days made it doubly impossible to hope for any kind of uniforms suitable for the Bantams. The organizing committees proceeded to make do.

This problem was partly solved by an energetic greengrocer called Fred Parsons who appointed himself as an unofficial quartermaster of the battalion. He proved to be a valuable man in finding and appropriating many supplies with a briskness that would have been the envy of the most ruthless "scrounger" on the Western Front.

An early and valuable contribution of Parsons was the provision of four hundred Boer War tunics which he uncovered and somehow prized away from a reluctant Army depot in Manchester. What these garments lacked in style and fit was overlooked by their merit as being at least military in appearance. As there were no khaki trousers to match the tunics, most of the men were to be seen wearing an assortment ranging from labourers' corduroys to banker's striped pants. Another outre touch was added by those men who improvised puttees around their legs with strips of red baize torn from seats of the Bebington Grandstand.

Members of the recruiting committee dug down into their own pockets to see the men kitted out. Mr. Bigland, Thomas McArthur, and his son Theodore Hunter McArthur, bought several hundred Post Office uniforms within ten days and issued them during a midnight parade.

Cyril Wright remembers how it felt as a new soldier to be dressed in this unexpected way. "I had rather shamefacedly been walking around in blue railwayman's overalls for a week or so, the best they could find for my platoon at the time. Now, I was dressed up as a postman."

"We were pretty disappointed at first, as we had been looking forward to khaki and brass buttons. But there we were, all done up in blue G.P.O. outfits with red piping around the edges. It wasn't long though before we began to see the funny side of it, and all manner of jokes started. We used to tell the girls Bantams dressed like that because we were going to be `posted' to France !"

Some of the more affluent recruits scorned the non-military clothes offered, and travelled to Liverpool to buy "Lewis suits." These were smartly-cut uniforms of officer-quality cloth, provided by a Mr. Lewis, a tailor who expressed his patriotism by supplying them at prices even some privates could afford.

Though the regulations specified the minimum height of Bantams to be five feet, there appears to have been a good deal of latitude applied by recruiters. It became common for men of well below this height to be accepted in the general rush to sign up two thousand men for the new battalions.

"I was exactly four foot ten inches when they accepted me," recalls Cyril Wright, a shipyard worker from Wirall, Cheshire. "I turned up at the Town Hall office with not much hope of getting in, but as I was a strong, healthy lad otherwise, they just said my heart was big enough to make up for height, and a soldier I became."

Other surviving Bantams proudly tell of being below five feet high—Jeff Pritchard, a miner, 4 ft., 11 ins., Graham Carr, a clerk, 4 ft., 10 ins., Nobby Streeter, a foundryman, 4 ft., 9 ins. But for the most part, the two Cheshire battalions were recruited from men close to five feet three inches, with chest measurements often much larger than minimum requirements. However, as the war moved on and the Bantam movement spread to other parts of Britain, the original standards were to be often ignored, with ultimately disastrous results.

Throughout the war, recruiters had a continual problem in watching for young boys, some no older than fourteen, slipping into the army. This was prevalent in every regiment, but was particularly difficult for the Bantams. Many mature men in these battalions were "boy-sized," and some eighteen-year-olds looked five or six years younger.

John Jones of Warrington recalled long afterwards, "I may be one of the very few Bantams still around now, because I joined up so young in the first place. I gave my age as nineteen years two months, although I was just sixteen at the time."

Harry Hurst said, "As for my being in France at the age of fourteen, my parents were dead and, of course, I falsified my age when enlisting. The A.B. 64 Paybook I still have shows my age on enlistment as nineteen. Being tall for my age, and the recruiting sergeant being presumably blind, I found myself on the Somme in July, 1916."

"I was very keen to get into the army," said Jeff Pritchard. "The only problem was my age, fourteen and a half. My mother was poorly in a county home and my father had six other mouths to feed. So one morning, I just walked away from my job as a cart-handler down the mine and went to the recruiting office. "How old are you, lad?" the doctor said. I looked him in the eye and said "Eighteen, sir." "Hmm," he said, "And what does your mother think of you going for a soldier?" I told him she was dying, and he just patted me on the shoulder and signed my acceptance without another word."

Most local recruiting secretaries saw the merit in Bigland's idea and campaigned aggressively to get small men to send to the Cheshires. Hundreds of Durham miners were inspired to follow their fellows who were the original Bantams.

"When the war broke out, I was seventeen and a half years old, working down the pit at Berwick Main," recalls George Embley. "I went to Newcastle barracks to join up but they told me I was under-age and too small (5 ft. 2 ins.). On my way home over the high level bridge, I saw a notice, "Join Bigland's Birkenhead Bantams!" Next day, I was in Birkenhead, at Rock Ferry school signing up with the 16th Battalion, and I still have the King's silver badge they gave me, engraved with "BBB" for "Bigland's Birkenhead Bantams."

From the start of the Bantam movement, many Welshmen came forward to join it. Being the major recruiting centre closest to North Wales, Birkenhead was a natural lure for Welsh would-be soldiers. They came in by train and foot every day, from Anglesey and Cardigan, from the Rhondda Valley and distant Cardiff. They were coal miners and farmworkers, most of whom were in excellent health and who made ready recruits. Among the miners, scores were below the minimum height yet tremendously toughened by their jobs underground which often had begun at the age of nine.

"When some of my oppos and me set out for Birkenhead, we had never heard of the Bantams," confessed Albert Lewis. "We were miners in our late teens, and we set out to join the new Tunnelling Companies that were being formed by the Royal Engineers. An agent had come to the pit and told us we could work as Army Moles, digging under the German lines, and be paid as much as five shillings a day. That was big wages in those days, so we set off to make our fortunes !"

Lewis and his friends arrived in Birkenhead and were about to take a train to London, when they were mistaken for Bantam recruits and directed to that unit's barracks. "We came across a lot of old friends there. When we heard they expected to be fighting Germans in a few weeks, we changed our minds and joined the Cheshires instead. We just laughed when we heard we'd be getting only one shilling a day."

With such an embarrassingly large number of rank and file recruits, Bigland and his committee were faced with the urgent need to find officers and N.C.O.s. [Non-commissioned officers—

all ranks with authority above private and below second lieutenant.] Many trained officers and NCO drill instructors had already gone away, either to the front or to join more fashionable units. Very few of the available remaining officers were keen to take on the new military venture of Bantams. Bigland shrewdly decided to take advantage of the local flavour of the battalion. Given a free hand to find and appoint his own officers, the resourceful Member of Parliament looked among his own circle of acquaintances.

Members of the Corn Exchange, managers of ship building firms, and the sons of business executives provided a ready core of officer candidates. He told each of those he selected to be officers they should buy their own kit, and their abilities would have to pass inspection after three months of training. He warned that if they failed to pass, they would be dismissed and any costs would be charged to them. It says something for the astuteness of Alfred Bigland that not one of the officers he selected failed the training course, and many of them had distinguished careers with the Birkenhead battalion and other regiments.

One of these officers was young Theodore Hunter McArthur, earlier a buyer of postal uniforms. He had been active since the beginning in helping to recruit the unit and was commissioned as a lieutenant. Tremendously popular with his men, McArthur played a key role in training the battalion, and in building the troops' morale as a disciplined fighting outfit. (Two years later, as a twenty-year-old captain, he was to lead his beloved Bantams into battle on the Somme.)

Not even the damp cold of early morning could subdue the two new battalions when they were paraded together for review on the Bebington Show Grounds. The eager recruits, dressed in their ill-fitting motley of Post Office blues, old-fashioned tunics, or railway overalls must have struck a strange contrast with the group of tall staff officers in immaculate uniforms who came to review them.

Lord Derby himself, in his silk hat and cutaway coat, was there to look over the Bantams for the first time. Before he had managed to make more than five minutes of his prepared lengthy speech, the enthusiastic men gave him a drawn-out roar of applause to signal he had said enough, a gesture which that dignitary must have received with mixed emotions.

It was obvious the Bantams did not need rousing speeches to get them into a fighting mood. They already fairly throbbed with martial ardour, eager to go to France tomorrow if possible, and asked only to be armed, trained, and shipped across the Channel without delay. They were in for a long wait.

CHAPTER THREE

Hard Up For Troops

By early 1915, it was obvious that the war had become a stagnant nightmare of killing that could go on for years. The opposing armies crouched shivering in an almost unbroken line of waterlogged ditches that stretched from the Swiss border to the Belgian beaches. Static trench warfare, with its massed artillery and machine guns, had already slaughtered most of the professional troops and created a new demand for huge citizen armies to feed a conflict of attrition. To accommodate this, Lord Kitchener announced that "Service" battalions would now have the same status as regular units.

Meanwhile, the authorities launched an even more intensive drive to boost recruiting. While volunteers still came forward, there was already a faint dulling of the original patriotic keenness, a hint of wary discernment among men of military age that odds of survival were low on the Western Front. One busy recruiting officer in Bristol rebuked, "I never thought I would see the day that young Britons would actually question the course of the war, and ask how long they would be serving !"

Newspapers in Britain did their editorial best to counter this trend by featuring front-line stories of high adventure: "Tommies Show Jerry What For!", "Boy Soldier Leads Gallant Raid!". Between these effusions—written second-hand by war correspondents forbidden by the General Staff to visit the trenches—the papers sandwiched lengthy appeals for volunteers. Using alternates of praise for heroes and contempt for "slackers," reporters described the enlistment of men into units forged from shared interests or origins:

The Legion of Frontiersmen, Sharpshooters, Tunnelling Companies, Soccer Rifles, Sportsmens' Battalions, Artists' Rifles, Golfers' & Cyclists' Company, and the many City Pals Battalions.

It is the volunteerism, the eager self-sacrifice, that so impresses anyone today looking back on that era. Wherever in the world there were people of British stock, the opportunity to serve formed a magnetic pull back to the Old Country. Five hundred men banded together under the name of the 'Australians of Western America' entrained from California, and sailed from New York to enlist in London. Five orphaned sons of British railwaymen arrived from Russia, and went straight from the boat-train to the Piccadilly recruiting station. Men came from the African veldt, from the far North of Canada, and from nameless islets of the Pacific, paying their own passage, giving up their livelihoods and offering their lives.

Despite this worldwide fervour, one could think of few more isolated or unlikely prospects for recruits than the wind-swept plains of Patagonia. There, in Chubut Province of southern Argentina, several hundred Welsh farmers and sheep-herders had settled over half a century before. Though scattered along the Chubut Valley, they were mostly concentrated around the towns they had founded, Rawson, Trelew, and Puerto Madryn.

Content to work hard, live free under a big sky, and mind their own business, these Cymric-Argentines had scant obligation to fight for a distant land that had offered little opportunity to their forefathers. Yet even here, the war's progress was followed closely through the English-language 'Herald' of Buenos Aires and month-old newspapers from Britain. Among these hardy folk, who discussed the war as often in Welsh and Spanish as in English, was a young ranch-hand named Jack Enrique Jones.

Argentine-born, twenty-year-old Jones had never seen the green hills of Wales described so often by his grandmother, and was on amiable terms with local settlers of German descent, yet he burned with the urge to join a Welsh regiment and fight in France. He was to set off on an Odyssey that brought him his wish within a few months, to survive the worst of the trenches, and spend the rest of his life in the United States, where he left a remarkable account of his career as a Bantam.

"What an exciting time that was to be a youngster!" Jones recalled. "The European War seemed to be on some distant planet, and to be fought by gods. Chubut was such a backwater to my mind then. I didn't have any parents left alive, my sister was married, and I was left to my own devices. I was strong for my size, and knew a lot about caring for sheep and cattle, so I never lacked for work. But all I could think of was how to get across the seas to Wales and sign up as a soldier."

"Some of the local old men had been in the British army many years ago, and the newspaper stories set their tongues wagging with memories of life in the ranks. Of course, there was more than a bit of embroidery of those stories, as I realized later on. However, at the time I was not to know that, and thought the army to be a fine life, especially the fighting part. Probably that's why there'll always be wars, as long as young men are excited by the idea of risking their lives and testing their courage against enemy bayonets.

"There was only one veteran who tried to warn me. He was very old, having actually been in the Crimean War, and I remember him saying, 'War is all murder, but trench war is the worst murder of them all.' I often thought about the truth of his words in the next few years."

Jones finally left his pampas homeland, running through a stormy night to jump aboard a coastal vessel at Puerto Madryn. He worked his passage to Buenos Aires, a cosmopolitan city which in itself was thrillingly different from anything he had known before. The British Military Attache was not impressed by the stunted, wild-looking youth who came back every day for a week before being allowed inside the Embassy. Though there were no funds provided for the many hundreds of Anglo-Argentine volunteers who had already set out for England, most of them had at least been given an audience and some kind of encouraging advice. When Jones finally gained entrance, he was allowed no further than the front hallway. There, an official voice brayed at the commissionaire, "Do get rid of the little fool. We're not that hard up for troops!"

At this point, it would have been understandable if Jones had gone back home, after a heartfelt "To hell with them!" Instead, his determination to go to war for Wales was only redoubled, and he set about making his own way overseas.

His first need was to get a job, as what small amount of money he brought was soon spent and he had been without food for two days. After a difficult time ("I wouldn't steal, not even food.") he found work at the cattle pens near the docks. There he learned that men with a knowledge of livestock could sometimes work their passage to Britain aboard cattle ships. These berths were in great demand, and it took some weeks of persistence before a skipper looked beyond his small stature to give him a job.

"It's funny, but I wasn't at all surprised when the captain told me that his ship would end the voyage in Cardiff, Wales. It just seemed meant to be. I fairly sang the whole way while I shovelled cow manure in the hold, working sixteen hours a day tending cattle that weren't as seasick as me, and one of which repaid me by standing on my foot hard enough to break it." So it was in the spring of 1915 that Jack Enrique Jones of Patagonia limped ashore at Tiger Bay, Cardiff, in the land of his fathers at last.

Though Wales was less inclined than other regions to turn away small men from the army, his 5 ft. 1 in. height kept him under the absolute minimum for acceptance. After being turned down at several depots, he was told by one jovial doctor to "Put some manure in your boots to help you grow." "I just tried that, boyo," Jones shot back. "It don't work at all!"

By the time he had arrived, there were already over a dozen units eager to accept men like Jones. Three famous Welsh regiments were among these, although it was to be some time before he learned of them.

It was a more openly inconsiderate time than today, and prejudice against short men was commonplace. The contempt voiced early on by some military spokesmen towards Bantam troops fell hastily silent after the favourable comments made by Field Marshal Kitchener. The authorities were further swayed to a policy of recruiting men below minimum height by a paper presented to the Royal Sanitary Institute in February, 1915.

Discussion of the topic "Tall men versus Short Men for the Army" was led by Dr. M.S. Pembrey, Lecturer on Physiology, Guy's Hospital. "When I was asked by the Council to open a discussion upon the question whether tall or short men make the better soldiers, I agreed because it appeared to be a suitable time," he began. "During the opening stages of the war, the standard for recruits was even raised for a short time, and this official action was interpreted by some as evidence that there were too many recruits, and by others that better material was required. The 5ft. 3ins. Minimum standard was soon restored, and later on was reduced when the so-called "Bantams" were enlisted. Can this lowering of the standard be defended, and if so, are there other arguments than those of necessity?"

"The official view that height in a soldier is an advantage is a reflection of the general view of the layman. There is often some truth in an opinion which is held by the mass of the people; it is necessary, however, to consider the evidence, for popular views may be based on insufficient data or traditions handed down from times when fighting was very different from what it is now."

"There will be no difficulty in proving that there is no evidence to justify a dogmatic opinion. The civilian has no experience of active service; the military men who have served in the field during the minor wars in the past have an experience based upon a highly-trained regular army, which was recruited in times of peace from a limited portion of the population."

"In peacetime, the need of employment is frequently the stimulus to enlistment, and height is then a recognized standard for recruits, for most men will agree that a tall soldier is more imposing, docile, and dignified than a short man. An unjustified bias may thus arise in favour of the tall man."

"A definition of terms is a necessary preliminary to an examination of the evidence. A man may be considered tall when his height is four or five inches greater than that of the average of his countrymen; on the other hand, he is short when his height is a similar number of inches below the average."

"All comparisons must take into account racial differences. A typical Scot would be considered a tall Welshman. The average height of the men of Great Britain and Ireland is uncertain, for there is not sufficient data; there has been no anthropometric survey of the country."

"According to the figures collected by the Anthropometric Committee of the British Association for the Advancement of Science, the height averages for 8,585 men between the ages of 23 and 50 years are : Scottish, 68.71, Irish, 67.90, English, 67.36, and Welsh, 67.66 inches."

"An adult Englishman of typical proportions has in the opinion of this Committee a stature of 67.5 inches, a chest girth of 36.5 inches, and a weight of 10 stone. 10 lbs. [150 lbs., or 68 kg. Avoirdupois scale: 'one stone' = 14 pounds.] Professor Parsons, from an examination of two or three hundred thigh-bones, concluded that in the 13th, 14th, and 15th centuries, the Midland Englishman had an average stature of 65.75 inches. There is no evidence of any sudden change in stature since, nor is there any proof of the somewhat prevalent view that the population of this country shows physical deterioration."

"The average height of the recruits for our Army during the period 1901-1910 was 66.1 inches. These anatomical data are of value, but are based upon too small a number of cases. Even if this objection were removed, it would be impossible to estimate a man's capacity by height. Physiological estimates must be expressed in physiological terms."

"It is now necessary to consider whether the greater stature of the tall man is distributed evenly throughout the body. It is not so distributed for the difference in height of men sitting down, but the individual differences become apparent directly they stand up. Thus a man 6 ft. 4½ in. in height was of course 10½ in. taller than a man 5 ft. 6 in., but compared in the sitting position, he was only 3½ inches taller. Height, therefore, is due chiefly to a greater growth of the lower limbs."

"What are the causes of difference in growth? In the first place, there is the racial factor already mentioned; as instances may be given the tall Russian and the short Japanese. Growth depends upon the correlated activity of certain glands, which produce internal secretions. Something is known about the relationship of the thyroid, pituitary, thymus, and the generative glands to growth; qualitative and quantitative changes in the secretory activity of these glands may result in retarded or defective growth, in the production of dwarfs, or on the other hand in excessive growth, such as that of giants."

"These two extremes are pathological and would be rejected by a medical man. Puberty is generally accompanied by a marked accentuation of growth. Associated with the influence of the glands are the effects of nutrition, muscular work, and climate. A good supply of food, active exercise and exposure to the stimulating effects of a variable climate, such as our own, will produce a sturdy growth, but all these factors are subordinate to the racial influence."

"These considerations show that the selection of recruits requires as much intelligence and experience as the selection of horses or cattle. The tap-measure can never serve as an accurate guide. The 'points' of a soldier are related to the functions which he has to perform."

"The duty of a soldier is to defend whole heartedly the interests of his country. The test of his efficiency is not his height nor his weight nor his girth, but his ability to bear the physical and mental stress of active service. To march, to shoot straight, and to subordinate his own interests to those of the race. If the question be reviewed in this light, it will be obvious that physiology and psychology, the sciences which deal with the working of the body and mind, are involved more than anatomy, which is concerned with structure."

"At the present time, the desire of the short men to fight is a psychological testimonial of their value. They are willing to give up good positions, to undergo hardships and to bear, what is often the hardest part of all, the slight regard or even contempt for the short soldier. The volunteer is better than the pressed man. Cromwell's army, on the 'new model', showed the value of the psychological factor."

"The essential organs are in the head and trunk. These are often better developed in the short man than in the tall man. During the period, 1891-1902, the chief cause of the rejection of recruits for our Army was not defective stature. Most men were rejected because they were under chest measurement and under weight. The weight of the brain is relatively greater in the short man, but this anatomical fact is no evidence of quality. The reaction-time of the short man is not so long, and associated with this may be his greater alertness and pugnacity. The tall man, of full proportions, is generally heavy, docile, and slow."

"The physiological reasons for the greater agility and activity of the short man are well founded in the relation between the surface and the mass of the body. The small man possesses a relatively greater surface, and this, in many ways, is an advantage. His small size is in favour of rapidity of action, strength, and endurance. During muscular work in hot weather, he would be less liable to suffer from heat-stroke, for he has a relatively greater surface to expose to the cooling effect of the evaporation of sweat."

"There are mechanical advantages and disadvantages in height, but a consideration of these in relation to marching, digging, and exposure shows that the resultant is not against, but in favour of the short man under the conditions of modern warfare. The short man has a smaller weight of body to carry, and the weight of his clothing and equipment is less; he is lighter upon a horse; he does not require so deep a trench, and offers a smaller target to the enemy. He is more firmly placed upon his feet, for his centre of gravity is lower. It is true that in relation to his size he requires more food, drink, and clothing, but his absolute needs are less, and thus there is a saving to the transport."

"The short man need not fear a comparison in relation to his capacity for work, endurance, and resistance to disease. Sir Charles Cameron, in his evidence before the Committee on Physical Deterioration, mentions that the big men of the Cameron Highlanders were always the first to fall out on the march. This is what would be expected upon physiological grounds, for the essential and resisting part of a man are in his head and trunk, not in his lower limbs."

"The evidence from the fighting capacity of tall and short races or of tall or short men of the same race is not against the short man. Numerous instances could be obtained from the military history of recent times. The following figures, which were kindly supplied by Mr. J. M. Bulloch from his forthcoming book on 'Territorial Soldiering in the North-East of Scotland, 1759-1814', are of interest, for they relate to the Gordon Highlanders whose fighting capacity no one will question."

"The prevalent idea that they were gigantic men is quite erroneous. The average height of 914 of the first recruits to the Gordon Highlanders in 1794 was 5 ft. 5 ½ ins. Dr. J. F. Tocher, who examined the lists, found that the figures for stature were very similar to those he had obtained for Scottish populations of the present day."

"In conclusion, I wish to point out the danger of extremes. The man who comes up to the average of his countrymen is, other things being equal, the man to select, for it is probable that his development has proceeded along normal lines. There may be some abnormality, present or past, to account for the extremes in stature, but in the absence of such, there are strong physiological reasons in favour of the short man."

Dr. Leonard Hill agreed with the physiological tenets put forward by Dr. Pembrey, and held strongly that they should have bantam regiments. He found from a Japanese military friend that the Japanese ordinary standard was 5 ft. 3 in., but in a national emergency they went down to 5 ft., for soldiers, and it seemed to him "this country could go down to that too. There was everything in favour of the 5-foot man in regard to his power of endurance and of his size for lessening the danger of being shot."

Then he required less clothing, his boots would require less leather. When he got into the trenches and was exposed to cold, he required less shelter and was more easily wrapped up and protected. A long lean man was more exposed to cold in the trenches, and the trench would have to be deeper to conceal him.

Surgeon-General Evatt of Camberley said, "As regards height, those who have served throughout the Empire knew that the Gurkha, who is a small-sized man, is a splendid fighter. The prejudice in favour of the tall man was a survival of the old days of shock tactics, but in these days great campaigns were not won by shock tactics, and the question of height could be largely neglected."

In his own regiment, extra-tall men used to be put into the Grenadier Company, as there was an advantage in having big men to throw grenades, but now the specific function of grenadier had been abolished. Evatt attached no importance to the question of height in the soldier, if otherwise he was of good physical type.

It was left to the Institute's chairman, Surgeon-General Sir Launcelot Gubbins, to put the conclusions of his colleagues in clinching military terms. He considered that the chief point they had to consider was, what was the typical height of the race? If they took officers and men, there was a difference of at least two inches. The average height of cadets at Woolwich and Sandhurst was about 5 ft. 9 in. Two years ago, he made an inspection at Woolwich, and was shown a junior class, one hundred and twenty strong, officer material whose average height was 5 ft. 10 in. The "private soldier class" averaged about 5 ft. 7 in. The only way in which Gubbins thought could account for the difference was the benefits of better feeding and better sanitary surroundings.

For the "officer class," he would look on the most useful type as 5 ft. 9 in., and his experience was that the medium man was the best on active service and generally. "With regard to the bantams," Sir Launcelot concluded, "It is ridiculous to refuse a small man if he does not come up to the standard height, provided his physical requirements are otherwise good."

Reassuring as these findings were, the Army had already issued instructions to regimental headquarters all over Britain to begin active recruiting of Bantam troops, "so long as rigorous standards regarding medical fitness are observed."

The intensive campaign which ensued in the next few months to enlist short men was followed with unusually close interest by a general public one would have thought already blasé towards any new efforts devised to sign up the nation's young manhood for war. As a result, the general public, the clergy, and military men began to debate the issue in the press. Because the need for more British soldiers was already acute, most debaters came down strongly on the "pro" side for the Bantams, drowning out their critics and urging fullspeed recruitment.

Reverend John S. Vaughan, of St. Bede's College, Manchester, wrote: "From Caesar to Nelson, from Napoleon to our own Field Marshal Lord 'Bobs' Roberts, some of the greatest soldiers have been some of the smallest men."

A military officer added his voice in a magazine article which foreshadowed the short Asiatic soldiers who conquered Singapore and Saigon in future wars. Major Darnley Stuart-Stephens observed: "The restrictions as to height have shut out from the fighting line a large section of our manhood. There still remains in military circles in this country the old-time and surely absurd prejudice against the little men."

"When Russia embarked upon that stupendous campaign in the Far East, I heard long-legged officers of the Tsar's Imperial Guard speak with most absolute contempt of the cheek of the little Jap daring to throw down the glove to the long, stalwart soldiers of Russia. We since know what these so-called under-sized Japanese soldiers have done, and their little sailors, despite their want of height, proved that under Togo they were admirably efficient in the handling of the newest forms of naval armament. The little man in that war established himself as quite as good a fighter as the longer 'Ruski'."

But the bantam-sized applicants themselves had few delusions. Some, like George Hughes, wrote with straightforward simplicity about their personal desire to serve: "I am willing to join the Bantams. I have been rejected on three different occasions for Kitchener's Army because I am only 5 ft. 2¼ ins. In chest measurement I am 39½, and I am thirty-seven years old. We don't kid ourselves we are likely to be as useful as the Grenadier Guards, but give the little ones a chance to show their worth to King and Country!" His letter published in the press resulted in his acceptance at London Bridge recruiting office one week later.

Even the stages of music halls began to echo the Bantam call. Entertainers had already found that any patriotic theme was popular with audiences, so when Stephen West wrote a new song, with music by Edward Watson, it was soon being sung in theatres all over Britain. To modern ears, it has a crudely obvious naiveté, but when considered in the atmosphere of early 1915, it was no doubt thought to be a cheerful ditty as well as being an effective singing commercial for recruitment.

> "Have you ever seen a Bantam in a fight?
> No other bird can 'stick it.'
> Like a Bantam, or can 'lick it,'
> And you never saw a Bantam taking fright!
>
> So what does it matter what the height may be?
> If it's five foot one or five foot ten?
> If a Briton's heart beats right,
> And he's longing for a fight,
> And the Dear Old Country calls out now for Men?"

It could have been response to the rooster symbol that appeared everywhere on hoardings, posters, and omnibuses, or perhaps something about the very jauntiness of the miniature soldiers themselves who offered to fight alongside larger men. Whatever the reason, the civilian population took the Bantams to their hearts. Bantam picture postcards, souvenir drinking-mugs, songs and poems, even embroidered cushion-covers blossomed in 1915 Britain to salute "the wee heroes."

This popular interest, so high at the time, makes today's scanty knowledge of the Bantams all the more puzzling. The commanding officer of a famed regiment, which once readily recruited an entire battalion of Bantams, evidently knew so little of his own unit's history he frostily dismissed my enquiries with, "It is very unlikely that we would have ever had such sub-standard men in our ranks."

Another unit's museum curator thought, "Such battalions were never used for much more than as labour or reserve troops." One regimental secretary was surprised when he doubtfully checked into the matter, and wrote, "We found after all that we did indeed have Bantams. Not much more than a couple of lines in the records about them, though." A Ph.D. research specialist in Leeds University military history department did not bother to do his homework, only sneering, "It is hardly worthy of study, as the Bantams were complete failures."

The sacrifice, the spirit, and the contributions of the Bantams are now virtually unknown. Yet they once proudly shared the exploits of some of the finest fighting regiments in the British army.

CHAPTER FOUR

The Devil Dwarfs

For years after after the end of the Great War, on each November 11th, at precisely at eleven o'clock in the morning, the haunting melody of bagpipes playing "The Flowers O' The Forest" would skirl across the hushed back streets around Lyons Road, Glasgow. Women and children huddled close in doorways and stern-faced men pulled off cloth caps while they watched the kilted pipemajor march slowly back and forth.

As the wailing tune died away, there would be a silence broken only by the sound of women's sobs and the fluttering of red, white, and blue bunting strung overhead. All eyes would turn to look at the corner of Garscube Road. There stood a giant black cross adorned with a wreath of poppies, and beside it a Roll of Honour in a golden frame, brought out from Kieran's Bar for the day.

The scroll had on it the names of dozens of Lyons Road men who had left that one short street to die in the First World War. It is said there were proportionally more killed from the small road than any other in Scotland. Among the names were over a score of men who served as Bantams. They and their comrades were remembered by this unique ceremony which was repeated each Armistice Day for over twenty years.

At the end of two minutes silence, another soldier would step forward, put a bugle to his lips and play "The Last Post." After the brassy salute died away, the two riflemen marched briskly back to Maryhill Barracks. The Highland Light Infantry had honoured its dead once more.

From Hong Kong to Halifax, wherever the British Army served, there were few warnings able to drain the ruddy cheeks of Sergeant-Majors or strike dread into Military Policemen as could the simple words, "The H.L.I. are coming!"

Recruited mainly in the streets of Glasgow and industrial towns along the Clyde, not many members of the Highland Light Infantry had so much as ever seen a heather-covered mountain. Yet if their regimental name belied their origin, it certainly described their ability. As infantry, the H.L.I. were arch-typical fighting soldiers. Zestfully as ready to punch-up a pubful of English soldiers as to storm a German trench, their quarrelsome reputation was legendary.

Though all the regiment had a special relationship with the civilians of Glasgow, there was a special affection for the "wee fellas" of the 18th Battalion. Over two hundred thousand men and women from the city were to serve in various armed forces during the Great War, yet few drew greater crowds than those which gathered to see the H.L.I. Bantams strutting along.

The onlookers would often call out jeers—"Look oot, laddies, there's a big cat loose!" and, "Dinna trip o'er yon matchstick!"—among the cheers, but the fondness was there for these men who seemed to represent the spirit of Glasgow's anonymous "little man in the street," and his cocky resentment of anyone placed over him in temporary wartime authority.

Local folk were also proud of the fact that the 18th was originally raised in direct defiance of the War Office. When an offer was made in early 1915 to recruit a Bantam Scottish battalion, the authorities in London curtly refused to sanction its formation. Not in the least discouraged, the Rotary Club, the Lord Provost, and the City Fathers set up a recruiting organization anyway. Within hours, over 1200 men sent in their names to join.

Setting a target of a full battalion, a Bantam Recruiting Week was inaugurated on February 16th, 1915. City tramcars were placarded with the slogan, "Bantams For The Front—3,000 Wanted—Apply 46 Bath Street." Soon after the drive was completed, the promoters were able to approach the War Office again, with two thousand recruits already formed into an over-strength battalion. The authorities this time graciously accepted, and the unit went into training at Girvan, Ayrshire.

Long before they reached France, the cantankerous 18th battalion had earned their nickname, "The Devil Dwarfs." It was soon awarded for their record for brawling and general mischief which almost eclipsed even the awesome reputation of their sister battalions in the H.L.I.

Alec Findlay witnessed over forty men being paraded for disciplinary sentences after a particularly riotous night before. The Company Sergeant Major added his own contribution to the C.O.'s punishments, by royally tongue-lashing the unrepentant group in forceful and obscene terms.

Exhausting his lengthy vocabulary of abuse, the CSM turned his scowling face away to hide a reluctant grin. "Ach, tak' the wee bastards away," he whispered. "There's no' a man o' them I wouldna' be proud tae lead o'er the top!"

For all their recalcitrance, they had proved to be readily trained into smart soldiers on the barrack square and the assault course. They excelled at foot drill and seemed tireless on route marches. One incident which particularly endeared the battalion to Glaswegians was when the 18th made a forced march from Girvan to Ballantrae.

They set out with a well-known police band in the lead, but when the march ended the police had all dropped out along the way. That the "Peelers" could not stand the pace set by the Bantams was a small triumph for the troops and for those of their back-street neighbours whose relationship with the police was not always cordial.

While these fierce Scots began training, greater impetus was put behind the campaign already underway to recruit several similar—if hopefully more manageable—battalions in England. The authorities had been impressed by the success of independent civic enterprise in Birkenhead and Glasgow in raising Bantam units so quickly. Such enthusiastic response and the evident surplus of volunteers spurred the generals to instruct several regiments to recruit enough bantams to form an entire army division.

This was an ambitious enterprise, as a division was composed of slightly more than twenty thousand men. Each division had three infantry brigades, plus artillery, engineers, medical and transport services. Brigades usually had four infantry battalions, of about one thousand men each.

The physical toughness of miners being already well noted, efforts to build the 35th and 40th Bantam Divisions were particularly directed towards those regions of England and Scotland where pit-workers were numerous. As the Welsh National Executive Committee was at the time looking after its own recruiting, that area was treated as a separate case. (The sensitive political situation in Ireland precluded putting in a further unit recruiting campaign there, and it was rightly assumed that there would soon be no lack of Irish applicants, anyway.) However, all counties were surveyed, whether they had collieries or not, to select the most likely regiments to host this particular type of Kitchener battalions.

Even in peacetime, crowded Lancashire had always been a ready source of recruits for the army. For instance, the Lancashire Fusiliers began the war with eight battalions, a large component of Britain's peacetime army. Before the Great War ended, the regiment had expanded to thirty-three battalions.

The region was the home of several famous county regiments, four of which were instructed in December, 1914, to raise Bantam units among other new Service battalions being formed. A large reservoir of suitable men was already known to be available in the mining towns and cotton-working cities there.

The Bantam recruiting drive through the Palatinate made frequent reference to a comment by one Dr. E. H. T. Nash, "The Lancashire miner is much the same type as the Welsh. They are sturdy and hard as nails, and better fighting and more quarrelsome men you could not find. The authorities could take five-foot two-inch men from among this class and raise some of the finest battalions possible." It became a phrase repeated so often that one luckless recruiter mouthing it in Salford was hooted off his street-corner platform by a group of miners passing by on their way to enlist at the Town Hall.

There was then still a strong tradition of local involvement with regiments, making the raising of military units an intensely personal matter. So it was that again one man spearheaded Bantam recruitment, as was often to be the case.

Sir Ryland Adkin, M.P., obtained the consent of the War Office to raise a Bantam unit in the LF regimental area, and formed a committee of powerful no-nonsense Lancashiremen to get the project moving without delay. Funds, supplies, publicity and industrial and civic support was assured with the impressive line-up of talent Sir Ryland put to work—Sir F. Cawley M.P., Sir G. Toulman M.P., Mr. T. C. Taylor M.P., the Mayors of Bury, Rochdale, Middleton and Heywood, the chairmen of the District Councils of Radcliffe, Ramsbottom, Whitefield, and Wardle, the Rev. J. C. Hill, Rector of Bury, Colonels R. W. Deane, G. E. Wike, and C. L. Robinson, and Major B. Smythe.

The committee named Colonel Wike, former C.O. of the 5th Battalion, to be the official raiser. When he opened his recruiting campaign on January 2nd, 1915, the response was overwhelming. The 17th Battalion reached its full strength of one thousand three hundred and fifty within five days, and assembled them at their depot in Oldham, under the command of Lieut. Colonel W. J. McWhinnie.

By January 20th, the 18th Battalion was also up to full establishment in their depot at Garswood, commanded by Lt.-Col.R. A. Irvine. There was such a volume of volunteers, that the Lancashire Fusiliers were able to form yet another Bantam battalion, the 20th raised by Mr. Montague Barlow, M.P. at Salford, with Lt. Colonel C. R. G. Mayne, D.S.O. in command. These units were grouped in the 35th Division's 104th Brigade, along with the 23rd Battalion, The Manchester Regiment.

The latter was raised by the Lord Mayor and placed under Lt.-Col.Sir Henry Hill at a separate depot in Morecambe. A famed city regiment, the Manchesters had been active in wars since before the American Revolution, where they first took their nickname of "The Bloodsuckers." This derived from the shape of their fleur-de-lis cap-badge, jokingly said to resemble the fever mosquitos which had thinned the regiment's ranks in the swamps of New Jersey.

Their Bantam component, officially known as the 23rd (Service) Battalion (8th City), The Manchester Regiment, reached full establishment by the end of December, 1914, largely due to the organizing ability of Mr. D. E. Anderson of the National Service League.

The Manchester Bantams filled their ranks so quickly that it caught the imagination of another newspaperman: "Many collier lads were forthcoming last evening. Some of them had gone straight to the Town Hall from the pits. As a class they were said to be a sturdy set of fellows, and men who will make capital fighters. Among the acceptances last evening was a youth from Glossop, who was drenched to the skin, and who had the appearance of having walked the dozen miles in the rain. The attestation form of another of last night's recruits showed that he was the father of no fewer than eight children under fifteen years of age."

Though there was a large number of coal-miners from Wigan in its ranks, the 23rd also attracted many city office-workers and prosperous businessmen. This mixture formed a highly disciplined unit, based more on friendship than on fear, a delicate balance which was typical of the "Pals" battalions being raised all over Britain.

The 105th Brigade was composed of the 15/16 Cheshires, the 14th Gloucesters, and the 15th Sherwood Foresters. The two pioneer Cheshire units were by now well established, under the respective leadership of Lieut. Colonels. F. H. M. Newell and R. Browne-Clayton. Proper military uniforms had been issued, some unfit men weeded out, and a programme of regular military training was underway. Living conditions had been greatly improved for the rankers, after being forced for a while to endure uncomfortable living quarters in bell-tents, relieved only by the kindness of local citizens.

Miss F. Musgrave tells how when her father heard of the Bantams being camped at the nearby Bebington Show Ground in very primitive conditions, he converted part of his home into a meeting place for the young recruits. "He had an extra bath-tub installed, complete with a huge boiler, so that the youngsters were able to come there for a hot bath. Afterwards, they could chat with their comrades in comparative comfort, play games, or read the books and magazines the family provided in an adjoining room."

The men were moved into a number of schools in the area, one of which was Ionic Street School in Rock Ferry. They were amused to note that they entered their billets through a door marked "Infants Department." Dozens of neighbours there adopted the men.

"I lived with my family alongside the Ionic Street School and I can still remember the Bantams marching down Lees Avenue," said Mrs. Harriet Williams, "They were a fine lot of chaps and my dear old mother was very good to them. She used to wash their shirts and socks, and many a jug of cocoa was given to them at nights when they would come on over to our house for a few hours for relaxation."

"They would cause much laughter among our family of twelve with their merry jokes and carefree disposition. They were stationed in the school for several months and I can still remember hearing the bugle playing reveille at five in the morning, and half an hour later the bugle calling the Bantams to the cook house."

"In 1914, I was a 15 year-old girl and employed at a confectioners' shop," recalls Mrs. Amy Swift. "One day we looked out of the window and saw a band of rather small soldiers marching by. We found out that these were the Bantams. They were stationed in a school very near to the shop. Most days or nights they would come in for a ham sandwich and a mug. of tea. Sandwiches cost two pence and the tea a halfpenny."

"They were a grand little band of men; always cheerful and bright, and flirtatious without being rude, but they did not seem to have much money to spend. I served them with sandwiches and many a mug of tea, for which I did not charge them. They sometimes joked about their own lack of inches, but they were the grandest bunch of men I ever knew."

"After a time, they moved on and we were outside the shop waving them goodbye. That was the last I saw of the Bantams.

Later we heard what had happened to them in the trenches, and remembered them with pity."

When the two battalions left Birkenhead for training at Masham, Yorkshire, and his original idea was adopted on a national scale, Alfred Bigland went on to aid Britain's war effort elsewhere. His administrative ability was recognized by the government, which appointed him a Deputy Director of Munitions. He set to work re-organizing Merseyside soap-factories in a massive programme to manufacture glycerine for high-explosives.

He was later sent to the United States as co-ordinator of food purchasing, a job he did so well as to be later credited with helping avoid what could have been severe food shortages in Britain. In any field, Bigland had a rare ability—he got things done.

This redoubtable Member of Parliament had his final moment of local glory on Sunday, March 21st, 1915. That day, Bigland stood with Lord Kitchener on the steps of St. George's Hall, Liverpool, to review a march-past of twelve New Army units, including the Cheshire Bantams.

. In the next couple of days, the Commander-in-Chief reviewed troops throughout Lancashire, paying flying visits to Salford, Bury, and Manchester. Each time, there were Bantams marching by, and Kitchener picked them out in his speeches as symbols of the nation's fighting spirit.

One witness was Harry Stanton, then a lieutenant in The Manchester Regiment. "After the march-past in Albert Square, Kitchener made a complimentary speech about the smartness of the Bantam troops. However, one-aspect of the parade disquieted Kitchener. While the men had been recruited in the Wigan and Manchester regions, the officers had been selected by the War Office. By some quirk of administrative planning, officers posted to the 23rd Battalion were mostly men of six feet or taller."

"FM Kitchener was devastatingly critical of this fact, pointing out that in action the officers would be immediately singled out as an easy target for snipers. It was therefore ordained that all the officers in the Brigade should be measured individually, and the thirty or so of the shortest (5 ft. 9 in. or so) should be drafted to the 23rd Battalion, and those of great height should be posted to other battalions of the Brigade."

About this time, the vagaries of army routine had also brought the 16th Cheshires an incongruous new recruit in the lanky 6 ft. 5 in. shape of Benjamin Pierson. After being rejected by several regiments because of his great height, he was finally accepted by the Cheshires, who assigned him to the Bantams, of all units. His disconcerted superiors responded by promptly making him a sergeant. Fortunately, he proved to be popular with the men, who accepted without resentment the tall rookie being promoted so quickly.

The incongruity of Sgt. Pierson towering over his charges became one of the entertainments of the parade-ground. As he was still somewhat vague about military matters, his platoon would good-naturedly chorus their own drill orders, then march and counter-march, slope and present arms, over and over until the privates had taught the sergeant. This turnabout method was so effective that "Lofty" Pierson eventually gained the skills of a first-class drill instructor.

There is a fine line dividing well-trained troops from over-trained troops. This comes when men are held under iron discipline month after month—marched, paraded, put through foot drill, rifle drill, bayonet work, and bombing practice, polished, spruced, and generally trained to respond immediately to any order. The intent behind such relentless drilling is ideally to make the men able to save their own lives in an emergency by responding to orders instantly, without conscious thought.

However, if the process is drawn out too long, men can become over-trained, and discipline tends to deteriorate the moment this feeling sets in. Some Cheshires had been moved again, and spent many months at Kinmel Park Camp in Wales. There, in cold rainy conditions, they began to feel the strain of training and the daily uncertainty of not knowing when they would be shipped to France.

Some of the instructors brought to the battalion late in the training programme had not settled in to share the feeling of esprit de corps with the Bantams. One such sergeant was a particularly vile-tempered disciplinarian. He began to pick on one soldier in particular, a young man by the name of Jenner. The sergeant took every opportunity to badger Jenner on the most petty details of discipline, from continual orders to get his hair cut to assigning him to the more dirty fatigue duties around camp. The charges laid by the sergeant against Jenner were more and more serious in their penalties, until Jenner was put into seven days detention.

On the last day of Jenner's sentence, the camp was electrified by the news that a large draft of men was due to go to France. The men began to crowd around the headquarters notice board, scanning it for their names. The bullying sergeant, towering above the rest of the troops, had just walked up to the board when a rifle shot rang out. The bullet narrowly missed the sergeant, went through a soldier's body, ricocheted off a tree trunk, then slammed into another soldier's chest. The men took full advantage of their training and scattered from the scene.

NCOs carried away one dead soldier and one seriously injured man. Company Sergeant Major James Swarburgh and Sergeant Brian unlocked the door of the nearby guardroom, and found Jenner lying on the floor moaning, "I didn't mean to hit them." He had pulled a ventilator brick out of the bottom of the hut wall and fired through there.

Before the court martial for murder, CQMS Swarburgh was called to see the Colonel, who said to him, "I'm sorry for you Swarburgh. You're a good man, but you realize it is your career on the line as well, as it was you who issued a weapon to the prisoner." The Supplies Sergeant went back to his office and spent the entire night studying the King's Regulations, and eventually found the regulation he had followed, stating that a prisoner must have his full equipment available for cleaning purposes when preparing to go on active service. As Jenner was on the overseas draft, Swarburgh had been in his rights to issue the man his unloaded rifle. How he obtained a live round of ammunition was a mystery.

However, the CQMS was a principal witness at the trial, which was soon held before Chief Justice Bray. The prosecuting counsel said in his speech, "The rifle was pointed in the direction of the murdered man." Jenner shouted from the dock, "Sir, the rifle was *pointing*!"

The "Prisoner's Friend"—an officer appointed as defence counsel—took up this point. The court chose to agree that there was sufficient ambiguity between the two words to cast doubt on any intent to murder, and Jenner's life was saved. He was declared guilty on the reduced charge of manslaughter, and received a sentence of eighteen years in prison.

The bullying NCO who was unofficially known to have been the real target of the shot, was quietly transferred to another regiment immediately after the trial. Months later in France, when the Bantams were stationed near the other regiment, Jenner's comrades could be seen fingering their rifles as they wistfully enquired about the whereabouts of a certain sergeant.

In May, attention was turned to the West Country and along the Bristol Channel, from where men of the Gloucester Regiment had left to gain battle honours in a dozen past wars. One adventure gained the regiment the exclusive right to wear its Sphinx badge at both the front and back of the hat, to commemorate their fighting back-to-back at the battle of Alexandria in 1801.

(A later distinction to the Glosters' uniform, added in 1951, was the blue ribbon of a U.S. Presidential Unit Citation awarded in Korea.) Their marching song, "The Slashers," is said to echo the time in the American Revolutionary War when some troops removed the ears of a judge they considered to have illtreated a woman.

The work was taken up with practiced-skill by the Bristol Citizens' Recruiting Committee, which had already formed seven new "K-Force" units for the "Glorious Glosters" as the county regiment was fondly known. Enjoying a glamourous local fame, the unit was able to quickly draw more than enough recruits to fill the ranks of the 14th (Service) Battalion, (West of England Bantams).

To bring in rural applicants, posters were displayed outside village pubs, put up near village greens, and even on trees at crossroads through the Forest of Dean, where many miners lived. The wording proved to be effective: "Lord Kitchener has heard that there are plenty of little and good men in Gloucestershire. The War Office has therefore instructed the Bristol Recruiting Committee to proceed at once with raising a West of England. Posters announced:

BANTAM BATTALION
Height 5 ft. 3 in. Chest expansion 34 inches
Enlist at the nearest recruiting office !

The response was particularly good in the city of Birmingham where there were then a large number of undersized workers. Officers were mostly Bristol men as was the original commanding officer, Major John Carr, previously the Chief Recruiting Officer for the city. A Birmingham teenager named George Palmer joined the battalion, "to see what I was made of." He was to change from a sheltered youth to a battle-hardened soldier within a year.

About this time the regiment also took on strength an unusually tenacious recruit. James J. Blake was a mere 4 ft. 10 in height and could not be taken seriously by any of the eighteen regiments he approached. For his nineteenth attempt, Blake wrote directly to the King, asking for Royal intervention. A few weeks later, he received a letter from Buckingham Palace which he took along to Bristol. The august introduction had the desired effect and, virtually in minutes, he joined the 14th Battalion as Private No. 27026. Suitably enough, Blake later became Champion Bantamweight Boxer of the B.E.F. in France.

After a few months of strenuous training at Ashton Gate, deliberately hard so as to shake out weaker men, the battalion was pronounced to be "a remarkably intelligent and smart body of men." They were dubbed "Bristol's Fighting-Cocks" by the local citizenry, who gave them a hearty reception when they marched through the streets. The 14th Gloucesters left the city in August, 1915, went off to Chisledon, Wiltshire to become part of the 35th Division. Training was increased in tempo, with unusually practical emphasis on trench warfare, and they were to find themselves in France just nine months after their formation.

"Robin Hood's Own," the jocular name for The Sherwood Foresters (Nottinghamshire & Derbyshire Regiment), recruited its 15th Battalion within ten days of April 10, 1915, when Nottingham city council authorized £1000 to fund a Bantam unit. The regiment kept alive its association with that romantic outlaw by wearing a green diamond "flash" on the back of their uniforms' collar. However, there was no memory of verdant woods for the nine hundred and fifty stunted men who left pit-villages and lace-factories in the two counties to enlist in the 15th Battalion at Normanton Depot, Derby. They were also joined by recruits from elsewhere in Britain, one of whom was a 19-year-old Oldham cotton-worker named John Taylor.

"We were sent to Nottingham Barracks, where we drew equipment at the near-by Lace Market. Each morning, all four companies had to fall in at the Guildhall, then march into the famous Sherwood Forest. There, we would do the usual square-bashing all morning. In the afternoon we were taken to the embankment alongside the River Trent and given more training."

"We were billeted in private homes; mine being on Huntingdon Street, with three other chaps. Our good landlady, Mrs. Hill, fed us well, and gave us a special treat each Saturday dinner. The two older men got a bottle of beer each, while we teenagers received a bottle of lemonade. When asked why we couldn't have beer, too, Mrs. Hill replied that we were too young for strong drink. Ten months later in France, we needed both strong drink and strong stomachs!"

The 106th Brigade was composed of Northerners—the 17th. Royal Scots, 17th. West Yorkshires, and the 19th. Durham Light Infantry, each a battalion in regiments famed for rock-like reliability.

The Royal Scots were the senior regiment of British infantry-of-the-line, of such early origin that they proudly called themselves "Pontius Pilate's Bodyguard." The raising of a Bantam battalion in Edinburgh was the personal project of Lord Rosebery. Before war was declared, that modest aristocrat had made several unpopular speeches appealing for a peaceful settlement with Germany, but when hostilities began, he gave his total support to the patriotic effort.

A tireless public speaker, he made a series of speeches at rallies throughout Scotland, urging that "The war must be fought to the bitter end, with no patched-up truce!" He daily addressed huge crowds in Edinburgh. At one of these gatherings, on New Year's Eve, he pleaded earnestly for more Bantam battalions to be raised.

As his opening theme, Lord Rosebery quoted exerpts from a Dublin pamphlet published long ago, in 1733, entitled "The Humble Remonstrance of the Five-Foot Highians Against the Unchristian Practice of Using A Height Standard In Enlisting Soldiers." In part, this read "We believe that it will not be very easy to show that an inch of a man's height is any substantial proof of his capacity to serve the government, or that a man will make one bit the better soldier for being as tall as a church steeple."

"Is not courage the principal qualification in a soldier? Is courage to be measured by the yard? And, since the invention of firearms, have not the five-footians a manifest advantage over your long-legged gentry? Cannot they draw a trigger as well as the tallest Guardsman in the Prussian service?"

There were eight pages in this vein, echoing some forgotten plea by British bantam soldiers of two hundred years before, and Lord Rosebery's practised tones read out every word to support his argument. He made the same speech several times, with the result that the 17th Royal Scots soon had more applicants than could be accepted and the unit was dubbed "Rosebery's Own." At first, there was neither uniforms nor billets for the men, so each was sent away after being signed up, with a primrose badge in his lapel and instructions to return when called. The unit could just as aptly have been called "Rotary's Own," as that organization's past-president, Mr. I. P. Dobbie had first proposed a "Short Stature" battalion on December 4, 1914.

The Edinburgh Rotary Club appointed a Lord Rosebery Royal Scots Recruiting Committee, headed by Mr. Dobbie and W. L. Sleigh. The executive committee mobilized 1000 men, paid for their housing in St. Leonard's School, arranged for old soldiers to drill them in King's Park, and tried to obtain suitable uniforms. Lacking an official supply, Rotarian Alex Wilkie cleared out his factory, brought in sewing machines and operators, and produced virtually tailor-made uniforms in a matter of days. Thus, yet another Bantam battalion had been quickly formed by individual enterprise. On January 20, 1915, the smartly dressed 17th. Royal Scots went on parade to be inspected by Lord Rosebery and their new commander Lt. Colonel R.D. Cheales.

Within three months of the outbreak of war, seventeen new Service battalions had been formed by The Prince of Wales' Own (West Yorkshire Regiment). The largest county in England, Yorkshire spawns tough, stolid folk who have manned a half dozen famous regiments for centuries. Like them, the West Yorkshires have always fought in a way that reflects their flat, direct manner; calmly warning enemies, "Tha'd best get out't road, or 'appen tha'll get a bloody nose!"

The regiment was raised in the West Riding, an area of open rolling moors and large wool-working cities. It proved a ready source of recruits who formed what was to be one of the most highly-decorated Bantam battalion of the war. The 17th. West Yorks was raised in December, 1915, by J. E. Bedford, Lord Mayor of Leeds. Shepherds, farm labourers, and miners came in from tiny villages to join up with hundreds of wool-workers from Bradford and Leeds, particularly from the Holbeck area.

In Yorkshire, it's not what you say that counts, it's what you do. That Yorkshire people have an unfounded reputation for being tight-fisted with money was again proven by their generous donation of funds and hospitality towards maintenance of the 17th. West Yorks. For many months, the 17th. battalion was a civic unit, even wearing the Leeds City coat of arms as its cap-badge. Not until August, 1915, did the War Department take over the battalion, when it began to wear the Hanover Horse badge of The West Yorkshire Regiment.

In the meantime, the Leeds Bantams drilled busily away on Holbeck Moor, under the stentorian orders of Regimental Sergeant Major Archer, an imposing figure with bristling red hair and waxed moustaches. By May, he had them smart enough to match even his exacting standards when the city turned out to cheer them on parade for Lieut. Colonel F. N. Atkinson and be marched off to Masham Camp.

The little men strutted jauntily away to the rousing music of "Ca Ira," the West Yorkshire's regimental march. A newspaperman commented, "There surely has not been a more sprightly tread of boot-heels since the West Yorks stole the tune from the French they defeated in 1793!"

Ringing in their ears was a speech by Lord Mayor Bedford predicting that the Leeds Bantams would one day be likened to Gurkhas when their turn came for fighting. This prediction was proven true time and again over the next two and a half bitter years, winning the battalion one Victoria Cross, a Distinguished Service Order, three Military Crosses, and two dozen Distinguished Conduct Medals and Military Medals. The cost of the stubborn courage of these tiny Yorkshiremen later sent entire villages and towns into mourning for the eleven officers and two hundred and seventy soldiers who were killed—a fatal casualty rate of over twenty-five percent.

Half a century later, on December 12, 1968, people stood in the streets of old Durham City weeping for the passing away of an entire regiment. On that day, the Colours of the Durham Light Infantry were laid to rest in the Cathedral for the last time. The ceremony marked the end of the 210-year saga of one of the finest fighting regiments in the British Army—a victim of financial constraints and bureaucracy which merged the DLI with three other disbanded regiments into The Light Infantry.

Soldiering has long been a tradition in County Durham, back to when it was the buffer-zone south of Hadrian's Roman Wall built to hold back the Scottish tribes. Viking raids and Danish settlers there instilled their descendants with enough warlike qualities of resistance to invaders that William the Conqueror's alien garrison at Durham City was wiped out. Norman reprisals were so severe that every town was laid waste and the population was decimated so that much of the region remains sparsely populated to this day.

It was a mainly local private army which defeated the invading Scots at Neville's Cross, as the post of Bishop of Durham was for centuries more a military than religious function. The Palatinate was virtually autonomous for centuries, and Durhamites and Tynesiders played such a key role in the successful cause of King George I against the Scots that they are to this day known as "Geordies."

Politically and geographically isolated for generations, and enduring a hard struggle for sustenance, it is not surprising that Durham folk developed their own distinct characteristics, almost their own language. Though markedly blunt in speech, which discourages conceit in others, their conversation is warmly sprinkled with the endearments "pet" and "hinny." However, it is often difficult for the uninitiated visitor to understand exactly what a Durhamite is saying in his rapid, singsong accent.

The Scandinavian influence is still strong in speech cadence, and many local words are not heard anywhere else—"plodgin" for wading, "clarty" for muddy, "haem" for home. They are also much inclined to assure one with "Why, aye, man!" rather than a mere "Yes." Overlaying dozens of these quaint words, is also "Pitmatic," an almost secret dialect developed among Durham coalminers who formed a large part of the county's inhabitants. So incomprehensible is it to outsiders, this language drove some Southern recruiting officers wild when the Durham Light Infantry began its phenomenal expansion in the Great War.

"The Faithful Durhams" had done well in scores of foreign wars, most recently the Boer War, when six battalions was considered a large body of troops. Always up to strength in peacetime, the D.L.I. had no problem in recruiting ten "K-Force" units in the last three months of 1914. By war's end, the Durham Light Infantry was to raise 37 battalions, a nigh incredible number from a small county which then had only about half a million males in the population.

A government health survey at the turn of the century commented on the short stature of people in Durham mining villages. "The typical miner is inclined to smallness, with short legs and the chest protruding." With a tradition of underground work from long before the industrial revolution, the Durham miner was shaped by heredity and generations of troglodyte employment. Poorly fed, worked hard from childhood on 12-hour shifts amidst dirt and danger, the Durham miners would emerge filthy from the pit, with hawk-like eyes and nothing much to look forward to each day beyond the ritual scrubbing.

Now, society was about to lure them out of the dripping coalmines and march them away from their long rows of one-up-one-down company housing to fight a bloody war. Even that escape might have seemed an attractive alternative to what they were used to, as the 19th (Bantam) Battalion, D.L.I. was fully mustered shortly after its announcement by the Durham Parliamentary Recruiting Committee.

Men streamed in from collieries at Percy Main and Esh Winning; from Shillbottle where men worked stripped naked because of the heat underground; from Washington, where had originated the ancestors of America's first President; and from pits at Morpeth, Cowpen, and Blaydon Main, and a dozen other coal-workings. Among them was 5ft. 2in. Joseph William Stones, a 23-year-old coal miner from Crook, who volunteered for service in the DLI, despite being married and having two small children. When he 'took the King's shilling' in West Hartlepool in March, 1915, it was his first fateful move towards a tragic destiny and public notoriety decades later. He would share this fate with two other Durham young men who joined the DLI Bantams in almost the same week—Peter Goggins of Stanley and John McDonald of Sunderland.

Doctors were horrified at the condition of a batch of bantam miner volunteers from Monkwearmouth Colliery, whose bodies were covered with carbuncles and huge open sores caused by years of working in hot salt water seeping down from the North Sea far above the mine tunnels.

Bantams also stepped forward from the shipyards of Sunderland and Gateshead, and lead-miners walked down out of the Pennines to converge on the battalion's depot at the Cooperative Building in West Hartlepool. There, the unit's first commanding officer, Lt. Colonel W. Thomlinson spread his energies between drilling his men and directing a colourful recruiting campaign.

The heady lure of enlistment fever prevalent then is described by Edwin Lofthouse, who joined the 19th D.L.I. at eighteen. "Just imagine a military band marching down the streets, all in bright uniforms and playing stirring tunes. One's eyes took in the regular pattern of the uniforms and the precise steps of the soldiers, and then the ear took special notice of the quick rhythm of the tunes, and one's heart started beating to the music. So much so, that one's feet were soon marching along with the soldiers."

"In this atmosphere, the crowd was drawn to some central place, where a recruiting address was given, and on the platform were some beautiful ladies who as their part in the war effort were prepared to give every man who joined a kiss. This then was the path which eventually led me straight into Hell itself."

Private Billy Watson of the 19th Durham Light Infantry was late in leaving his home in the mountains near Wearhead to return from embarkation leave. "When I started walking back down the road towards Durham, the sky turned dark and before very long I was struggling with my full pack, kitbag, and rifle through a heavy blizzard. The snow got thicker and thicker, it became dark, and there was not another soul on the road. I kept hoping that someone with a horse and cart would come by," he recalled. "But thre was nobody on the highroad, nor a light to be seen anywhere."

"Just when I thought I was going to freeze to death, a woman's voice called out, 'You look perished, hinny.' She said. "Better come haem with me." She was a farmer's wife from the look of her, and we walked a long way across fields and moorland, than over a couple of short hills, until we came to a cozy-looking farm-house. We were greeted at the door by the canniest [prettiest] lass I had ever seen. She had red hair and lots of freckles, you know. She greeted me shyly and I followed her inside where there was an old man sitting with his dog alongside a roaring coal fire."

"He welcomed me and handed me some pipe tobacco, which was a great luxury at that time, and told me to keep the tin for mysel. The two women prepared a meal of boiled poatoes mashed with milk, and cups of strong black tea. There was a strange smell in the room and a strange look to the old man that I did not recognize at the time. Later, when I had seen active service, I knew the look and smell to be that of a man who is about to die soon."

"Although none of us spoke much, I remember that night as one of the happiest I ever spent in my life," said Watson. "The girl and I got on well together, and I can say now that I fell fond of her right on the spot and sensed she was feeling the same way about me. I remember how her mother, the old woman—although she can't have been that old really—seemed to spot what was going on, and I would catch her smiling to herself as she looked at the pair of us. Even the dog took to me, and he would spend a lot of time with his paw on my knee as I rubbed his ear and stroked his neck. I took notice of the handmade collar on the dog. It had bronze studs in an old strip of leather."

"I slept there by the fire in a chair that night, as they had not a spare bed for me. I awoke next morning to find the lass making me breakfast of porridge. I said goodbye to the old man and was walked to the front gate by the mother and the girl. The old woman said her goodbyes first and walked back to the house leaving me with the girl. We didn't say much, but I touched her hand and said, 'I reckon I'll be back.' She smiled, sort of shy, you know, and said, 'I do hope you will.'"

"I walked away laden down with my army kit, plodgin through the deep snow which was still falling. I turned back once and she was still there, a little figure waving to me though the flurries. I went over the hill the way they had pointed, and after a long time found the road again and marched off to war."

Private Watson fought in the trenches for over two years with only one leave in all that time. He managed to get home in the summer of 1918 for seven days. He spent all of that time walking across the hills in the area he guessed the farmhouse would be, vainly searching for the family that had been so kind to him during the blizzard.

"You see, I know it sounds strange now," said Watson, "But I had never thought to ask their last name and they never asked for mine. So I didn't know even their name to ask neighbours whereabouts the farm might be. I thought about that lass every night and every day while I was in the trenches. As soon as I was released from the army in 1919, I came home to Weardale and started to look about for her. I searched for many a night and every weekend, for I was back at my job of mining, one of the lucky ones. But no matter how much I roamed thereabouts, I couldn't find anything that looked like their farm."

"After a while, I gave up looking properly, but of a Sunday, I would still find myself taking a walk up and down the high road still half-searching. A few years later, maybe 1922 or so, I was sitting on a bank having a smoke, thinking about that girl as a matter of fact, when I looked down and there was her dog. Sure as I stand here, it was her dog. The same black and white old dog with the same copper-studded leather collar. I was so startled, I could hardly speak for fear the dog was a ghost."

"Then I began to talk to him and he wagged his tail, and put his paw on my knee as he had done five or six years before. All that afternoon, I tried to get the dog to walk away so that I could follow him, but as much as I shouted to him, the more he wanted to stay. In the end I walked away back home and he followed me for a while, but when I looked around, he'd gone into the dark. So I never did find that canny lass again, and all my life I've felt sad about losing her and wondered how it might have been if we had met up again."

By mid-1915, the three infantry brigades were ready for grouping as a division, and in June they began assembling at Masham Camp, Yorkshire. The 35th (Bantam) Division was officially formed on July 5th, 1915, under the command of Major General R. J. Pinney.

The decision to place General Pinney in charge of the unconventional new force was a remarkably good one. Among the general staff officers at that time, there were few others who could have better utilized the Bantams or even seen their potential. Pinney was a man who looked on war with a clearer eye than many of his Blimpish colleagues. While serving with the 23rd Infantry Brigade

at Neuve Chappelle some weeks earlier, Brigadier Pinney had saved
his men from total annihilation by the simple method of personally
going into the front line to see what was holding back their advance.

There, he found men of the Scottish Rifles, the Devons, the
Middlesex, and West Yorkshires piling up their dead and dying on
the uncut German wire. Their orders, despatched from comfortable
headquarters far to the rear, had sent the men of the 23rd in repeated
charges to certain death. General Pinney struggled through shellfire,
smashed trenches, and a carpet of dead and wounded until he was
crouching with his men in enfiladed positions. He called off the
troops, ordering them into more sheltered positions, and
telephoned the divisional gunners. He demanded heavier and more
accurate shellfire on the wide sheet of barbed wire entanglements,
now fringed with the tatters of khaki corpses. The directed barrage
quickly blasted a path through the obstacle and gave the 23rd a
better fighting chance when ordered forward again.

This open-minded and experienced soldier settled into his new
job of moulding his new Bantam force into a fighting unit, despite
the derision and negative expectations of visiting medical officers.
"It is quite impossible to expect undersized men to be useful as
soldiers in the British line in Flanders," one reported. "It is well-
known that such little men cannot bear the physical and moral
load of modern warfare. One has just to see their unsoldierly
appearance on the parade-ground to realize the total unsuitability
of Bantams."

Lieutenant Colonel MacQuarie's views were not untypical of
the time, when staff officers were still ordering men to go over the
top in parade-ground marching order to attack barbed wire and
concrete machine gun emplacements. Pinney preferred a more
optimistic approach, putting his faith in a programme of hard
battle training.

The practicality of all training was reviewed by the 106th's
new Brigade Major, a previously-wounded member of the Royal
Warwickshire Regiment, named Captain Bernard L. Montgomery
DSO. He later became better known as Field Marshal Lord
Montgomery of Alamein.

Trench-digging, musketry, and artillery co-operation exercises began to show the men what tactics to expect on the Western Front. Though nothing but experience itself could demonstrate the grisliness the troops would find out there, some veteran NCO instructors did their best to simulate it. However, after complaints by the camp laundry, orders were given that instructors must desist from splashing warm cattle blood onto troops to imitate gory battle conditions.

Thus trained and honed, the 35th moved south in late August to Pereham Down on Salisbury Plain, Hampshire. They stayed there in mouldy bell-tents or leaking huts, being endlessly trained and watching hundreds of thousands of troops crowding the huge Plain and then leaving in draft for France. As the months rolled on and the chilly sky poured ceaseless rain, the Bantams began to feel they would never get to war.

Donald Gray was then a young private in the 17th Royal Scots. "By the time we waited on Salisbury Plain, we had been in uniform for eight months and more. We had lived sheltered lives far removed from the dangers of trench warfare and were nothing more than second-class soldiers. We might as well have enlisted in the Boy Scouts for all the good we were doing for our country."

On a miserably cold morning in December, the Division was cheered to be notified it was about to sail off to sunny Mesopotamia. Full tropical kit was issued, including voluminous shorts which were so large that the men clowned by walking about with two of them in each garment. Even more hilarity was provoked by the solar topee helmets which made the Bantams look like giant mushrooms.

Within a month, orders were changed again. In late January, 1916, the tropical gear was changed for long woollen underwear. That made it official. The Bantams were destined for the Western Front after all.

Scale

Ostend · ·Bruges

·Dunkirk

·Ypres

St Omer·Cassel
Meteren· Bailleul
Hazebrouck· Quesnoy
Steenwerck· Armentières
Roubaix·

CALAIS

GHENT

Poperinghe ·

Courtrai

Pecq
·Velaines
·Ath

LILLE

Tournai

Bethune·
·La Bassée

·Loos
·Lens

·Vimy
·Douai

·Mons

Fosseux
·Arras

Maubeuge

Bullecourt Quéant
·Lucheux Inchy
Achiet-le-petit Bourlon·Cambrai
Beaumetz
Noullens
·Bapaume Ginchy
Haplincourt Haplincourt
Villers Plouich·Heudecourt
Vaux Albert· LeTransloy Gouzeaucourt
Rancourt
Corbie· ·Bouchavesnus ·Ronssoy
·Mont St Quentin
AMIENS ·Péronne
·St Quentin

British Sector on Western Front

CHAPTER FIVE

Extracts From An Officer's Diary.

The Cheshire Bantams, though first of such units to be raised, had waited fifteen months before being given their chance to fight. In the meantime, they had been endlessly drilled and trained, their ranks combed repeatedly to remove all but the very fittest physical specimens amongst them. When the 15th Cheshires finally reached France in early 1916, they were sent to the front almost immediately.

We are able to study first-hand the battalion's fortunes through the memoirs of Lt.-Col. Harrison Johnston, DSO., a compassionate, clear-eyed soldier who later privately published "Extracts From An Officer's Diary." It reveals the day-to-day experiences of his men, written down while they happened and told with modest, straight-forward simplicity. Among his matter-of-fact descriptions of trench warfare, mud, and death, Lt.-Col. Johnston also brought out how the troops faced such horrors with a patient good humour which gained his warm affection.

"31st January, 1916. The CO marched the Battalion through Le Havre and about three miles outside, all the way uphill, to a so-called rest camp! A pretty name given to a number of tents in rows in a wet, muddy field on the crest of a high, bleak hill. We told the men off to tents; the camp very dirty. Twelve men to a tent. One tent to each Company Officer."

"The people seemed very interested in our men. They are splendid, so cheery and bright under all circumstances, and I know they will show the world that the little men were not given their chance in vain. You'll see the money spent on their training has not been wasted."

"Thursday, 10th February, 1916. (Molingham) This place is very damp. Canals, ditches, waterways, stagnant water, smells everywhere. I had chloride of lime put down all over the place, and it smells yet. Should not care to live here. As I finished this, I heard horses' hoofs. Looked up, and there was a full-blown General, with some of his staff coming down the lane, followed by a Lancer complete with flag. I went out. The guard on the next billet did not turn out. The sentry presented arms. I saluted as they passed, and the General wished me good afternoon."

"As soon as they had passed, I rushed up and asked why the guard had not turned out? A man called McLellan was the sentry, and he said "I asked him if I should turn out the guard, and he said 'No'." My goodness, to think that a sentry in my Company should ask a General if he would like a salute!"

"McLellan was a waiter in the Sergeants' Mess and has not been on parade much until we left England. They seem to have got all the real dead-beats on guard today. It is enough to make one weep."

"Monday, 21st February, 1916. We had first parade 10 a.m. One hour's physical drill and one hour's bayonet fighting. The latter had to be done under cover in barns, so that aeroplanes could not see the men. Airmen were busy this morning. Our fellows brought down a Taube about two miles from here. He had ventured too far over our line. Some of our officers and men saw the fight and saw the German fall."

"This morning we have drawn fur coats (jackets) for all officers and men. We will look like a lot of Teddy Bears! The coats are nice and warm, and if the weather keeps like this we will need them. It froze all night, and has been snowing until now, 1 a.m. We've been at physical drill and bayonet fighting and now we are off for a route march, just a short one."

"Weather very severe. Everything frozen stiff. Ice so strong that I saw a man stand on a deep ditch this morning. It was a beautiful day. Sun out for five or six hours. All officers had to visit Brigade concentration point today. They went separately with one Sergeant as orderly. These Sergeants will take out patrols of eight men each;

first leaves at 6 p.m., last at 7.15. Each patrol should be back here in two hours. An officer has to be at the point to take times of arrival and check any noise or chattering."

"Kynaston volunteered for this duty and has just gone off. He will have a cold wait in bleak spot, so have made him wrap up well, fur coat over overcoat. He has taken an NCO for company."

"6.20 p.m. Cold is not the word for it. This is the worst drop of weather I have ever tasted. It is snowing hard and I have been out talking to the poor little fellows whom I am sending out on patrols. They have five or six miles to march, and I feel mean coming back to this warm room after chasing them out, but it has to be done. Partington is out at some lonely crossroads taking the times they arrive. He offered to go. I don't ever need to order my boys out on these unpleasant stunts, they always offer to go. I am truly thankful I was so lucky with my Company officers. They are a grand lot of fellows."

"The CO and Major Shaw paid a visit to the trenches today with two snipers out of my Company. They returned safely, but did not think much of the trenches we have to occupy. We started for the trenches at Givenchy with an officer to take us the first bit."

"Thursday, 2nd March. I found we had to provide three more fatigue parties, each of forty men and one officer, to go up near the line and repair trenches. I sent Robert, Kinny, and Partington on these. I have just heard that we are sending out a big bombing party tonight to strafe the enemy. I wish I could be up to see it. That's the proper thing to do. I hear we are also sending out bags of rations, as samples of our grub, each containing a German letter describing the nice comfortable rest camps in England for German prisoners. This is supposed to tempt the Hun to come and surrender!"

"Friday, 3rd March, 5.15 p.m. I met "Sambo" (the CO's servant) this morning standing outside the estaminet, so I asked him where he was off to. "Up to the trenches with the Colonel, Sir." I said "Sambo, if anything happens to the CO, you're for it. I'll have you put against the first tree and shot." He said, "Quite right too, sir, and serve me right. But nothing can happen to him whilst I'm with him. I'm his sniper." Sambo is a good lad, he's always smiling, and a chap who's always merry and bright is the man for my money every time."

Mud of Nomansland: Stretcher-bearers struggle to carry a wounded comrade through the glutinous quagmire formed by continuous shellfire along the rain-swept Western Front.

"Saturday, 4th March, 1916, 11 p.m. This morning when we wakened up, it was snowing hard and had been most of the night. Everywhere is white. It continued to snow until 3 p.m. and as we had to be knocking about all morning we got very "fed up" and wet. The relief was completed by 8 p.m., after being held up on the way whilst people in front drew gum boots. We got none, but some had been left here for us. Unfortunately, most of the men were wet through before we reached the boots. In places, the water comes well above the knees, and some of my boys have been up to the thighs in it. There are some decent dug-outs, however, which is a blessing. We have no rum but have sent for some."

"Sunday, 5th March, 2.40 a.m. We stood-to just after 5 a.m. and I went round the Company's line. Returned at 6.15. for the tea which had been promised, but none was forthcoming, so I lay down for a snooze on one of the wire frames on the floor which form beds. The bally brazier had gone out long ago, and it was very cold."

"Immediately after breakfast, I started my morning tour. I found all my men cheery and had a word with each. Their feet were cold and wet, but there was no grousing. Each had a smile and a cheery word in reply to our bits of chaff. Lads who'll stand last night will stand anything. Up to their knees in snow water, most had been nearly up to their middles coming in. It froze during the night."

"I gave the necessary orders for our withdrawal. It turned out that we were the only Company of the 15th leaving the trenches that night. Remainder had to wait until 4 a.m. yesterday morning, the reason being that a great stunt was to take place in front of the bit of line we occupied. A big mine was to be 'popped off' at midnight, which necessitated all the front and support trenches being cleared of troops."

"The mine was in three parts. It should not have been fired until the end of the week, but owing to the saps [tunnels] having collapsed, through bad weather, the RE decided to poop it right away. The show was elaborately arranged and Major Campbell came up to our dug-out to explain the operation orders to the officers concerned. Of course, the mine was the star turn, but there were a good many other side-shows."

"At 10 p.m. a bombing party were to go out and throw bombs where we cut the Germans' wire the day before. A pretty thin job, as the Huns are sure to have machine guns trained on these breaches in their wire. Later, an officer and eight men were to light smoke bombs and throw them over the parapet. This was to make the Huns think we were treating them to a gas attack, and get them out of their dug-outs with gas-helmets on. Of course, all our saps and front line trenches had to be evacuated whilst the show was on, and reoccupied later. Coloured rockets had to be fired from the keep. Artillery were to commence a big strafe at midnight exactly."

"It was near midnight when I got on to the bed in my billet. I heard the mine go up and then the artillery got on the job. Until 12.30 there was a terrible row, then went all quiet, and I tried to sleep. It was very cold and the rats were noisy and running about over my legs. I don't mind rats, but they kept pulling papers off the table and making quite a noise. I could not sleep well, I suppose I was too tired. However, I slept some, and shivered a lot."

"Wednesday, March 15th. We went to Brigade HQ. where a motor-bus picked us up, and after a long drive we arrived at our destination. Here we witnessed a great display. Lines of infantry attacked lines of trenches and set up different kinds of smoke as they captured different lines (with no enemy). We enjoyed the spectacle, as it is the first time we've watched others do the work."

"When this was over we had a firework display. All kinds of signal rockets and flares, even some mortars fired bombs which burst very high, releasing balloons shaped as fish, men, tigers, and dogs. These are known as 'Rockets, Japanese, liberating animals." Flare lights descended slowly on parachutes, stars of all kinds were thrown. But in daylight, it seemed a waste and not very instructive."

"Monday, 20th March. We left our billets at Comet Malo yesterday morning at 9.00 a.m. and marched seven miles to Epinette. The roads were very bad. One particularly, which is marked a first-class road on the map, was about a foot deep in mud and full of jolly holes. Glad I had my horse. All the men were carrying full packs, plus fur coats, ground-sheets, and mackintosh capes. This, with rifles and one hundred and twenty rounds of ammunition each, is a heavy load for little men."

"I only had one man fall out. He was ill and has been taken off in the ambulance this morning with high fever. Influenza, I think. He is a Scottish laddie (O'Neil) and I am sorry to lose him. I had quite a number of disciplinary cases for office hours today. Nearly all for dirty rifles. Nobody got less than the limit of my powers, seven days punishment. We have now to be extremely particular about the rifles being always absolutely perfect. The least bit of carelessness on the part of a man might cause a jam at a critical time."

"We are to have a concert tonight, and are inviting the officers and men of the Gloucesters to come. We go into the trenches with this regiment, so the CO wants us to get to know each other. Very wise."

"Monday, 27th March, 1.15 a.m. Each man carries two sandbags up to the trenches, also rations for next day, but now we have only to carry one hundred rounds of ammunition per man. We started our march as a Battalion and got into different formations at different points as we approached the front. Companies left after the long halt at ten minute intervals; then platoons at two hundred yards' intervals; then formed two-deep and kept to the side of the road; then single file into communications trench. Roads quite close up are in good condition—rough concrete. Our men marched in and relieved a regular regiment of the line like real old soldiers."

"I reported relief complete (by telephone) at 8.26 p.m. I had then to send a few messages and make various arrangements. Captain Earle, Brigade Bombing Officer, came up this morning. I told him our grenades would not quite reach, so he offered to bring up a few that would reach there. He came up with them and a lot of men, rifles (for grenades), etc., this afternoon, also a cake in a box and invited himself for tea. We were glad to see the lad. Earle's strafe came off all right, and he fired nineteen Newton grenades, nine of which landed plumb in Fritz's trench. Not bad, eh?"

"Saturday, 1st April, 3 pm. Relief commenced to arrive about 8.45. Relief of my Company complete 9.30, but we had to wait for "W." They completed 10.15 and moved off, we followed. We had to leave by different communication trenches after passing along "W's" sub-sector. Men all loaded up, dark night, strange country, mostly overloaded, in single file along very bad tracks, through wire, mud and water. Our men were silent and discipline good, but frequent halts necessary owing to losing touch."

"We were not shelled at all coming down, but many stray bullets continually about. They seemed almost to follow us as if they could see us. Ricochets hum and whiz overhead. I think going up and coming back from front line is the most nervy part of our business, but I've never seen anybody of ours show funk yet. Arrived Battalion H.Q. 12.30 a.m. and when I went in to report the CO wanted to know why we were so late!"

"Sunday, 2nd April. A beautiful hot day, such a treat. I sent out two patrols at night, or rather at 1 a.m. One, under Lance-Sergt. Slavitz, had to go towards a certain spot in the Hun line, report on the condition of the ground between (ditches, cover, etc.) This information specially required, and each Company has to make a separate report this trip."

"4.15 p.m. We had two patrols and one wiring party out last night from 11 p.m. until 12.15 a.m. One, under Sergt. Brittain, brought useful information about condition of No Man's Land. They lay by the Hun wire for a quarter of an hour and heard a working party busy on a new fort the enemy are building. When it is finished, the artillery will blow it out. A Hun surrendered to the Battalion on our right last night. He was a young Jaeger about eighteen years old."

"Saturday, 8th April, 2.45 a.m. I have had a reward of £20 cash, an offer throughout this trip, for a live German brought to my HQ. A number of the boys were very sick that I had restricted their movements and would not let them raid the enemy trench to get one. Such action would defeat the scheme for a rather bigger stunt, to take place shortly, of which they know not."

"Here's Kynaston with his Lewis Gun, to which is attached a hyperscope. This excellent arrangement enables the gun to be fired over the parapet without any of the crew exposing themselves. It is a wooden frame attached below the gun and fitted with a periscope."

"Sunday, 9th April. The strafe was a great success, but it is very evident that we will have to get a stronger rifle, or some better arrangement for firing these new grenades. First shot, the stock of the rifle broke. This is the last we have left, as two broke yesterday. However, the boys tied it up with string and we were able to use it, although it had to be refastened at each shot."

"We were firing it with a long lanyard, and everybody had to take cover when each shot was fired for fear of accidents. It was a great success. We fired 35 grenades out of which 23 landed either right in, or just behind the enemy's trenches. Two landed plumb on top of a dug-out."

"Meantime Wilson, with his Lewis Gun, was making a nasty mess of some snipers' loopholes, which we had marked. We all quite enjoyed the fun. Old Fritz took it very quietly and did not retaliate. No doubt he will prepare some little treat to give us back."

"The Bantams Comforts Fund is sending us out a splendid lot of stuff, and their parcels are continually arriving. We all feel very grateful to the ladies who are working so hard for us. The men know where their new socks, pipes, mufflers, &c., are coming from, and they are very thankful."

"Sunday, 29th April. We used Lewis guns with hyperscopes to good effect during the afternoon. It is a grand arrangement for upsetting old Fritz. Our snipers have rigged up a splendid telescope in a loophole running through the parapet and it is fixed on a gap in the Hun line. A fat Hun worked there for a while, but we could only see his helmet. He was too careful."

"Last night, there was a terrible strafe on our right a few miles away. The Hun used gas two or three times, and I hear that although he reached our trenches he was turned out in less than a quarter of an hour with heavy losses. We had no casualties from the gas, which speaks volumes for the efficiency of our gas helmets."

"Sunday, 30th, 2.30 a.m. It's jolly cold in this new dug-out, very draughty. I had three wiring parties out between 11.30 p.m. and 1.30 a.m. I find that our wire is not so good as I thought. I was over the top twice tonight and had a good look round. The wire on right is fairly good, but left flank is very bad for 30 or 40 yards and will need immediate attention. It is now 3.20 a.m. We will stand-to. It's getting quite light and the larks are singing."

"Wednesday, 3rd May. At stand-to on Monday evening, the Boche sent three shells simultaneously over the Strand trench. I was at the extreme right flank of my Company frontage, when a message came to say that ten of my boys were hit. I was talking to Capt. Morgan, who is holding a bit of the reserve on my right flank."

"I asked him to send his stretcher bearers along. As I was returning I met Billy, so sent him off to Strand. I then telephoned the Dressing Station to warn the MO that I had cases coming along, and doubled down the communication trench to see what I could do. I went and had a word with the lads and felt proud of them. One boy was dead and five were wounded. Everybody was cool and stretcher bearers worked quickly and well."

"On the Saturday evening, I was very surprised to meet the CO coming round. He had been in London at 11 a.m. and was here at 5.30 p.m. Pretty quick, eh? Of course, he had been driven here straight from the boat on a good motor-car. It shows what can be done. The other way, he took three days to get home!"

"Orders came announcing an inspection for next morning, by the new Brigadier. He has really arrived and is not the officer we expected. He is Col. A. H. Marindin, late Black Watch, now temporary Brigadier-General."

"Near Chappelle, Sunday, May 14th: My first impression of the line is a good one. The breastwork is quite good, parados good, but no administration trench. Dug-outs not very good. There are a few danger spots, where the Boche sniper may bag a few of us, but on the whole the line seems comfortable and cushy. The communication trenches are not good."

"The battered fragments of a few houses stand between us and the front line. The mess is a French steel dug-out of the usual type. The usual small offices and sleeping places all round. Signallers, orderly room, kitchen, sleeping quarters for the CO. Myself and Graham-Barnet have a bed in the orderly room. The RSM, officers' servants, orderlies, runners, orderly room staff, pioneers, are accommodated near by."

"It has been a delightful hot day. The evening is beautiful. A cloudless sky and no wind. Partridges are calling, blackbirds singing. A yellow-hammer quite near is singing his chirpy little song. An occasional shot is fired and a ricochet sings over occasionally."

"About 8 p.m. last night, one of our planes flew along the front, passing over the Hun line at a height that was too low for the Archies [anti-aircraft guns] which can't fire below a certain height. All the Huns fired at the 'plane with machine guns and rifles, a perfect fusilade. The pilot was priceless, and we all turned out to watch the display and thoroughly enjoyed it. He would fly over the Hun line, just where his friends fell this morning. He would turn round and fly away over our line, then back again, and each time he swooped down quite low and fired his machine gun at the trenches of the Hun."

"About 7.30 p.m., I went down to "B" lines with the CO. He has had a rifle battery rigged up there. We tested the rifle battery and it was going later in earnest all night, and every night it sends its jolly messengers along a road behind the Hun lines, and we can shoot straight up it from here."

"I found that in addition to the wiring parties, Billy had a patrol of five out. There was some confusion while this party was out. They met six Germans. Bombs were thrown from sap held by W. Company and two of our own men wounded. One, especially (Tunstall), behaved splendidly, searching for the men who had been hit. His name has been forwarded to Brigade for commendation. The men are all in now."

"I got up in good time and went off to the dressing station to see these men in the morning about 7 o'clock. I got a lot of good information about the construction of the Hun obstacles, his sentries, the position of the M.G. and the strength of his garrison in the front line. They all insisted that the enemy trenches are quite as strongly held as ours. This is rather useful, as we had an idea that they were very thinly held. The wire was very strong and deep, consisting of double apron fence and then 20 feet of low wire about 3 ft. high fixed on wooden frames, like our concertina wire, but held on the frames firmly and well picketed down."

"A new draft arrived from depot and also a small draft (67 to the Battalion) of cyclists. These are big men, and I feel it is a pity for them to have sent the chaps to us, as it rather spoils the 'Bantams' business. However, we frequently have to send men away, and we may be able to pass them on."

"We have got a gun back here, which gets Fritz ripe every day. She is called 'Silent Sue.' The explosion of the gun is not loud, but she throws a big shell. She is a 'six inch, and fires continually. The Germans frequently shell where they think she is, but most of their stuff is going into a nice big field and doing no harm."

"Captain Gibbs was up today, and he showed me some of the Huns' latest shrapnel. He had just dug it up. Three pieces in one hole, two round lead bullets and one marble. You know, what kiddies call 'olleys.' They are the cheapest kind of marble one can buy. Gibbs told me that his men had repeatedly reported that the Hun was using a mixture of stone marbles and leaden bullets, but he doubted it until he saw it. Fritz must be getting short of even the baser metals."

"Friday, 9th June. At stand-to, Willy was going round his Platoon when he heard sharp words of command coming from one of the bays. He halted and listened to the following amusing performance: Shield, who was my servant when I was attached to the artillery, was bossing the show. He had four men on the parapet.

He called, "Battery action."—pause—Number Three gun stand fast. Salvo fire!"—pause—Voices from the top—"Number One gun ready, sir!—and similar reports from other guns. "Fire!"—pause—"Repeat fire!" His crew worked as though they were on a serious job, but when Willy walked into their bay, there seemed nothing unusual. All at their posts and never a smile."

"Don't you love these little men who can play amidst the serious business o war? There's not a dry shirt in the company, and we're here until next Saturday. We're very cold, yet Captain Johnston is grousing about the condition of the men's webbing equipment. How can our chaps be expected to keep their equipment clean in this? But we're in the Army, and we've got to keep smart as possible."

"Major Shaw called at 4 a.m. He is getting as regular as the Hun. The latter gentleman started firing A.T.'s [aerial torpedoes] yesterday, and he fired every quarter of an hour to the minute for two and a quarter hours, then finished."

"A Patrol sent out by Z Company got bombed. They went up an old trench, intending to sit and listen at a certain spot, but Fritz was sitting there first, heard them coming and bombed them. Lieutenant Alexander and three men were hit, but all got back."

"I'll tell you a story that is true to finish off this little lot before I post it. A certain Brigadier in our Division is very keen on gas helmets, and severely strafes anybody he finds without one. One day, he was going round the front line, and suddenly discovered that he had forgotten his own. He asked a Tommy to give him his gas helmet, but the Tommy refused and said that his Captain had told him that he must not part with it on any account. The Company Officer stepped forward and told the man to give the General his helmet-bag at once, and he'd see it was replaced. The General marched off with the helmet slung on. As he came out of the communication trench, he met a subaltern without a helmet and gave him gyp, saying that he would not have officers and men going about without gas helmets. He finished up with, "Here, take mine," and gave him the one he had borrowed. As the subaltern turned away the Brigadier said, "Now you have one, do you know how to put it on?" "Yes, sir." "Well—do so!" The youth opened the satchel and revealed a dirty pair of socks ! The poor Tommy responsible was crimed."

"Friday, 23rd June. Up at nine, but no parade until 11.15 for the march to the place we were to be inspected at. We passed Battalion starting point 11 a.m. and Brigade S.P. 11.30. The men felt the heat a good deal as we were in marching orders."

"The 19th Northumberland Fusiliers, a Brigade of Artillery (which now consists of three batteries of 18-pounders and one battery of howitzers), one field company R.E. divisional cyclists, 106th field ambulance, and the four battalions of our brigade, were all massed on the large field. A long wait before our inspection, but perhaps not quite so long as usual. At last, orders came down. General Pinnie: "The parade will come to attention and slope arms," repeated along the line, the 'General salute,' 'Present arms." Bugles played 'General salute,' and all infantry presented arms. "The parade will slope arms and order arms," repeated, then "The parade will stand at ease.""

"General Sir C. C. Munroe commanding the First Army is a short, rather stout man. He looked rather severe and had a black shade over one eye. He went round the artillery 'like a cooper round a barrel,' as Fred would say. He then came round us (on his horse). General Pinnie mentioned Col. Newell's name as he reached him and explained that he commanded the 15th Cheshires, then I heard him say to the CO, 'Your men look very well,' and so he passed on."

"When the General had finished, he went to a small table in front of which stood a group of heroes. He presented medals. Five officers received the Military Cross, and a number of NCOs and men received the Distinguished Conduct Medal and Military Medal. [The DCM is particularly prized, considered to be close behind the VC in merit.) Then the General took his stand, and the march-past commenced. Artillery led and they looked splendid. We followed, and the boys were on their toes. As we passed, the General remarked, 'These men are wonderfully steady.' Such praise from an Army Commander was very gratifying. I believe General Pinnie was pleased."

"I met a funny character for the first time on the Brigade march on Tuesday. He is a 2nd Lieutenant and commanding a battery. He was in the main guard with me. He's a Lancashire lad and a very capable officer. Talks broad Lancashire and does not care a— for anybody. He's the sort of chap one could absolutely depend upon in a tight comer. Funny tales are told of him, but I'll just give you one or two. An official notice came round on one occasion, 'Please state by retreat tonight exactly how many trench boards have been broken up, and used by your battery as firewood.' He just wrote across it, 'Scores!' Another time, he was put under arrest and his Sam Browne belt taken away. He promptly wrote to the Brigadier, complaining that he could not strop his razor, as they had taken his belt away. His belt was returned to him."

"Monday, 3rd July. Morning, 8.30 a.m., and here I am in a smelly, bumpy, third-class French railway carriage. Already, we have left the flat country and are passing through undulating country pretty and, as usual, every available bit is cultivated. The crops are growing rapidly and look very well indeed. Let's hope the crops of the Central Powers are not so good. The people are all waving and shouting to us from the houses and fields. They wave handkerchiefs and the children throw kisses. Nearly all the children salute smartly in the English way. Our Tommies teach them wherever they are billeted."

"We arrived at the station, Bouquet Maison, to find a fivemile march to Sur St. Leger in front of us. A a hot day, roads dusty. Nobody knew our destination until the C.O. got his instructions at the station. The march to billets was rather trying and told on the men, who were carrying packs and greatcoats again. We arrived about 2.30 p.m. We were all tired and went to sleep once we were fixed up and the men settled. The people are nice, real French, not Flemish."

"Two new drafts arrived for us, one of 103 men from the 11th Cheshires and another of 61 from the 10th Battalion. These men are Bantams, and had been sent to the other battalions during the last two months. Now they are returned to our Bantam Battalions, and they put us miles over strength."

CHAPTER SIX

Into The Line

At night in February, 1916, you could stand on the cliffs at Folkestone on England's south coast and sometimes be able to hear the war going on. If the sky was clear and the wind was right, the eastern horizon would ripple with pale light, the glow alternating with the faint sound of gunfire. When the troopships reached Le Havre, the "wump-wump-wump" was a steady drumming in the air, a close reminder of what lay ahead. By the time the 35th Division went into camp in the Foret de Nieppe, near Merville, the noise of bombardment 12 kilometres away was so loud that some of the men were at first convinced that they had actually reached the firing line.

But before a group of fresh brigades could plunge into battle, there was a whole ritual of settling in to perform. Like some huge dog turning around and around in new grass, the Division had to be reformed, billeted, and marched here and there, while its medical and signals units, gun parks, and supply-trains were organized.

The artillery, engineers, pioneers, and signallers of the 35th Division were standard-sized troops, not bantams, who had been assigned from other formations. They brought with them brand new guns and other support equipment which was readied for use by the 157th, 158th, and 159th Brigades of Artillery, 163rd Brigade of Howitzers, three Royal Engineers companies, a Signals company, and the 19th (Pioneer) Battalion, Northumberland Fusiliers.

One of the 17th Battalion was Frank Heath, an eighteen year old Yorkshireman. He looks back on his early days in France with clarity, "We were first billeted in a paper mill, and our boudoir was a large warehouse filled with paper bales ready for pulping, on which we slept. As it was warm there, we were able to undress. When the women came to work at 6.30 a.m., and caught us nearly naked, they loved to wrestle with us and touch us up a bit. One lad named Felton was much younger than any of us and had a baby face with rosy cheeks. He was a particular favourite with all the French women, and they called him their *"cheri piccanini."* The madameselles paid him very special attention every morning, each in turn loving to embarrass him by touching him in a certain intimate way."

To ease the Bantams into the war, they were first allotted to XI Corps, which contained the 38th (Welsh) Division and the Guards' Brigade. Each battalion was marched towards their encampment in stages, and encouraged to mingle with the seasoned troops of the local parent units in the hope that some individual experience would rub off on the newcomers. As is often the case, a strong liking immediately grew between the very tall and very short soldiers, when Bantams and Guards met.

"There was a lot of chaffing going on today," wrote Guardsman Alec Thames to his brother at the time. "After we finished telling the Bants they had duck's disease, we had to take a lot of very funny insults in turn, about us looking like long drinks of warm water, and so on. Very sharp tongues they have, and we've taken to the scrappy little chaps right away."

The newcomers soon learned that in volunteering to fight, they were accepted as equals in a purgatory which was a great leveller, and where survival was the only real priority. On his first day at the front, Private Harry Tillotson's unit was marching up a sunken road to relieve some Grenadier Guardsmen.

"As we were going up the line, they were coming down the line," he recalls. "The big fellas looked at us with grins all over their faces. At first we thought it was because they were so tall and we were so small. But it wasn't, they were smiling just because they were coming out of the line and we were going in."

On the 11th of March, Lt. General Sir R. Haking awaited Lord Kitchener on the reviewing stand at Wardrecques, where the entire division was to be inspected once more by the Commander-in-Chief. "I shall never forget it," says Jack Paget, at the time a seventeen-and-a-half year old 2nd Lieutenant with the 18th Lancashire Fusiliers. "It rained in sheets all day and the whole Division just stood there, drenched, waiting for Lord Kitchener to turn up. When he did, he was hours late."

Just before dusk, Kitchener arrived to watch the parade of each battalion through the downpour, then made another congratulatory speech about the turn-out and appearance of the men he had been interested in since their origin. Still wet, the battalions went back that evening to hauling ammunition and supplies through freezing rain and snow, as the division pressed on to ready itself for front line service.

While logistics were being put in place, cadres of officers and NCOs were selected to gain some first-hand experience of trench warfare. They were attached to fighting units, given a taste of the real thing for a few days at a time, then sent back to convey their scant knowledge as best they could. It was the method used by military machines throughout history, but the individual results were not always of practical use.

"Some of our officers didn't seem able to put into words what they'd seen," believes Nobby Streeter, by then a lance-corporal. "We had three or four days of it with the Welsh Division, and came back to set up a training course. Thank God, we had a few old sweats with us."

"Two of our officers had been sergeants in the South African War, and were able to get across the facts to the rest of the battalion. But by and large, our other officers thought it 'wasn't good form' or something to talk about what they'd seen. They stood there fingering their swagger-sticks and mumbling about how things were a bit sticky up there, old boy. They were good fellers, mind you, but they'd been brought up to keep a stiff upper lip, and not to seem to show off ever, so they never passed along any useful advice."

"One young two-pipper [1st. Lt.] stumbled along this way for a bit in the middle of a training exercise, until a South African veteran who had been made up from sergeant to a captain stepped in front of the company and said, "What he means, lads, is don't bunch together, keep your rifle clean, and your arse down at all times!"

Members of the experienced cadres were more often the subject of interest for the personal stories they brought back. On February 14th, Lt.-Colonel Harrison Johnston of the Cheshires wrote in his diary, "Here's Billy Brown come back. He is full of terrible tales of the wicked Huns, but he's glad to get back to the fold. The experience has been invaluable. It has given him renewed confidence in our men, and he says 'Well, Johnnie, I know our boys will do well.' I've been telling him and others the same thing for many moons, but he knows now. The best little men in the world, you will see."

"Billy brought some pretty stories back with him. One being that a Sgt. Major of the company he was with captured a Hun officer in the last show they had, and shortly afterwards was found carefully strangling the chap with a pull-through [cord.] I don't quite see the point of choosing that special mode of disposing of the gentleman, but we all have our different forms of amusement."

The green units began to learn methods of how to save more lives, often at the cost of the few for the many. Fusilier Frank Harris describes how it worked. "Troops in the line were strung out; just a Lewis gun post about every hundred yards. Should the Germans come, the outposts were sacrificed, but gave alarm for most troops held further back. During the day, nothing moved, but after dusk you could hear the hoofs of mules and jingle of harness, cursing drivers, and see shadows of men moving up and down the duckboard tracks. Men had to be relieved every forty eight hours, or they would have died of exposure."

Some shivering Lancastrians in one such outpost on the night of February 23rd heard a large group of Germans approaching. They determined to wait in ambush, calmly laying out a row of grenades in front of each man, and being careful to quietly hold bolt-tension while the Lewis gun was cocked to avoid that tell-tale clatter. The enemy advanced in open order, beginning to eagerly run forward when it seemed they would be able to invade the British trenches unseen. The listening-post crew opened up a close range, killed or wounded several intruders, and drove off the rest.

A few days later, the 17th Battalion received a note from the area commander, Brigadier-General, L. A. Price Davies, VC. "Please convey to the battalion my appreciation of the spirit they showed in the recent encounter with the enemy. The readiness of the listening patrol allowing the enemy to approach and then dealing with them is also an excellent sign."

An hour and a half after going into the Welsh trenches, the division had its first battle casualty on February 18th, when Private Caxton of the 17th West Yorkshires was shot in the head at Neuve Chapelle. More observers from the West Yorks and the 17/18 Lancashire Fusiliers were wounded in the next couple of weeks, three of whom later died. Around this time, the Cheshires began to take casualties during their first sampling of trench warfare.

Colonel Johnston led his men into the sector where they were to learn their trade. He wrote in his diary, "On entering the communication trench, we stepped into a foot of water. The 'duck-walk' planks were narrow and along the centre of the trenches only. The consequence was that when one's foot slipped off the boards, a leg would miss the duck-walk and sink three feet into the filthy water which filled the trenches. The planks are on piles which are driven into the bottom of the trench, but in places they had become loose, one would step on one end, the other end would tip up and in one went! The sides of the trenches were wet and slimy, and people frequently fell in."

"Absolute silence was observed. No cursing or exclamations, just the splashes. Any noise would have drawn fire on us at once. As it was, I had one lad hit by a stray bullet before we left. When we arrived at the trenches, we found them in very poor condition. Narrow, badly kept, very wet owing to the snow-water, and almost without dug-outs."

"The dug-out occupied by the officers, otherwise named 'Company HQ,' was a smelly hole in the earth, which had to be entered by crawling on all fours through a tunnel with a floor of sticky mud. During the strafe, a 60 lb. trench mortar shell fell just outside the door. This completely wrecked the officers servants' quarters and kitchen, which was a light dug-out next door where food was prepared. The three servants were buried, but got out all right and unwounded, although badly shaken. A large water-filled crater formed in the space between the trench and the dug-out, as it was raining heavily. 'C' Company on our left lost eight men, four killed and four wounded, by a rifle grenade. One man at 'D' also got hit on the head this morning by a splinter from a whiz-bang, but it was only a light scalp wound."

Frank Heath was sent for his first taste of war: "We were moved along the La Bassee canal bank at night to the trenches at Givenchy. The Welsh Fusiliers were to give us instruction as this was our first time in the line for us. As we entered the communication trench, we were challenged 'Who goes there?' followed by cries of 'Make way for the dead and wounded!'"

"When it was dawn, we moved into the front line, which was merely composed of shell holes. It was pretty quiet, except for a few bullets and an occasional shell whining its way to a target well behind. I was detailed to go to a trench a few holes away to bring breakfast for six men, a rasher of bacon and a hunk of bread. When I got out of the hole, a bullet whizzed just past my leg. It put the wind up me and I ducked with my head buried in the snow."

"After two days of this, we Lancashire Fusiliers were withdrawn, as it was assumed we had learned enough to be able to hold the line on our own. We marched three miles to a barn for a rest and a sleep. You could hear the guns thundering away and see the Very lights. Whichever direction you looked, those coloured lights seemed to encircle you. After we had been asleep for all of two hours with our boots off, we were awakened by Sergeant Nightingale shouting, 'Come on lads, we are going on a working party!' The job was to carry barbed wire and duckboards for the Royal Engineers in the front line which we had just left."

Raised on accounts of mass slaughter on the Somme where 60,000 casualties were suffered in a single day, and on tales of whole battalions wiped out at Passchendaele, Lens, Vimy, Verdun, and Belleau Wood, we now tend to think that was how it was that so many died in the Great War. But the French General Mangin summed up the dreadful truth best: "Whatever you do, you lose a lot of men". Most of the time, they died in a steady trickle—here, a green young lieutenant sniped near the latrines; there, a wiring party caught by a Spandau; a squad wiped out by a sudden trench mortar bomb; a volley of shrapnel hitting a crowded cross-roads, or perhaps the morning sun brewing up dormant phosgene gas from the bottom of a trench to send an exhausted platoon lying there into the deepest sleep of all.

Trench raids, sniping, salvos from the routine morning "hate," small local skirmishes—each killed thousands of men every day by the multiple handful. You could waver off the duckboard and quietly drown in liquid mud without anyone being the wiser, catch your death of cold, or die from one of a hundred other mishaps. At Suzanne, three Bantams fell asleep at the side of a deserted road and their remains were found at dawn, pulped under the heedless wheels of a passing ammunition wagon.

Accidental wounds and deaths were common where millions of loaded small arms lay casually everywhere. One such incident was seen by Fusilier Frank Heath. "A chap by the name of Willet was on the firestep, cleaning his rifle. He asked Jack Darraque to grab the end of his pull-through cord, which Jack did. Willet then closed the bolt and pressed the trigger. Darraque was shot right through the heart. Willet was court martialled, not only for killing Darraque but also for cleaning his rifle without first removing the bolt and magazine as laid down in regulations."

The same training cadre had another tragedy the next day, just after they came out of the line into reserve. A popular officer, Captain Tyas, was putting a detonator into a Mills bomb which then exploded in his hands. His men sadly buried him the same day in the village cemetery at Savigny and were marched back to the line that night as a rations-carrying party.

Even training courses well behind the lines took a small but steady toll of men. Their next-of-kin wept no less bitterly over the fruits of a badly-aimed practice salvo or of a shortfall during mortar-bomb instruction. Over 30 officers and men were killed from a variety of such non-battle causes, in two months in France before the 35th Division officially went into action.

After intensive preparation, in which detachments from each battalion were given a taste of trench conditions, the Division was considered to have been "blooded." On March 10th, the entire 35th was sent in to occupy portions of the front line east of Festubert and bordering Neuve Chapelle.

The sector chosen for the Division to hold lay between Festubert and Laventie, in the lowest-lying part of the wet Flanders Plain. There, trenches tended to peter out every few hundred yards into quagmires impossible to dig, so that breastworks of sandbags and brick rubble were as common as conventional ditches. Lacking firm lines, both sides tended to raid back and forth more frequently than elsewhere, tempted by the flimsy battlements of each other. By deliberately withdrawing from low ground, the Germans did have the advantage of better drainage, as was their more intelligent strategic habit throughout the war.

So much water on the surface or just below ground made Flanders and Northern France the very worst places on the face of Europe for trench warfare. The neat picture shown on military maps of an orderly line of trenches was not possible in reality. Streams and marshes constantly interrupted the lines all along the battlefield, making any form of dug-out almost impossible. Even on apparently firmer ground, the desperate shovels of infantrymen soon encountered permanent saturation close below the surface, which kept most trenches in a constant state of wetness. On higher ground, the problem was that rainfall could not drain off through the clay. As a result, men were often forced to spend their time in the line standing up to their ankles or knees in cold water and liquid mud. For the smaller Bantams, this problem was that much more severe.

"We were issued with two empty sandbags each before we went into the front line, the idea being to fill them so we could keep out of the mud and reach over the firestep more easily. The only trouble was, the wet soil and muck available for filler soon collapsed flat as a pancake. I've seen us up to the waist in slush and wet muck," recalled Cyril Wright. "We tried all kinds of tricks like cutting shelves in the trench wall high up to get us out of the water. This wasn't too good an idea, as it made it too easy for snipers and also reduced protection against shellfire. But the misery of standing in deep mud would become so bad, we would risk a bullet or a Jack Johnson just for a bit of respite and dry feet."

During the first week of March, 1916, the three brigades began to take over their sector. The 104th Brigade relieved the 58th Brigade from holding the sector around Plum Street, while the 106th Brigade relieved the 57th Brigade next door. The 105th Brigade had been in reserve under instruction in the trenches of the 38th Welsh, and it was decided to now let them take over in full.

A signaller with the 38th Division, Edgar Pursell, was repairing telephone lines in an observation post that night. "It was a fairly quiet part of the front," he said. "We had been there several weeks, and scarcely heard from the Germans. All was dark and quiet as the Bantams filtered in from the road, along the communications trenches, heading for the front line. Suddenly, all hell let loose."

"Until the Somme battles later, it was the heaviest bombardment I had experienced. Shells poured into the sector, blasting the new troops at the very moment they started to man their position. Within minutes of arrival, dozens of dead and wounded Bantams were being carried back along the C.T.'s."

"It was uncanny," Pursell thought. "Our baptism of fire was particularly savage and devastating. How? Why? On a well-known quiet front? As usual, us rookies had been given that inactive front to gain experience. It was everybody's opinion that the Germans somehow knew full well that the Bantams would be going in to man that sector that night. And they obviously knew the time to the very second!"

This devastating welcome was the Division's first experience of the apparent German omnipotence in matters of military information. Next morning, survivors swear they had another demonstration that the enemy knew the Bantams had moved into the sector. "A very scary thing happened the first morning we were getting ourselves sorted out at stand-to," Graham Carr recalled. "Listen to that!" one of our sergeants said. Clear as could be, we could hear the Jerries crowing—"Cock-a-doo-arroo-arroo-arroo!" then laughing fit to bust. We didn't think anything of it beyond promising each other we'd soon make Jerry laugh out the other side of his face, but our sergeant made quite a fuss of it, and kept saying, "How do the buggers know already?"

There is a persistent story that every time the Bantams occupied sections of the front line, the Germans opposite would begin to make derisive rooster calls to show they knew which troops had moved in. The same type of thing is mentioned by Scottish and Irish regiments who were greeted by Teutonic shouts of, "Hello, Jock!" and "Top 'o' the mornin,' Paddy!"

Though the British troops may have developed an exaggerated awe of German military intelligence, there is no question that the enemy did frequently seem to know an uncomfortably detailed amount about local British troop dispositions. This may have been due to their being able to form a well-developed espionage net amongst the French population, a few of whom were apparently subverted by a combination of bribe money and old feelings of hostility towards Britain.

A few weeks after their arrival, the Division was able to solve one such problem, as Colonel Johnston described while writing home in April. "Did I tell you the story of the spy who gave our artillery away? When I was attached to the Battery the other day, an officer called my attention to a civilian ploughing in a large field. He was using two horses, a black one and a white one. It seems that some days he would plough for perhaps an hour without an alteration of the position of his horses. He would then change the horses over at the end of each furrow. It was noticed at last and he was watched. The gunners became convinced that he was giving information to Hun aeroplanes who were observing for their artillery. We had three or four Batteries close together, which were frequently moved slightly, but the Boche always got the range and chased them out of their new positions. The man was continually watched, and two nights after I left he was found in a hedge with a rifle watching the road. A number of troops had been shot on this road at night by a sniper. The man is dead now."

The first Bantam unit to experience the full weight of the enemy was the 18th H.L.I. They were occupying trenches which straddled the Duck's Bill, a salient bulging forward about 500 yards north of Neuve Chapelle. Some of the men were miners, and had reported hearing sounds of underground work there the night before. However, they were still in position at dawn on March 13th when the Germans fired a mine under the salient. It is believed that the explosion also touched off the British counter-mine, doubling the blast effect and sending up an entire section of the forward trench. When the smoke and dust cleared, there was a long mound of foul-smelling clay where the men had been crouched on the firing step, caught at stand-to as the enemy had planned. Though several survivors were quickly dug out, it was found that 30 Scotsmen had been killed, and another 30 were wounded.

Deafened and groggy from the eruption, the troops on each side of the crump stood firm at their posts, loosing off such a volume of fire that the enemy follow-up raid melted away. The officers and NCOs showed remarkable coolness in the fire fight, running along behind the trenches in full sight of the enemy to rally the men. Among them, 2nd Lt. St. George Yorke was awarded the Military Cross for his leadership.

A few days later, the Corps Commander sent a message to be read to all ranks: "I am very pleased with the action taken by all ranks to deal with the situation at the Duck's Bill on the morning of March 14th (sic). I am also glad to hear that there was no sign of giving way amongst the men of the 18/Highland Light Infantry, who were exposed to the full effect of the mine. This shows that although these men have only recently arrived in this country, they are to be trusted to maintain their positions even in the most dangerous and difficult circumstances."

The 17th Lancashire Fusiliers were given a swampy section of line outside Richebourg to hold. As no trenches could be dug, the principal strong points were three sandbag forts named Boars Head,

Post Number One, and Post Number Two. "We had our first casualties here," recalled Frank Heath. "Lieutenant Nuttal was hit with a bullet, then Dick Cannavan was killed running 200 yards from Boars Head to Post Number One over open ground while trying to get a stretcher. When we got him in that night, we found a bullet hole straight through the middle of his forehead."

In mid-March, it was decided to give the 17th Lancashire Fusiliers some experience in a large trench raid. They were withdrawn from the line and sent to Richebourg St. Vaast, and rehearsed for the raid against replica trenches. Selected to go over in the attack were three officers and fifty other ranks under the command of Captain E. T. Cowan.

An artillery barrage was started the day before, intended to cut wire along the enemy front. The men bunched in a forward trench for several hours, delayed by a German searchlight, that was only put out after a prolonged fusilade. Finally, they went forward at 9.30 p.m., in a raging blizzard which blinded them while crossing No Man's Land, bridging ditches with a ladder they carried, and managed to get through the shell-torn wire.

The Germans were understandably on the alert after so much attention and when the snowstorm halted to clearly reveal the Fusiliers, the attackers were forced back by a shower of grenades at the very lip of the trenches. Machinegun fire killed two Lancashiremen, and wounded ten more, before they had to withdraw. A limited allowance of 30 rounds prevented artillery from giving much support, and the raid was judged a failure.

Trench raiding was a way of life for British and Commonwealth troops throughout the Great War. Though every bit as warlike, the French and Germans did not raid as frequently, considering it to be an expensive and bothersome activity. The British High Command constantly badgered front line regimental officers to send out raiding parties, "to present an aggressive stance at all times to maintain the men's fighting spirit."

Raids were ostensibly made to capture prisoners to be interrogated for intelligence gathering purposes, but their high cost in casualties, which often provided the enemy with exactly the same kinds of information, in reality negated their stated aim. Many officers who had to lead men on such dangerous sallies believed they were more for the purpose of justifying Staff Officers' existence at the cost of other men's lives.

Yet the average Tommy seldom thought of such subtleties, and did his job without much question. The pugnacious Bantams seem to have been very ready participants in raids within a short time of their arrival at the front, and there was never a lack of volunteers when a "stunt" was announced.

"We were continually sent out on trench raids, wiring repair parties, and listening patrols in No Man's Land," recalled Patrick Cassidy of the 18th H.L.I. "On trench raids, we had our faces blackened, put scarves on our heads, and then were each given a tablespoon of rum before setting out. I always found those raids to be a bit hectic. We would creep right into the German lines to take a prisoner or throw a few grenades, then got back as soon as possible to our own side."

"One night on a raid, we were caught by a Very light. As we took cover, a Spandau started to fire at us. We'd been spotted and bullets hummed close all round us. I felt a blow and a sudden wet feeling on my back and legs. I thought I'd been hit for sure, but made it back to our lines. There, I found that a tin of condensed milk in my haversack had been hit and I was unharmed."

"Dutch Courage" was an important ritual before starting out on a raid. Rough brandy for the Germans, gnole spirits for the French, and "Services Rum, Diluted" for the British. As Private Cassidy mentioned, men were hardly given enough SRD to warm their stomachs, let alone send them roaring drunk into combat, but even a tiny drink of it was always welcomed when carefully doled out before a raid.

Because of the dash and initiative needed by men taking part, a raiding party usually was composed of volunteers. However, some units would order men to also take part if it appeared that they weren't generally pulling their weight in the trenches. Between 25 and 50 men would go over, with their positions and functions well defined in advance. A small section armed with Lewis light machine-guns and hand-grenades would bed down just outside the British wire to wait as a covering party. The rest would go on in small teams of bombers, bayonet-men, and rear bodyguards.

Cold steel was emphasized, bayonets and daggers, as was a variety of clubs, iron bars, and knobkerries for purposes of stealth. The main weapon of raids, though, was the Mills 36 grenade, that deadly egg-shaped bomb with a sectioned cast-iron case which remained in British army service for another 60 years.

George Palmer of the Glosters tells how, "If we met a Jerry patrol in No Man's Land, it was mostly a set-to with bayonets and entrenching tools and pick-handles—quite a useful cosh they made. Of course, there were casualties on both sides and we would take back whoever we could. There was no time to waste, as when Jerry got wind of us he would try to make sure we never got back if he could help it. Safe home again, it was time for a good supper of bully-beef, dog biscuits, and a sip of water out of a petrol can which was never washed out, the dirty buggers. So to bed until stand-to just before dawn."

The Battalion Diary of the 17/West Yorkshires tells how they spent that month of March. "No attacks. No raids. Heavy manual work, keeping trenches dug, pumping water, revetting trench-walls, carrying Engineer supplies. Bitterly cold which at least reduces the mud, then warm weather which miserably thaws the ground, then cold sleet and blizzards. Fewer casualties from enemy snipers, as men learn survival skills and counter-sniping. Constant bombardment by enemy guns and trench mortars."

They were relieved at month's end by the 19th Durhams. The Geordies were still recovering from a mine and gas attack which caused seventeen casualties on March 14th while they had been in trenches with the 59th Brigade. "We were under bombardment all the time after we relieved the Yorkies," says Billy Watson. "You couldn't just spend all day hiding down on your hunkers, so we would stand on the firestep by the hour watching Jerry's parapet for a chance to hit back. I didn't get a chance until I reckoned how to get him cross [angry.] I fired off five rounds rapid, then moved quickly aside about ten feet and watched near where I'd fired at.

Sure enough, a bare head popped up behind a rifle, and I shot him while he was firing at where I'd been a minute before."

Several battalion commanders had offered cash bounties of up to fifty pounds sterling for the first prisoner to be brought in. The Sherwood Foresters captured the division's first German on April 6th, when a fed-up deserter from the 17th Bavarian Regiment wandered through their wire. This voluntary PW did not pay a prize, and though a few more daring individuals strained for the chance to claim a bounty, most were content to forgo trench raids for the moment. There were other dangers enough as it was.

Some men of the 15th Cheshires at the bombing school narrowly escaped death on April 9th, when a student dropped a Mills-bomb after pulling the pin. Sergeant-Major Shooter scooped it up and threw it clear a moment before it exploded. He was wounded in the thigh, the only one hurt among the nearby group of officers and men whom he saved.

The entire division now received orders to move slightly south to the Ferme du Bois sector, and several changes in command were arranged en route. At this time, the 104th Brigade received a new commander, Brigadier-General J. W. Sandilands, who stayed with them from then on right until the Lancashire unit disbanded in March, 1919.

The Bantams had been instructing the 1st Australian Division in trench warfare. Now, they turned over the sector to their students and marched off to the quiet trenches in front of Richebourg l'Avoue. Immediately, the Germans greeted their arrival with a heavy bombardment of high explosive, gas shells, and smoke canisters. Five members of the 15th Sherwood Foresters were killed, including the popular Major H. T. Thirlwell.

The accuracy of German intelligence was again demonstrated when they shelled the British reserve battalions out of their rest camp at Croix Barbee. The shellfire swept on by plan the next day, smothering a trench salient called The Neb and causing a dozen Cheshire casualties.

The division struck back with a series of night raids, sending men against the German listening-posts, with orders to "kill or demoralize the enemy." A fifty-man patrol of the 23rd Manchesters went over on May 1st to silence a machine-gun post at Les Brulot. They destroyed the guns, inflicted some casualties, and returned with only two men wounded.

Enemy bombardment continued unabated for the next month, despite the strong counter-fire of divisional artillery. The Manchesters attempted to repeat their success and set out on another raid. This time, they were caught in the light of flares at the enemy wire, were fired on, and had to withdraw, carrying back their casualties. Four men covered the retreat and evacuation of wounded so valiantly that the Military Medal was later awarded to Sergeant Hare, Corporal O'Connor, and Privates Townley and Lee. German retaliation gunfire was very heavy, catching the raiders and their comrades in the forward trenches. In a half hour, eight Mancunians were dead and 15 were wounded, including the fatally injured Major Bannatyne.

The Germans preferred to make more massive attacks in larger numbers, and on the night of May 30th, they came close to breaking the 35th's line. Recently, the weather had grown warm, raising the men's spirits and increasing the tempo of combat. Several British units decided to send out fighting patrols under cover of a rain squall, unaware that the enemy was planning to launch a major assault.

The German attack was partially foiled by one of the raids setting out from the 15th Cheshire's position, as later described by their war diarist:—"The Colonel thoughtfully sent up a feed for the men who were to go over the top, tinned tongue, cakes, etc. They fed at 10.00p.m. Officers supervising dealing out of bombs and wire cutters, and at 11.45 p.m. all go over the parapet from a bay in W. Company's line."

"At 11.50 to the tick, the lid of hell was suddenly lifted, and Old Nick seemed to vomit an inferno of fire and noise. As I stood on the fire step I felt the whole breastwork heave. Trench mortars were all around and the air was full of shell. Spurts of flame seemed to come from between my legs, from each side, and behind me, 18-pounders screeched overhead. Machine guns and rifles cracked out, but seemed very insignificant. Heavy rods from our TM [trench-mortar] bombs whizzed back over our heads. Time passed very slowly. The little drain pipes from which TM bombs are fired seemed like pipes from the nether regions spitting fire. At last the artillery lifted and the TMs stopped."

"A strong impulse seized me to go out to those lads, but I had to stop behind. I felt a worthless thing, but we can't all go, can we? I knew our lads were advancing then and I prayed for them as I stared out into No Man's Land. Time never passed so slowly, minutes seemed like hours, straining my eyes to see what was going on, but nothing to be seen. Our shells passed in one hissing procession over our heads."

"Then Schofield's voice, 'Is that Capt. Johnston? Can you see anything?' Next, Barnett with a message from the CO that I must immediately send a runner to him at W. Company's HQ directly after I saw the OK flashes from Partington, which would mean that the raiding party had passed through the covering party on their way back."

"Time dragged on. Artillery stopped firing. My brain was busy with names of men I must take out with my search party. I gave an order for stretcher-bearers to be brought up to the bay in readiness without taking my eyes from the front. A flash from the darkness, Only a Hun rifle, then another. A few dull explosions (one's lips formed the word 'bombs') a few rifle shots, then a few flare lights, but nothing more."

"It was just after one o'clock. More rifles crackled out from the Hun parapet. A few more dull explosions somewhere out there among the wheat and long grass. Companies on right and left are giving covering fire. W. Company's rapid fire is good. No sight of a flashlight. The rain pours down and the smoke hangs about everywhere. Bamett's voice asks if I'm keeping a sharp lookout for the signal. I say 'Yes.' I must be civil. The boy doesn't understand that my lads are out there. Suddenly a scuffle at the end of the bay and a voice 'Tell Capt. Johnston they're coming in!'"

"I sprang over two men, who were crouching down on the duckboards, and with a loud 'Make way!' hurried to the end of the next bay. Here I found congestion, largely men who had pals out, and a few curious sentries from the next bay. They melted at my first remark. The two parties came over the top as a drill movement, in their sections, just in the order in which they had left, except that all the officers came last. I checked the party and bustled them back to our lines as fast as I could, after sending word to the CO"

"Taking advantage of the dark, wet night, old man Boche had a big working party out, with a strong covering party in front of it. Our barrage on his parapet prevented their return. They had taken shelter in deep ditches. The first our chaps knew of this was a rustle in a ditch and the explosion of four bombs right in the middle of the party. The chaps scattered but were reorganized at once by the officers, who led them to the ditch. Willie threw the first bomb and the Huns retired as the others pasted the ditch, which runs diagonally into another big one near the German wire."

"As our party reached the second ditch, they again met opposition and had to bomb the blighters out of that as well. One Hun fell in the ditch and was seen by several of our men. There seems no doubt that others were also scuppered, but as our artillery had ceased fire altogether, and the Germans were lining their parapet and firing rifles, the party returned. Whilst the strafe was on, I distinctly heard the horn blown [for stretcher-bearers] several times in the German trenches, and I have no doubt that we accounted for a few. We were very lucky and our few wounds were trivial."

The brunt of this German attack fell further along the line where the 18th Lancashire Fusiliers had found themselves crouching in their trenches under heavy bombardment at the very hour they were expecting to be relieved by the 17th Battalion. Telephone lines were cut and there was no means of knowing what was happening on each side of their position or if this was part of a major attack. Corporal H. Bloor and Private Dunn set out through the shellfire to learn the true situation on the left of the Lancashires. Though Bloor was wounded, the pair managed to return with information that the neighbouring 15/Sherwood Foresters had been forced to vacate about 200 yards of front line. A Lewis gun section of the 17th Battalion already in the line under command of 2nd Lt. R. J. Tyhurst had moved to cover the gap.

The Lewis gunners received support from a company commanded by Lieutenant J. W. Strong, who organized the defences there just in time to repel a storming-party sent across by the vigilant Germans. A bomb fight ensued, followed by hand-to-hand combat in the trenches before the enemy was repulsed. The struggle for the thinly-held trench gap went on until 4.00 a.m. next morning, when reinforcements arrived from the 14th Gloucester Regiment. Congratulations and thanks for holding the line arrived from Lieut. General L. E. Kiggel, Chief of General Staff, along with awards of the Military Cross to Lieutenants Gardiner and Tyhurst and a Distinguished Conduct Medal to Corporal Bloor.

Next day, word spread through the Division that it had been a near thing. The Germans had intended this major raid as a counter-offensive to delay British preparations being made for the Somme offensive. They took back with them one officer and thirty-seven men of the Sherwoods, many of whom were already dead, wounded, or shell-shocked from the massive bombardment which obliterated their trenches. Some idea of German intentions was gained from the large stocks of abandoned picks, shovels, and bags of hand-grenades. One other interesting find was also described. "When the Hun got into our trenches the other night, he left behind many things, including a cat-o-nine-tails. This showed signs of much use. It is evidently a form of encouragement used upon infantry who are not over-anxious to get upon our bayonets."

Night after night, the Bantams continued to harass the enemy; raiding across the festering real-estate, to kill Germans and to die themselves on the wire or in the inevitable counter-bombardments they provoked. One raid in particular, on June 8th, 1916, was to enter the folklore of the division and provide colourful material for the busy war-boosters in Britain.

The 14th Gloucesters sent a 60-man raiding party against the enemy trenches south-west of Les Brugots. A box-barrage isolated their target at 9.00 p.m., and they set out just a few steps ahead of the German artillery counter-fire. The raiders split into three groups and advanced despite machine gun fire. They blasted their way into the trenches where the courageous Germans still held on after enduring the softening-up from artillery. The fight became a hand-to-hand brawl with every man for himself—confusion of bursting grenades, shooting, stabbing, and clubbing, while men screamed with the vile murderous voices of close combat. At the end of it, thirty Germans and eight British lay dead, and the enemy fled into the box-barrage where many more were killed. The Bantam raiders scampered back to their own side, dragging a heavy Maxim machine-gun with them.

Lt. Meldrum later told the story of how the Glosters captured the trophy: "We halted halfway until the barrage was lifted from the front line up to the support trenches, then the raiding party went into the enemy trenches. When I got in, I made my way along with my party to the right, bombing dug-outs as I passed them, and found the gun between an open emplacement on the parapet."

"The crew of six were trying to fire, but it had evidently jammed. My first bayonet man charged the crew and accounted for two and my bomber accounted for the rest with four or five grenades. One man who was scrambling over the parados, I shot in the back. I then tried to dismount the gun, so as to carry it back more easily, but could not, so with the help of two men, I lifted the whole thing and rolled it over the parapet. After doing some more damage, I and my party made our way back to our trenches."

"Captain Butt, who was in charge of the raiding party, was wounded in the enemy trenches. While making his way back to our lines, he was unfortunately killed by a shell. Lt. Brown, who also led a party over, was wounded just as he reached the enemy trenches, but before he went back he emptied his revolver into a crowd of Germans and also threw all his bombs. As I learned afterwards, Col. Roberts was hit by almost the first shell when the enemy retaliated, and died almost instantly."

Bantams trophy. Wounded soldiers eye German Maxim machinegun on display in Bristol. Weapon was presented to the city by the 14th. Gloucesters after capturing it in July, 1916.

For personal reasons, Major-General Pinney decided to present the gun to the city of Bristol, as he was a grandson of the Mr. Pinney who was Mayor there in 1831. As the battalion had been raised in Bristol, it was felt that the trophy was a useful method of publicizing the unit's adventures, and might help to stimulate more recruiting in the area. Ten days after the raid, crowds of Bristol people turned out to see the Maxim on display at the City Art Gallery in Queens Road, which justified the effort made to gain a propaganda coup with local flavour.

As part of the ceremonials, Lt. Meldrum was introduced to the Bristol City Council by the Lord Mayor. The dignitaries were surprised when they entered the council chambers to see the Maxim gun on a table in front of the mayoral chair. Mayor Baron read aloud a personal letter from Major-General Pinney : "To the Lord Mayor of Bristol, June 19th, 1916. The 14th Battalion Gloucestershire Regiment wish to present a German machine gun recently captured by them to their raisers, the Mayor and Corporation of Bristol. Lt. Meldrum who led the party is bringing you the gun. May I be allowed to express my personal thanks to your Lordship and Corporation for the good battalion you have given my division."

After reading aloud General Pinney's letter, the Lord Mayor asked the sword-bearer to bring Lt. Meldrum into the chamber, where he saluted the Council and took a vacant aldermanic seat. The embarrassed young officer sat through a good deal of the fulsome praise, though he probably thought it a small price to pay for a few days of blessed leave from the trenches. After what must have seemed like an endless spate of oratory, his Lordship said that he thought the Council would desire that they all should send back their lively sense of gratitude to the men for the magnificent heroism they had displayed. He asked Lt. Meldrum, who was leaving for the trenches again in a couple of days, to take with him the city's sense of gratitude and every good wish for the battalion and that they would surely keep up the reputation of the old city.

"Some day," said the Mayor, "we will have the pleasure and honour of receiving these men back in our midst. In the meantime, the gun will be a cherished possession of the Corporation."

When Meldrum returned from his brief well-earned home leave, he found the Division humming with rumours of a Big Push being prepared, and read the personal letters posted on all notice boards conveying the congratulations of Army commanders for the successful repulse in early June:

"Corps Routine Orders by Lieut. General Sir R.C.B. Haking, K.C.B., Headquarters, 9/6/16. 360. The Corps Commander has much pleasure in publishing the following letter received this morning by First Army: 'The Commander-in-Chief is of the opinion that the behaviour of the troops of the 35th Division was most creditable. Signed, L. E. Kiggell, Lieut. General, Chief of General Staff.'—To 11th Corps. The G.O.C. First Army has great pleasure in forwarding the above letter for your information, and in adding compliments for the gallant manner in which troops of the 104th and 105th Infantry Brigades withstood intense bombardment and delivered an immediate counterstroke to drive the enemy back. Signed, S. H. Wilson, Lieut. Col. G. S., First Army."

Evidently the courageous behaviour of the Bantams had enhanced their reputation and helped silence their few remaining critics. All through their first five months of active service, they had staunchly done as well as other troops in front-line duties. Now that they had beaten off a major strategic attack, they were conclusively proven to be reliable fighting material, so long as their sturdy quality could be maintained by reinforcements. But, the 35th was being steadily drained of its original Bantams by death, wounds, and illness, and already grave concern was being expressed by Divisional medical officers at the declining physical and mental standards of new men coming out from Britain.

In retrospect, it is obvious that the Bantams' problem was part of a larger malaise affecting the British Army as a whole in mid-1916. Already, unsettling thoughts were being expressed about physical standards of recruitment in general, regardless of height.

When the concerns of front-line commanders reached the calcifying levels of London-based review boards, the worthy aims of military or medical men fell into the trap of rigid categorization. At the War Office, troops were seen simply as either "sound" or "unsound" types. The Southborough Committee did much good work in striving to ensure that more care would be taken with medical examination of recruits, yet itself oversimplified the human consequences of battle.

"We are of the opinion," reported the committee, "That adoption of the new measures we recommend would result in the admission of a fewer percentage of recruits mentally and nervously unsuitable for military service. Such types of men are likely under the strain of war to become the subjects of varieties of hysteria and neurosis commonly called 'shell-shock'."

While it is obviously true that nervous or unfit men make poor soldiers, even the bravest warriors could and did crack under the hideous conditions of the Western Front. No amount of earnest committees could mitigate against the nightmarish conditions that the "soundest" of men faced month after month in the trenches. Contrary to the modern-day impression that all generals were ignorant of trench conditions, General Aylmer Hunter-Weston wrote about personally seeing how bombardments could reduce men to gibbering idiots : "The ding-dong fighting and constant exposure to fire night and day has an effect on most men's nerves, and more than one of the senior officers, brigade and battalion commanders, have broken down under the strain. It is marvellous how quickly most officers and men, who have not gone over the breaking point, recover after a good night's sleep and a couple of day's rest." But not every man was as resilient or recovered mental balance so easily.

Though the War Office in 1916 officially recognized "shell-shock" as a genuine consequence of exposure to modern warfare, especially artillery barrages, most military doctors and army officers regarded the term as at best "fiddlesticks," and at worst an excuse for deliberate cowardice. Senior commanders safely far from battlefields despatched orders that "Malingerers claiming shellshock must be treated with the utmost severity." Even frontline fighting officers who were compassionate in most things towards their men with whom they shared danger, felt an obligation to be stern against anyone giving in to nervousness at expense of his duties.

"The Brigadier gave us his views of the officers and men who 'take ill' when things get hot in trenches," wrote Lt.-Col. Harrison Johnston, 15th. Cheshires. "I agreed with every word he said. I am truly thankful that our battalion has been so free of this 'shellshock' business, but regret that isolated cases have occurred. Revolvers will stop any men leaving in future when funk is their trouble."

Johnston was referring to a few incidences when soldiers who retreated against orders were shot out of hand by officers to discourage other troops from abandoning their posts. During the Great War years, most people regarded any soldier who claimed to be traumatized to justify failure to carry out his duties as simply a chicken-hearted malingerer. This attitude was widespread among the ordinary troops themselves, who generally despised any comrade who let down his "chums" in a fight. There was growing official recognition of "shell-shock," but it was rarely accepted as an excuse for acts of cowardice at the front. In 2003, the preferred term is "post-traumatic stress disorder," and is recognized as a valid psychological condition brought on by reaction to horrorific combat experiences. But in 1914-1918, the world was a harsher and more judgemental place, when execution was still the common legal punishment for civilian capital crimes.

The British Army and Royal Navy were even more unforgiving about what were then considered heinous offences. The General Staff was convinced that only the implacable certainty of death by firing-squad could maintain iron discipline in battle. Commanders believed that fear of being shot at dawn by one's own comrades would stiffen the resolution of any soldier who might otherwise be tempted to "show a yellow streak," as it was called.

Years later, in 1930, Britain would abolish army executions, but during the Great War, there were still several military offences punishable with death. They included murder in a war zone, mutiny, cowardice before the enemy, disobeying a lawful order, desertion from the front lines, sleeping or being drunk while on post, striking a superior officer, casting away arms in the presence of the enemy, abandoning a position without orders, or in any way treacherously assisting the enemy.

Under military law, soldiers accused of these offences faced immediate trial by Field General Courts Martial. Such hearings were in no way "military kangaroo courts" as alleged later by sensationalist critics. In fact, all courts martial followed detailed rules of strict procedure set out in the 908-page *Manual of Military Law*, and considered testimony presented by witnesses and interpretations of evidence. During World War One, FGCMs were mostly held hurriedly just behind the front lines and usually presided over by officers of the accused's own regiment.

Few of the FGCM judges, prosecutors, or defenders (an officer assigned as the "prisoner's friend") had any legal training. However, as the war went on, more attention was paid to the need for legally-trained officers to attend courts martial, and brought in if availble. Whenever a FGCM condemned a man to death, the court papers were required to be then passed up the chain of command—brigade, division, corps, and army HQ—to allow senior officers to add written opinions whether the sentence should be commuted or confirmed. Finally, the case was placed before the Commander-in-Chief for his ultimate decision.

Official statistics show that 3080 death sentence verdicts were handed down by British courts martial between 1914-1921. However, only ten per cent of these execution orders

were ever actually confirmed and carried out. Most of them
were commuted to lesser penalties by order of Field Marshal
Sir John French and Field Marshal Sir Douglas Haig, the
successive C-in-Cs. Contrary to his modern portrayal as being
entirely heartless, records show FM Haig refused to confirm
nine out of ten death sentences submitted to him, usually
preferring terms of penal servitude instead.

However, senior commanders refused to stay the sentence
of 346, the total number of British and Empire soldiers who
were officially executed during the Great War. Thirty-seven were
executed for murder, but the majority were shot for desertion
in the face of the enemy. Virtually all were private soldiers or
NCOs; only four commissioned officers being executed
throughout the entire war.

Not at all secret at the time, the pros and cons of military
executions were repeatedly debated in Parliament and British
newspapers while the war was going on. Though many voices
spoke out against the shooting of soldiers for being found
wanting on the battlefield, public opinion was generally in
favour of punishing any men who "showed the white feather."
Virtually every family in Britain had relatives in military service,
which naturally biased most civilians against any soldier who
tried to avoid the dangers being faced by their comrades.

Evidently, many trench veterans themselves gave scant
sympathy to fellow soldiers who were executed for cowardice.
Decades later, Frank Palmer wrote, "I can't say I'd have liked to
have been in a firing-squad myself against one of our own
blokes, but there were too many good friends who were killed
while doing their duty for us to care what happened to any
bastard who ran away and left us in the lurch."

Jack Jones had a similar opinion. "We were all scared stiff,
all the time, in the trenches. But you had to grit your teeth
and soldier on, no matter how bad it got, because the very
worst thing you could do was let down your mates. Anybody
who did, though, the bugger deserved to be shot."

Such was the stigma of having been shot for cowardice,

names of victims were kept from the public for seventy years, mainly to protect their families from disgrace. When a book identifying the condemned was published in 1989, purportedly to expose historical injustices by ruthless military commanders, it deeply shocked many families who learned for the first time that ancestors long revered as heroes had in fact been court martialled and executed under dishonorable circumstances.

The Public Records Office disclosed for the first time the names of 305 soldiers who had been executed—not including those shot for murder and other criminal offences—and their case files were fully declassified in 1993. Of these, 18 men were shot for cowardice, and 266 for desertion in the face of the enemy. In addition to British troops, 25 Canadians were tried and executed by their own regiments on charges of cowardice or desertion, as were five New Zealanders and 11 South Africans.

Considering that approximately 5,000,000 men served with the British Army during a relentless four-year-long war, 346 is relatively not a large number to have warranted execution. (There was even a similar precedent half a century before, during the American Civil War, when the Union Army put to death 267 soldiers for desertion.)

Of course, it was still an individual tragedy to each of the executed soldiers and their relatives. Viewed within the context of the times when the events ocurred, such punishments were perfectly acceptable behavior to averagely honorable people during the 1914-1918 era. But social attitudes have changed radically over time since, so that many standards and consequences that prevailed in the past are deplored in the 'politically correct' 21st. Century as having been outrageously inhumane.

The piteous revelations in the 1990s sparked latter-day moral outrage and anti-establishment attitudes, fuelling protest campaigns for Parliament to declare retroactive blanket pardons for Great War military execution victims. Organized protesters made repeated demands for revisionist pardons to be declared by two successive British governments—under both Conservative and Labour administrations.

Armed Forces Minister John Reid expressed a "deep sense of regret" at the loss of life but ruled out the possibility of pardons for the troops shot by firing squads. He opined: "The point is that now, 80 years after the events, we cannot distinguish between those who deliberately let down their country and their comrades in arms, and those who were not guilty of desertion or cowardice."

Not included in the official total, are the unrecorded and uncounted additional incidences of troops being shot out-of-hand by officers and Military Police which also took place in the trenches. This summary form of execution on the battlefield was euphemistically known as "being sent behind Dickie's bush," a play on the name Dickebusch, a village in Flanders.

"Battle police, MPs, Redcaps—the ordinary soldier regarded them as his natural enemies, more so than the Jerries," recalls Harry Hurst. "Though I was not an eyewitness, others who were told me that a few Tommies found wandering behind the line after running away from combat did not live to face court-martial, receiving on-the-spot execution from battle police."

Though such drastic action was fairly uncommon, the threat of dire punishment was very real, a nagging fear the men had to consider whenever their nerves were close to breaking under the strain of constant warfare with no hope of rest or escape.

"The first time I saw a man on Field Punishment Number One, I couldn't believe my eyes," said Edward Scales. "A youngster of less than eighteen by the name of Barton, who had been in the thick of the fighting, disappeared soon after. When the Military Police found him, he was sent back to face Major Yatman. This officer had just arrived from India, and he was very strict. 'Shell-shock is cowardice, and will not be tolerated!' he told us on parade."

"Young Barton was the first one to be punished. We were marched past him in single file so we could see what to expect. The poor lad was spread-eagled across a gunwheel, his wrists and ankles tied with rope and a sign "Coward" on his chest. He was kept like that in the pouring rain for hours at a time. We Bantams were all volunteers from Tyneside, and we could not understand how anybody could treat one of our own men so badly. We would never ill-treat German prisoners like that, and certainly not torture them. Yet after the company was marched past Barton, we were told by Major Yatman, 'He got off lightly. The next coward will face a firing squad!' We private soldiers began to wonder who our real enemies were."

Soon afterwards, the grim threat was carried out nearby on a young private who had already once endured Field Punishment No.1 for neglect of duty. James Archibald was 19 when he volunteered in Edinburgh the previous year to join the 17th. Battalion, Royal Scots Bantams. He served in the trenches at Richebourg off and on for a couple of months, and the battalion was sent back up the line on May 14, 1916. That night, he disappeared into the darkness shortly after being told he was to become a sentry when their forward trench was reached.

The following afternoon, a local Frenchwoman asked two Lancashire Fusiliers to speak to a soldier who was sleeping in her barn. He proved to be Pte. Archibald, who was not armed or wearing any webbing equipment, indicating an obvious absentee from his unit. He was immediately arrested, and brought before a court martial to face trial for desertion. Even though he had been absent for less than 24 hours, Archibald clearly had intended to avoid front-line duty, and was briskly sentenced to death.

From the language used by prosecutors, one might wonder whether he was as much detested for his puny physique as he was for trying to desert. Court records describe him as "a typical slum product, of poor intellect." Lt.-Col. Cheales added, "From a fighting point of view, Pte. Archibald was not of much consideration . . . an unreliable man."

He was seen to have one last use, though. Brig. Gen. O'Donnell commented, "The 17th Battalion Royal Scots contains some rough characters and lately there has been a certain amount of insubordination especially when orders are issued for heavy work in the trenches. I am reluctantly compelled to state that I think an

example is necessary in the interests of discipline of the Brigade."
Pte. Archibald being handy and expendable, he was shot at dawn
in front of his comrades at Loisne on June 3, 1916.

Despite "I told you so" sneers by a few critics of the Bantam
experiment, the charge against hapless Pte. Archibald was scarcely
typical of the majority of his comrades' performance in battle. A
congratulatory letter written on July 2nd by Gen. Sir Charles
Munro, General Officer Commanding First Army: "I should be
glad if you will convey to all ranks my appreciation of the fighting
qualities they have displayed since they have been in France. The
35th Division has carried out four successful raids into the enemy's
trenches and has developed a fine fighting spirit."

The Bantams kept up making aggressive night raids against
fiercely-defended enemy strongpoints, and the 15th Cheshires
destroyed a strong enemy raiding-party. Units particularly
distinguished themselves during a successful assault on German
trenches at the Boar's Head. Then in early July, 1916, the 35th
Division received orders to move at six hours' notice to a new front—
the Somme.

CHAPTER SEVEN

The Gamecocks

When the 40th (Bantam) Division was first constituted in September, 1915, it was feared that most of the suitable human material had already been siphoned into the 35th Division. Recruiting for the latter had just received a boost when the National Registration Act was passed in July. Then it became evident that their battalions were already filled and could take no more applicants until combat thinned their ranks. The proponents of the 40th Division went ahead with renewed confidence, which further increased with news of the Derby Scheme.

Under this system introduced by Lord Derby—"The King of Lancashire" and newly appointed Director-General of Recruiting—all men of military age were enlisted for one day then immediately passed into the reserve with liability to be called up when required. Half of these 2,000,000 Derby registrants were married men, and the hint was clear that national compulsory service was in the offing.

Conscription eventually did receive Royal Assent in January, 1916, but in the meantime there was still definite social pressure on men to volunteer before being forced to go.

Helpful as this climate was for recruitment of new formations, the particular physical requirements of the 40th Division still presented problems. The authorities had learned from the experience of the 35th, and were leery of opening the doors to substandard men not up to the sturdy levels of the original Bantams. Medical boards were strictly warned against this when a number of British army regiments were given their guidelines for Bantam battalions.

The 40th Division was headquartered at Aldershot, with the

administrative arrangements set up in a more orderly way than the ad-hoc origins of earlier units. It was placed under the command of Major-General H. G. Ruggles-Brise and planned to be a deliberate blend of English, Welsh, and Scottish troops. The new 119th Brigade under Brigadier C. Cuncliffe Owen would consist entirely of Welsh battalions—19th The Royal Welsh Fusiliers, 12th South Wales Borderers, and 17/18th Welch Regiment. The Anglo-Scottish 120th Brigade under the formidably-named Brigadier-General Hon. C. S. Heathcote-Drummond-Willoughby was intended to receive the 11th King's Own, 13th Btn. The Cameronians, and the 14th Highland Light Infantry. Originally, the all-English 121st Brigade led by Brigadier J. Campbell was to get the 12th Suffolks, 13th The Green Howards, 12th South Lancashire Regiment, 18th Sherwood Foresters, and 22nd Middlesex Regiment.

The Welsh units of the 119th Brigade were expected to provide the most promising quality of bantam recruits, because of the very large proportion of hardy miners available and the local capability for enlistment. The bureaucratic machinery had been in place there for some time, so that the formation of Bantam units in the Principality was a swift and smooth operation. A meeting of the Welsh National Executive Committee in September, 1914, had set itself the task of raising a Welsh Army Corps, and had reached that goal within a few months. Ever since their ancestors stopped the Romans cold, and later used their longbows to win the battles of Crecy and Agincourt for England, Welshmen had been renowned as soldiers. They were keen to get into this latest war—which promised to be a good one—and filled every new battalion within a few days.

By origin and employment, the average Welshman was then inclined to be slightly shorter than a Scot or Englishman, and the coalmines of the Rhondda Valley and other colliery regions bred hardy men who were born to strenuous activity. Elsewhere in Wales, from the sheep farms of the Brecon mountains to the crowded homes of Cardiff and Newport, and among the coalpits and ironworks of Monmouthshire and Gwent, men stepped forward by the thousand to enlist in the Great War.

What became the South Wales Borderers had a fighting record that went back to the 17th Century. After service in many campaigns, the Borderers' battalion acquitted themselves so well against Napoleon it was awarded a Sphinx badge and the word "Egypt" in the cap-badge. It is probably best known for the tragic defeat at Isandlwana in 1879, when the entire 1st. Battalion was massacred by Zulu impis, and for the immortal defence of Rorke's Drift next day. In that gallant stand, 140 British soldiers held out against 4,000 Zulu warriors, and were awarded eight Victoria Crosses for their valour.

At time of the Rorke's Drift battle, the unit was still designated the "2nd Warwickshire, 24th Regiment of Foot," and did not officially become the South Wales Borderers regiment until one year later in 1881. (In 1969, the SWB were amalgamated with The Welch Regiment into The Royal Regiment Of Wales.)

The still-extant nominal roll written by Lt. Chard on the day of the battle, states that about one third of the gallant defenders of Rorke's Drift were actually Welshmen (most others being English-born troops.) However, now that school-houses have been supplanted by movie-houses as sources of information, the popular film "Zulu" has transformed public perception of Rorke's Drift into a glorious Welsh-only event.

All through its history, the SWB has been a regiment that expects nothing but the best of its recruits, and at first it faced the prospect of "bloody dwarfs" with something less than enthusiasm. The Borderers braced themselves at Newport Depot when news arrived that they were to expect drafts of bantams for the 12th Battalion, (3rd Gwent). "I'll have no Tom-tiddlers in my regiment!" roared one giant Company Sergeant Major, and even refused to retract his remark after catching the eye of a somewhat diminutive Captain who was also the unit Medical Officer.

Among newcomers on parade that day in May, 1915, was Albert Lewis, the miner who had given up the chance to be a well-paid Tunneller by joining the Birkenhead Bantams instead. He and a company of his fellow Welshmen were transferred to the 12th SWB to infuse a group of trained soldiers into the unit's recruit instructional programme. "They promised us we'd all be sergeant-instructors by month's end," said Lewis. "Fat bloody chance, boy-oh! Every one of us left alive was still a just shilling-a-day private at war's end." Another eager youngster who had finally managed to become an SWB soldier was the ex-sailor, William Parkes. He was destined to become a ferocious night-raider, survive the war, and live out a very long life in the United States.

Though the nucleus of ex-Cheshires was available, the battalion temporarily borrowed a number of drill-instructors from the local police to provide some modicum of barracksquare knowledge. Military training was slow until July, when veteran officers and NCOs were transferred to the 12th, and the unit was moved to Prees Heath Camp in Shropshire.

It was here that the fiery Argentine Jack Enrique Jones arrived for training, a Welsh soldier at last. "I don't know how many regiments had turned me down before I got into the Borderers," Jones said. He added as disgusted evidence of his desperation, "I even tried to join some bloody English regiments, but they wouldn't have me either!"

"There was a bit of let-down at the recruiting office though. The officer looked at the form I'd filled in and gave a sneer. 'What sort of dago are you? This isn't the flamin' Foreign Legion, you know!' I told him I was as Welsh as he was and I'd come all that way to fight, and I'd just as soon start with him. He quietened down a bit at that and signed me up without any more of his lip. But from then on I kept quiet about Argentina, and dropped the Enrique part altogether after being called 'dago' a few more times."

"I'd just got a steady job in Cardiff when I found I could get into the Borderers, so I drew my week's pay and blew it all on beer to celebrate. I wasn't a drinking man then, so I felt pretty bad the morning after when I arrived at Prees Heath."

Jones' bleary eyes saw entire trainloads of Welshmen arriving with uniformed companies from Newport and drafts of civilians from Ebbw Vale, Pontnewydd, and Tredegar. As well, there was a train filled with Welshmen recruited overnight in London and with a batch of twenty caught on the rebound after being turned down by the Royal Navy at Chatham. These men from different backgrounds were united by their Welsh origins and proved to be readily trained into a smartly disciplined unit with high morale.

Their pride was further heightened when orders were posted later in July by Lt.-Col.E. A. Pope, their new C.O. He announced that the battalion was struck off the rolls of its original 115th Brigade and was now officially part of the 119th Welsh Bantam Brigade.

The second regiment to raise Bantams for the brigade was The Royal Welsh Fusiliers. (In 1921, it changed its name back to tradional spelling, becoming The Royal Welch Fusiliers.) The RWF wore one of the army's best-known dress distinctions. This is a fold of black ribbons stitched on the back of the coat collar, a hold-over from the days when soldiers' hair was tied in a queue. Such a traditional a regiment selected St. David's Day, March 1st, 1915, as the appropriate date for announcement of formation of their 19th (Service) Battalion.

The RWF observes a number of colourful ceremonies on that day of their national saint, including "Eating the Leek." This ritual has the commanding officer visit the enlisted men's dining hall, accompanied by a drummer, the Goat Major, and the regimental mascot, a white goat. The animal is traditionally supplied to the regiment from the Royal herd, and is prominent at all ceremonies of the unit. On this particular day, the mascot is dressed in his splendidly decorated apron and has his horns painted gold for his duty of supervising the youngest officer who must stand on a chair and consume the Welsh national vegetable non-stop before the drum stops rolling.

According to David Jenkins, this was the spectacle which the first 19th Battalion recruits saw when they arrived at the barracks near Deganwy. All the uniformed troops wore green leeks in their caps and paraded around behind the pampered goat, which doubtless eyed the newcomers with contempt. Ceremonies ended with the civilians awkwardly clumped along the edge of the barracks square to witness the garrison lustily singing, with leek-laden aspirates, the stirring anthem "Men of Harlech."

As the last pungent chorus died away, a drill-instructor turned to the wide-eyed recruits and bellowed, "'Ow am I ever goin' to make real soldiers like them out of 'orrible little men like you?" An ex-miner called back, "Easy, Corporal. Start feedin' us all on onions like that bloody Billy-goat, an' we'll be able to gas the Jerries to death!"

Though this irreverent newcomer spent his first night in the army at cleaning latrines, he may have been gratified that his wisecrack was later often repeated by comrades to draw a laugh even under shellfire.

Their county of origin is recorded in the sub-titles of two Bantam battalions recruited for The Welch Regiment—17th (1st Glamorgan) and 18th (2nd Glamorgan). They had been quickly raised in the Rhondda Valley in January, 1915, and sent respectively to Rhyl and Porthcawl, first attached to the 43rd Division. There, the recruits were trained by old soldiers of the regiment brought back as instructors. Under such grizzled leaders, the Glamorgan men learned how to become adept at rifle-drill and the weapon's more important use on the firing range.

Like most Kitchener battalions in training, the Welch Bantams were issued with the old-fashioned Long Lee Enfield, Mark II, which weighed 9 lb. 4 oz. and was 49.5 inches long. As these rifles were not much shorter than the men themselves, they caused some difficulty in attempts to master arms-drill. When marching at slope-arms with 18-inch bayonets fixed, the long weapons were downright dangerous for all but men in the first rank, and there were a number of nasty head wounds inflicted until troops learned how to hold the rifle at a rigid safe angle.

Firing the Long rifle was also difficult for any short-armed man, because of the butt length. The .303 Lee Enfield fired a 174-grain bullet with a muzzle velocity of 2,440 feet per second, with a proportionately vicious recoil. Even trained soldiers can experience a bruised shoulder after rapid fire with the "Lee-En." This punishment must have been much more severe for any short-armed Bantams who were unable to hold the butt properly, pressed tight against the shoulder.

Traditional goat mascot parades with drum and bugle band
of the 17th. Battalion, Welsh Regiment (Bantams,) at Rhos
on Sea, Wales, 1915. Two years later, after the battle of
Bourlon, this battalion lost so many men killed in action, it
officially "ceased to exist."

This was an important consideration at a time when the entire British Army training was based on fielding soldiers able to fire at least ten aimed rounds a minute. (Trained soldiers of the Regular Army could fire over 20 shots a minute. So devastating was rapid fire from the Lee Enfield that, during the retreat from Mons in 1914, the Germans believed it was from machine-guns). This problem with butt-length was recognized early, and musketry training overcame it for Bantams through special instruction and practice.

When they embarked for France, their aged weapons were exchanged for the Short Magazine Lee Enfield, then the standard active service rifle. The SMLE was 5 inches shorter and more than a pound lighter, thus a more comfortable weapon for all troops, but particularly so for Bantams. The Royal Small Arms Factory, when told of this problem for smaller troops, introduced a rifle modification with a half-inch shorter butt. These were identified by the letter "S" stamped into the brass heel-plate. Further modification which reduced the butt by one inch, marked "B" for Bantam stock, was not officially introduced until September 1st, 1918, long after most Bantams were dead or gone.

In the summer of 1915, the 17/18 Welch Regiment arrived at Aldershot, each now also accompanied by an obligatory Welsh mascot goat, and caused a good deal of comment among the civilians of that Army-dominated town. The Welch settled alongside their fellow-countrymen in the 119th, and weighed up the other battalions in the 40th Division. "I don't know which is worse," Jack Jones declared, "Both bunches of them talked sort of funny, look-you!"

The units whose speech he maligned were English and Scots, who were having enough trouble without the prospect of fighting a three-way brawl every pay night as well. The 120th and 121st Brigades were undergoing a series of drastic weeding out of sub-standard men which was to continue until early 1916 and for a while threaten the existence of the whole division.

Not everyone found the Bantams to be an admirable body

of men. One disappointed observer was the poet Isaac Rosenberg, himself a new recruit to the 12th Suffolk Battalion. Though not in the least warlike, London-born Rosenberg had returned from South Africa to join the army, just as his writings were gaining him a growing reputation. Originally turned down by the Royal Army Medical Corps, he commented in a letter, "I could not get the work I wanted, so I have joined this Bantam Battalion (as I was too short for any other), which seems to be the most rascally affair in the world. I have to eat out of a basin together with some horribly smelling scavenger who spits and sneezes into it, etc. It is most revolting, at least up to now. I don't mind the hard sleeping, the stiff marches etc. but this is unbearable. Besides my being a Jew makes it bad amongst these wretches. I am looking forward to having a bad time altogether."

He scathingly referred to his fellow volunteers, mostly Cockneys, as "A horrible rabble. Falstaff's scarecrows were nothing on these. Three out of four have been scavengers; the fourth is a ticket-of-leave." The sense of fellowship seems to have caught him later however, when he wrote to joke that "The King inspected us Thursday. He must have waited a good while for us to stand up. At a distance we look like soldiers sitting down, you know, legs so short." Rosenberg left Bury St. Edmunds with a draft of Suffolks which went to help make up yet another Bantam unit being formed in Lancashire.

There had been a large number of under-sized volunteers still on the rolls of the Warrington recruiting committee in September, 1915. Lacking only a battalion able to accept them, the authorities created the 12th (Service) Battalion, South Lancashire Regiment. Lt.-Col. W. B. Ritchie, DSO, was appointed as commanding officer, and he initiated a vigorous training programme when the battalion went to Blackdown Camp, Aldershot. It formed part of the 120th Brigade, 40th Division, and "showed fine spirit in the traditions of the South Lancs."

However, the new battalion was no sooner trained than it was disbanded in April, 1916. Most of its fit officers and men were transferred to the 11th Battalion, King's Own Royal Lancaster Regiment, and Lt.-Col.Ritchie was given the command. So it was that cadres of Londoners, East Anglians and Lancashire miners found themselves melded into a regiment mainly formed of tough moorland men from Cumbria. When The King's Own Royal Lancaster Regiment announced the urgent formation of the 11th Battalion, it made no mention of the word "bantam." The height standards were given as between 5 ft. and 5 ft. 2 ins., chest expansion 33 ins., and age between nineteen to forty. The posters did promise "You and your friends will be kept together and trained at Lancaster as far as is possible."

The recruiting base for this new battalion was the same as for the previous units raised by the King's Own, a semicircle of towns from the Lancashire coastal resorts of Blackpool and Morecambe to Barrow, Ulverston, and Garstang, and the mountain villages of Cumberland and Northumberland. It was evidently a region which had not been previously combed for bantam-sized men, for the response was overwhelming in numbers, considering that by then the first flush of enthusiasm for war had ebbed across Britain.

The regiment made an extra aggressive drive to fill the unit by touring the countryside in motor coaches. The missionary party consisted of a brass band, an adjutant, quartermaster, medical officers, recruiting sergeants, and parliamentary speech-makers. The resulting flock of recruits were looked after by a local retired officer, Major F. V. Churchill until the arrival of a permanent C.O., Lt.-Colonel G. W. Priestley. Together, they did their best to make the men as comfortable as possible in a collection of tents and hutments in Coulston Road field behind the Depot.

One of the first to walk between the granite pillars of Bowerham Barracks, past the regimental dogs' burial plot, and into the arrivals office, was Harry Stansfield. "The place was bedlam," he recalled.* "Groups of soldiers and civilians mixed together were being drilled on every patch of open space inside and out. They were so mixed up, I was given two medicals and two sets of uniforms. Strangely enough, they both fitted me well, so I guess the army had the Bantams' clothing problem licked by then."

"We were well received by the regulars at the depot who worked hard enough on our training that we won the regimental prize cup for general smartness at our passing-out parade eight weeks later. Our drill sergeant was a Liverpool Irishman, an amusing character who said we would never be sent abroad as we wouldn't be able to see over the parapet. How wrong he was." [These memories were bravely recounted to me during Harry Stansfield's terminal last weeks in Ottawa's Tri-Services Hospital, in late 1978.)

The Highland Light Infantry had by now recruited a second Bantam unit, the 14th Battalion, but was also experiencing difficulty in maintaining physical standards. "We had a lot of wee lads who never should have been accepted," says George Cunningham. "Short and wide was the style we needed, and here were weedy boys and old men. I was fair disgusted at the medicos for taking them in at all. We youngsters with a bit more heft to us could see there wasn't much chance of building a fighting battalion until they got rid of the runts."

The same concern was expressed for the 12th Battalion, Royal Suffolk Regiment, whose officers now regretted having passed along some fit men to the King's Own. One wrote, "Among them had been well-knit men from Suffolk, Cambridgeshire, The Isle of Ely, and Essex. The promising start of the 12th Battalion was set back not only by the drafting away of some fit men, and medical discharges but by the further loss of 133 'men' who were sent home after a careful check proved they were well under minimum age."

The Suffolk Regiment was founded in 1685, and always took pride in retaining its county character as much as possible. However, when faced with the need of additional small men, the regimental depot at Bury St. Edmunds had to tackle their recruiting drive with more widespread efforts, directed by Major

A. James. Deputations were sent into Yorkshire and Rutland in search of suitable applicants, and a draft of two hundred Bantams was gratefully received from the Middlesex Regiment. Elsewhere, other regiments were suffering similar problems.

Twenty-three Gaelic speaking fishermen sailed from the Outer Hebrides to the mainland when word reached them that The Camerionians (Scottish Rifles) was forming the 13th (Bantam) Battalion. They arrived at Hamilton Depot in mid-July and were signed up in turn after brief interviews conducted via their one English-speaking member. He was made a Lance-Corporal on the spot, with the sole job of interpreter while herding his fellow-islanders through. their training.

Other bantam recruits included schoolboys and black-smiths, sailors and clerks. The largest occupational group was again composed of miners, who walked in from all over Lanarkshire to join the new battalion of this historic regiment.

Originally named after the Presbyterian followers of Robert Cameron, The Cameronians was raised in 1698, and for many years afterward each man in the regiment was required to carry a Bible in his haversack. Such religious fervour was coupled with a redoubtable military skill which in modern times is reflected in their unique custom of carrying rifles during church parades.

One of the appreciative recruits was James Robertson, the coal-heaver who had been rejected by the London Scottish on the first day of the war. Though Cockney-born, Robertson was proud of his heritage, and determined to serve only in a Scots regiment. The day after he drew his railway warrant and issue bag of cheese sandwiches for the journey from London, he was in Hamilton Depot being happily fitted with Cameron plaid "trews" (trousers.) Wisely perhaps, the authorities had decided that kilts somehow just wouldn't look right on short-legged Bantams. The 13th Battalion was formed in two months, and moved down to Aldershot in September. However, it was steadily reduced in numbers by frequent weeding-out inspections. By February, 1916, the Cameronians had abandoned the experiment, sending Robertson among with 200-odd survivors to join the 14th H.L.I.

The Middlesex Regiment—nicknamed "The Diehards"— was mainly composed of Londoners, and its officers decided to tap some of the large number of undersized Cockneys who were enlisting in various other regiments. Accordingly, the 22nd (Bantam) Battalion was formed at Mill Hill in June, 1915, "There never was a battalion more buggered about than we was," said Tommy Dickson. "The poor old 22nd had no sooner been trained to a "T", when it was disbanded and off we went to the Suffolks. Then back we all came to the Middlesex again, this time in the 21st Battalion, a half-Bantam outfit."

Several hundred short Londoners thus found themselves in the city regiment after all, with a sort-of Bantam unit.

Marching in the 21st Battalion was a 34-year-old New Yorker who claimed to be the shortest corporal in the British Army. Barely 4 ft. 9 ins., high, Henry Thridgould had emigrated from Britain to upper New York State in 1911, and was so happy with his new home, he declared he'd never leave. However, when war was declared in 1914, he paid his own way back across the Atlantic and managed to join the British army within days of arrival. Thridgould's powerful voice and demanding grasp of parade-ground drill made him a popular figure during Middlesex Regiment ceremonials until he went off to fight in France.

In the spring of 1916, Major General Ruggles-Brise faced the reality that his division was unfit to go overseas in its present state. Lacking the uniform hardiness of the Welsh miners, the Anglo-Scots brigades had lost the struggle to obtain enough fit men from the material sent by their parent regiments. In the 120th Brigade, the King's Own and the H.L.I. rejected over 1,400 men and could muster only one reliable battalion each. The 121st brigade had disbanded the Sherwoods and Middlesex and managed to form good battalions for the 12th Suffolks and 13th Green Howards.

The Divisional Commander insisted that he needed at least

four additional battalions of fit men before the 40th could go
on active service. The War Office agreed to send him the 13th
East Surrey, 14th Argyle & Sutherland Highlanders, and the
20/21st Middlesex Regiment. With the exception of part of
the 21st Middlesex, these reinforcements were regular-sized
men, and it was decided that despite the majority of the division
still being bantam-sized, the fighting-cock divisional sign would
be discarded. While retaining its title of 40th (Bantam)
Division, the sign would now be a non-committal white
diamond. As we shall see a year later, though, the valour and
bloody sacrifice of Bantam soldiers at the battle for Bourlon
Wood became immortalized in the divisional sign by re-
incorporating their fighting-cock symbol.

For the numerous remaining Bantams, survivors of repeated
medical examinations which were curiously more exacting than
those given to men of average stature, the prospect of active
service was suddenly near. Morale soared when orders were given
in early June for the division to move towards Southampton for
embarkation to Le Havre. The 11th King's Own were heard to
march aboard the *SS City of Benares,* singing to the tune of
'The Church's One Foundation' with confident self-mockery,

> "We are the Bantam sodgers,
> The short-arse companee.
> We have no height, we cannot fight.
> What bloody good are we?
> And when we get to Berlin, the Kaiser he will say,
> Hoch, Hoch, mein Gott, what a bloody fine lot
> Is the Bantam companee !"

The last units of the 40th Division sailed across the Channel
on the evening of June 5th, 1916. That same night, far to the
north, *HMS Hampshire* hit a mine off Scapa Flow, sinking into
the black waters with all hands. Among them was Field Marshal
Lord Kitchener, the nation's top military leader and the
Bantam's most powerful champion.

The 40th Division was placed in the First Army Corps, commanded by General Monro, who inspected the 121st Brigade on June 12th. One of his staff aides loudly chortled, "I suppose the little chaps will do alright once they manage to get over the parapet!" An apple-cheeked captain of the Green Howards loyally riposted with a dare, "And perhaps you'd like to give them a leg up and come along yourself in their first battle show, sir!" From his youth, rank, and outspokenness, one gathers this officer was a veteran of previous hard duty in the trenches, with not enough expectation of surviving combat to give a damn about being insubordinate.

The division had arrived in some of the most pleasant weather seen in northern France for almost a year. The eternal leaden skies had cleared, and brilliant sunshine tried to give even the Western Front a more cheerful appearance. "Larks and other songbirds were everywhere," David Jenkins remembered. "Singing away with no fear of the guns, a beautiful sound they made. Shelling died down for a few days, as if the gunners didn't want to shatter the peaceful sounds. When an officer set off with a shotgun to hunt partridges behind the lines, we all actually booed him."

The majority of officers were concerned with bloodsports on a larger scale, as they worked to organize the fresh division into fighting order. The three infantry brigades were marched into position in easy stages, drawing a somewhat more respectful response than their predecessors from civilians who now opined, *"Comme ils sont solides."*

Concentrated west of Bethune, with their headquarters at Bruay, they were joined by the non-bantam troops and equipment of their support brigades. Three field artillery brigades, the 181st, 185th, 188th, and the 178th howitzer brigade were under command of Brigadier H. L. Reed, who had won his VC during the Boer War. The Royal Engineers provided the 224th, 229th, and 231st field companies. There was a Signals Company, and the 135/6/7th Field Ambulance units.

Early in the war, General Haig's initial opinion had been, "The machine gun is a greatly over-rated weapon." In grim fact, within months, the machine-gun had become the most fearsome infantry weapon. Now, the 40th Division was forming its own 244th MG Company., and the 12th (Pioneer) Battalion, Green Howards, was attached for trench working and as a reserve of riflemen.

While this organization went on, the familiar pattern of training and attachment for front line experience began. Brigades sent sections to Maisnil-les-Ruitz for training in bombing, wiring, sniping, and patrolling. Other groups marched to the Bois-du-Froissart for training in woodland fighting. Each battalion in turn sent cadres into the trenches alongside veteran units. Within three weeks of entering the war zone, the Bantams had sustained 250 casualties, 47 of them fatal.

Eighteen of the Division's first casualties were members of the 18th. Welch undergoing trench instruction with the Munster Regiment near Maroc. One of them was Trevor Jones, who observed, "There was no mud to speak of when we first went into the line. The area quite reminded me of home, all slag-heaps and pitheads. I recall we were having a bit of a sing-song in the trench, when an Irish voice shouted, 'Look out, toffee-apple on the way!' I just had time to see a mortar-bomb like a big round ball with a stick in it come twirling across the sky when there was one hell of a bang. I dug myself out and helped the others recover six dead men lying right beside me. They didn't look dead, really, and I expected them to start singing again the next minute."

Isaac Rosenberg was among the new arrivals, now transferred to the King's Own, and wrote to a lady friend in June, 1916, to describe his first impressions of combat. "We made straight for the trenches, but we've had vile weather, and I've been wet through for four days and nights. I lost all my socks and things before I left England, and hadn't the chance to make it up again, so I've been in trouble, particularly with bad heels; you can't have the slightest conception of what such an apparently trivial thing means. We've had shells bursting two yards off, bullets whizzing all over the show, but all you are aware of is the agony of your heels."

Just as the Somme offensive started further south in early July, the 40th Division was given its own sector to hold at Loos. When the battles first began in 1915 for possession of Loos, the objective had been to gain control of the coal workings there. Soon the area was devastated, the mineshafts blocked, the railways destroyed, and the miners had fled or lay dead under their ruined villages. Both armies then settled down to a mindless slugging match across the bulging salient in the Black Country between Lens and Hulloch, a futile killing ground.

Here the line ran through the dreary landscape called the Gohelle, a chalk plain dominated by Vimy Ridge to the west. In peacetime, a few woods and treelined roads had relieved the flat monotony. There had been many small villages, too; ugly *corons* of red-roofed miners' houses in linked rows. Towering around them were huge black piles of stone waste from the coal mines.

Now, only a few splintered tree stumps and piles of rubble marked the sites of human settlement, and the slag-heaps took on a new importance. From their summits, even a 100-foot elevation provided a commanding observation view of the surrounding Gohelle. All these mounds were dominated by the Double Crassier, a mountainous slag-heap through which ran the front line of both enemies. Because of their observation value, these mounds were constantly being fought over, men dying every day for temporary possession of a few piles of stones.

At night, fighting patrols circled the heaps at ground level, pausing to listen for the slither of gravel above, which betrayed the slightest movement. Then bombs would fly, either the fat Mills grenade or the skimming oyster bomb and stick grenade of the Germans. Bayonet parties would scramble up to finish off survivors, the dead and victors often sliding down together in miniature avalanches.

The Double Crassier was where the first decoration was gained by a member of the 40th Division. Lance Corporal A. C. Handy of the 12th Suffolks received the award of the Military Medal for single-handedly attacking a German patrol.

This desolate environment of rubbled villages, mining equipment, and shale-tips generated its own savage style of roving warfare. The Bantams were sent out day and night on fighting patrols to meet Germans on similar missions. It became a meeting place for war-parties with no more strategic purpose than to inflict death on the enemy. "We didn't really think about the big aims of the war," said Morgan Davis. "All we knew was the job of killing Jerries and stopping them doing the same thing to us."

So many potential strong points to provide cover or observation gave these ruined features a spurious importance on staff commanders' maps, and resulted in the Division receiving a continual series of such fatuous orders as "A show of force must be made to retain control of Fosse 8 coal-works," and "You will send a strong patrol to penetrate beyond Hill 70."

Raiding was a constant activity along the sector as the Division probed through the heavy belts of German wire in search of prisoners or combat. The enemy learned how to turn this aggression to their advantage by strewing the area with booby-traps or simply lying in ambush for British raiding parties.

"We were out one cloudy night covering a raid, when everything went wrong," Jack Jones recalled. "I was waiting with my Lewis gun and two bombers for what seemed like hours. We'd just decided that our patrol had got lost or captured when the bright moon broke through clouds. Clear as day, I could see our officer and his party running forward all crouched over. I could also see three Jerries lying in a shell hole aiming a machine gun."

"I hadn't time to tell the bombers where to throw, so I just loosed off with the Lewis. I fired a short burst, then the Jerries opened up and hit some of our lads point-blank. I fired two drums at the machine gun crew and we sent a few bombs over too. Our officer was just seeing to our wounded when another bunch of Jerries arrived, firing as they came. Most of the raiding party went down in a few seconds. Luckily for me as it turned out, I could not fire until I reached the other pans of ammo. Before I had a chance to pull the trigger, there was a noise behind me and about ten more Jerries passed a few feet away. They would have got us for sure if I'd been firing then and given away my position."

"The two large groups of enemy turned over our lads, looking for prisoners or identification. None of our wounded can have been able to walk, because the Jerries began to finish them off, one by one. Horrible it was; the sound of rifle butts and bayonets, and the odd crack of a pistol. We didn't want to commit suicide, so could do nothing to help. We didn't let them off Scot-free, though. When they moved away and were bunched up to pass through a gap in their wire, I fired three pans of .303 into them and the two other chaps emptied their rifles. After a long wait, we crawled over and found eight Welsh dead and some Jerries scattered here and there. We did not go to examine the enemy bodies near the wire, because there would be a Spandau trained on them for sure."

A second raid by the 12th. South Wales Borderers had better luck, and managed to enter the German lines. They ranged left and right of the entry point, bombing dug-outs as they went. The enemy fought back with grenades, one of which badly injured Captain Pritchard. While withdrawing, this officer spotted a Bavarian attempting to hide and leaped back down into the trench to take the Division's first prisoner.

Though weak from his wounds, Pritchard refused assistance and insisted on keeping charge of the captive. Soon afterwards, he was wounded again, and only then handed over the PW to 2nd. Lieutenant Wood. Pritchard made it back to his own lines, but died from his wounds soon afterwards. Lt. Wood delivered the prisoner, who was found to carry useful documents, and returned to the German trenches. He saw to it that all the SWB wounded had been evacuated and was the last man to come back. For his actions, he was awarded the Military Cross. Strangely, there is no record of any medal for the resolute Captain Pritchard.

About this time, the 18th. Welch Regiment captured a prisoner who arrived under bizarre circumstances. While retiring from a raid in which they blew up some mines, lost three men missing, and carried back their wounded Lt. Salisbury, a German was seen scuttling along the rim of Double Crassier. He was expertly winged and brought back bleeding but alive. Under interrogation, he proved to be co-operative in giving information about his unit, but vague about how he came to be wandering alone around the slagheap. From what he could recollect, it was deduced that he had been blown up by one of the mine explosions, hurtled across a fifty-yard-wide belt of wire, and was dazedly roaming on the wrong side of the line when shot.

Raiding continued to be the obsession of High Command, yet which never issued any special equipment to help make the commando-style sorties more effective. Troops were left to improvise; lead-weighted coshes, sharpened entrenching-tools, or for some officers, privately purchased automatic pistols. One notable exception was Lord Howard de Walden, who commanded 9th Batt., Royal Welsh Fusiliers in 1916. Being both wealthy and generous, he often provided his men with extra comforts and equipment paid for out of his own pocket. Interested in historical arms and armour, de Walden commissioned his friend and fellow collector Felix Joubert to design a knife especially for trench-fighting.

The fearsome result was a dagger with an 18" long leaf-shaped blade, 3" across at its widest, and a pointed hilt that could also be

Fearsome trench-knife specially designed for Welsh soldiers was adopted by the Bantams for use in night raiding.

used as a weapon. The unique circular hand-guard could be folded flat when the knife was sheathed. Each blade was engraved with an intertwined "Jo", Joubert's mark, and lettered, *Dros Urddas Cymru* ('for the honour of Wales'). Folklore had it that Joubert's knife was based on an historical Welsh design used by archers at Crecy. According the RWF Museum though, "This is romantic nonsense, and there is no evidence to suggest that any specifically Welsh form of sword or dagger existed."

Lord Howard issued his knives to his 9th. Battalion, who soon employed them effectively for night raiding. Before long, a few of these daggers turned up among Welsh Bantams, too, either by barter or recovery from dead previous owners. Jack Jones recalls hefting one, which he called his "cabbage cutter." He wrote, "Very useful it was, too. The main idea of a raid was to capture a Gerry prisoner and bring him back for interrogation about the opposing enemy. But once we had bagged one, any others we came across that night were surplus to requirements, you might say. In which case, our sharp knives could finish off the poor blighters with a minimum of noise."The many miners in the 40th Division found they had reached a sector ideal for their talents. The chalky ground was perfect for trench-making, but even more so for mining. Wherever such ground allowed, military tunnelling added another dimension along the Western Front, as miners sank tunnels to lay explosives under each other's lines. So prevalent was this warfare and so feared was its result that front line units detailed men to do nothing else but listen for sounds of mining below. Stethoscopes and microphones were developed for this task but, for the most part, troops relied on their own sharp hearing or on such crude listening-devices as an empty petrol-can half filled with water sunk into the trench floor.

At Loos, underground war was at times more destructive in its results than the bombardments. Time and again, whole sections of trench earth would erupt skyward with bits and pieces of human flesh, then fall back to bury men who had escaped the blast itself. The British Army employed special Tunnelling Companies to push mining saps forward and tamp ammonal in place for detonation before attacks. Too often, the resulting craters would only form new magnets of death as troops from both sides would rush forward to occupy them and fight duels around their muddy rims.

"We had three shafts going at once in our trench," smiled Morgan Davies. "It had been a year or two since we'd used a pick and shovel underground, but if anything we worked harder than ever we did down the pit. Officers warned us to go a bit slower, as too much excavated chalk was a dead giveaway of what we were up to. We had to cart it away or dull it down with mud, or Jerry would give us some extra attention."

"Their lines were sometimes only three or four days digging-distance away. Things got tense near the end, as you never knew if Jerry was sinking a counter-mine. We would dig and lay explosives in a mad rush to beat him to it. The worst part was that we had to get permission to blow from the Senior Trenching Officer. If he delayed the okay too long, up we could go on top of a double load of TNT, his and ours together. That happened every few weeks."

One German miner worked so loudly underground that he became known as "Old Bill." So long as he clinked his tools, coughed, and generally indicated his position, the British could trace progress of the enemy minework. Listeners became so fond of him that they would delay firing counter-mines until his distinctive clatter ended and he was well clear of the blast. Finally, this unseen chivalry had to end, when the opposing camouflets were so close that it was dangerous to delay, and Old Bill was regretfully blown sky-high by his Welsh opposite numbers.

Night raids and mining gave the infantry brigades some sense of being able to hit back at the enemy and helped alleviate the constant strain of artillery bombardment. Shellfire was the ever present fear. Whether the projectiles came singly to shatter a quiet moment or in thousands during a major cannonade, men's flesh would cringe at each vicious explosion and sense a helpless vulnerability. A lone shell would crack a ranging air-burst, there would be a bowelchurning pause, then the sky would fill with screaming metal and plough earth, mud and humanity alike into a ghastly paste.

The troops devised their own half-comical names for the different types of missiles. There were "minney-werfers" that threw 150 lb. missiles, "screaming-meemies" that howled before they killed, and "daisy-cutters" that exploded a thousand razor-sharp blades at knee height.

There was the slow rumble of "Big Fritz," a railway-gun 12 miles away, and one could follow the 16-inch shell on its slow way to devastate a 500-yard radius. Whiz-Bangs and Jack Johnsons were fast, flat-trajectory shells that arrived before you knew it, while fat Rum Jars and Oil Drums [types of heavy shells] sailed over lazily, fuses fizzling to give time for the alert or the lucky to run elsewhere.

At Maroc, sentries were permanently detailed to stand, well-hidden, on high pit-heads to listen for the hollow "chung" of a trench mortar. They would then blow a whistle and point to each bomb as it curved across the sky, so that its point of arrival could be anticipated well in advance. But no one could anticipate all the high-velocity artillery shells that hunted men hourly and tore their bodies.

The grim realities of being a medical orderly under shellfire are recalled by Phillip Brereton Townsend, then a 17year old private in the 135th Field Ambulance, RAMC., attached to the 40th Division.

"Shortly after arriving in France, I was detailed to be on duty at a small advanced dressing station in the ruined village of Maroc, not far behind the front line in the Lens-Loos Salient. Together with another private, I was detailed to go to the mortuary which was in a partially demolished house. In a rear room on the ground floor, lay eight bodies, two of which had been recently recovered from No Man's Land. My comrade and I had been given a bodkin, string, and eight old army blankets. We were ordered not to inspect clothing or pockets but to place each man's identity discs in a docket envelope and sew up the body in the blanket, then sew the docket to the blanket."

"When we moved one body, which was green with age after being in Noman's Land for a long period, onto the blanket, I fainted, and my comrade had to bring me round before we could proceed on our task. This was my first job as a medical orderly in the theatre of war, and at my young age I could not quite cope. It took us nearly all afternoon and evening to complete the task, after which the bodies were ready to be loaded onto a mule-drawn ambulance for transit to a cemetery behind the lines."

"Later, when we were about to go back to the line, my section of the Field Ambulance was resting near the forward area. We were partaking of a stew concoction from our field kitchen just as a platoon of Gordon Highlanders came marching out of the line. Each man was lumbered with a load of equipment, all covered in mud, sadly in a filthy condition. Suddenly, we heard the whine of a heavy shell, and it exploded very near the platoon, detonating with terrific force."

"The result was that out of about two dozen men, seven were killed and eleven wounded. We rushed over to the casualties, giving instant succour. I with two comrades came on one soldier who's left leg had been shattered by a piece of jagged metal, and the leg was hanging by only an inch of flesh. We were unable to handle him as a stretcher case until I had cut through the inch of flesh with my jack-knife. After which, we were able to lift him onto the stretcher and into a motor ambulance. His kilt was roughly weighed later and we found it to be about fifty pounds including blood, flesh, mud, and water."

Andrew Gilmour was a sixteen-year-old private in the 14th Argyle & Sutherland Highlanders who served in the 40th Division. "After having one spell in the line, we were detailed to go back to defend some four or five sectors—thinly occupied lines in extended salients like Hulluch and Loos, deadly legacies of the previous partial successes. With all too many casualties, we were still expected to keep up the impression that the trenches were fully manned, with all the usual activities of patrols and raids, trench extensions, repairs and saps manned within forty yards of the German lines.

"During these months, I never heard it suggested that the Bantams were not every whit as good as ourselves (a normal height unit) or as any other division, though we in the Argyles did have one grouse. With an average difference in height of some eight inches, it was not unknown to find that the Bantams had pulled down the parapet and used it to build up the firestep."

"At a place near Loos known as Fosse Calonne, on a hot day in August, 1916, the Argyles were in support waiting to take over the front line from the King's Own. Word came down to us via the bombing platoon that a German raiding party had taken away as prisoners the King's Own section manning a sap close to the enemy lines. The sap had been re-occupied, but would the Argyle bombers please come and help take over as soon as possible?"

"I happened to be the first to arrive ahead of three or four others who hurriedly made our way into the forward listening-post. I stole apprehensively towards the sap-head, expecting to find a sentry with a periscope watching the German lines and someone there to give the usual information about bomb-stores and ammunition supplies. Instead, I found one solitary Bantam, half naked, his tunic, rifle and equipment strewn nearby, busily chasing lice along the seams of his shirt. He cocked a mischievous eye at me and remarked in broad Lancashire tones, 'Ee, Jock, 'ee wants fookin, doos t'Kaiser!' With that, he grabbed his belongings and scampered away along the trench."

A strong bond of affection and mutual confidence was forged between this Scottish battalion and the Lancastrians. In September, when the latter were taking over a trench from the 14/Argyle & Sutherland Highlanders, they found posted up a piece of paper inscribed with a poem written by Major Maxwell Rouse:

> There's a regiment of Bantams, in a place I mustn't name.
> Who, for cussedness and courage, stand alone,
> You'd pass 'em by in Blighty with a look of mild surprise.
> You'd calculate the column was a'wantin' p'r'aps in size,
> By glory on the other side you'd hand 'em out the prize
> —King's Own.

> With kits abunched around them, and a bushel load of bombs,
> You'd barely find the owner on a phone,
> With picks and packs and Lewis Guns, they get there every
> time,
> A-walkin' on the parapet, to miss the ruddy slime,
> The stiffer task afore 'em, the cheerier the climb.
> —King's Own.

> When shells and other trifles scream their passage through the
> night,
> And Very lights a-twinkle in our zone,
> When snipers pick a penny from our pockets at their ease,
> And enemy machine gunners are cuttin' life as cheese,
> We ring up reinforcements, and we say to Bisset, "Please,
> —King's Own.

> And when the units muster in the Grand Review above,
> When God to every Tommy lad is shown:
> With picks and packs and Lewis Guns, you'll see 'em swinging
> by,

Just little men—not giants—but their chins are carried high,
And kindly He'll look down on 'em, and whisper
"They are My King's Own."

The weather began to badly deteriorate towards the end of the 40th Division's stint in the line. Temperatures dropped to freezing and cold rain turned the coal-dust everywhere into a black abrasive slime. When word arrived of their impending relief, officers decided to step up aggressive activities to give the enemy a last salute. Each battalion during its final four day rest in reserve was required to plan for raids during its last four days up the line. As each took its turn in the trenches it was with the knowledge that they had to go out looking for danger, as if the routine shelling was not hazardous enough itself.

Four raids went out on the night of October 8, two each by the 18/Green Howards and 20/Middlesex. The Yorkshires blew gaps in the enemy wire around Long Sap, and sent in two raiding parties led by 2nd. Lieutenant L. A. Venables and A. W. Simpkin of "B" Company. The Germans had not been occupying the tunnel and rushed forward along the communications trench into a shower of hand-grenades. Two Germans were captured unharmed, and the raiders would have then withdrawn content if more of the enemy had not arrived. A vicious hand-to-hand struggle began, with men leaning over comrades' shoulders to stab or shoot at the shadowy figures within the narrow trench walls. Five Germans were killed with no loss to the 13th Battalion, and they returned with their prisoners.

The next night, it was "C" Company's turn, under command of Second Lieutenants Hodgson and Perkins. They blew their way into the German trenches and held them for 58 minutes. This time, no prisoners were captured, but 20 of the enemy were killed in a drawn-out fight which raged at each end of the occupied section of trench. Bantams stacked enemy dead at the traverse angles, firing across these human barricades. As intelligence material, they brought back identity discs, maps, and unit shoulder straps taken from the slain. The raiding party carried away their seven wounded, one of whom later died. Though wounded himself, 2nd. Lt. Hodgson continued in his duties and was the last man to leave the German line. The raids brought congratulations for the battalion from the Corps, Division, and Brigade Commanders, along with exultation over "the marked increase of success on our side."

The Germans were not to be outdone, and proceeded to shell, gas, and raid the Yorkshire sector with increasing fury. Deaths and wounds increased among the Green Howards, but they held their line until relieved. Another battalion was caught during the relief, when a mine was exploded under them, and the Germans temporarily gained possession of 70 yards of the Division's line. Pride was assuaged next morning when the enemy was ejected by the 17th. Welch Regiment, though at the cost of losing its popular commanding officer, Lieutenant Colonel Wilkie, who was killed.

On November 2nd, Divisional Order No. 28 detailed the relief of the 40th. Division, and prescribed the route march south west towards their new host XV Corps, Fourth Army. The march was a miserable trek through blizzards, sleetstorms, and very heavy rain. Much resentment was caused when the troops were ordered to march at attention, as the easy leadership was tightened once the men left the front.

James Pringle, 12/Suffolks, wrote his memories of their withdrawal. "Soon as we weren't fighting their war for them, senior officers started appearing and barking remarks about what slack soldiers we were. We were dog-tired, constipated, in rags and holey boots. We'd been shot, shelled, gassed, scared stiff, and worked like slaves, but now all they could call us was slackers."

"Our own officers and N.C.O.'s hadn't much choice but to crack down, too, and they went at us, shouting 'Straighten up!' and 'Left-Right-Left!' We had a bit of fun for a while; making sheep-noises, singing dirty songs, and deliberately staying out of step. We kept this up long enough to show we resented being bollocked about, then we settled down to marching as smart as could be. Soon, all you could hear was the tramp of boot-heels and the pouring rain. Already our cheerfulness on leaving the line had gone. I marched on, soaking wet, wondering what new hellhole the Gamecocks were being sent to."

Private Edgar Robinson (seated) left a written memoir of his combat experience as a teenaged Bantam with the famed Green Howards Regiment.

CHAPTER EIGHT

One Green Howard's War

Before the First World War, the sparsely-settled North Riding of Yorkshire had always found enough men to enlist in the Alexandra, Princess of Wales' Own (Yorkshire) Regiment—more popularly known as The Green Howards.

Strongly local in favour and with a valiant reputation, it had originally been known as Howard's Regiment, following the 18th. Century practice of naming units after their colonels. However, when the 3rd. Foot and 19th. Foot Regiment each were led by colonels named Howard, the regiments became distinguished as "The Buff Howards" (later "The Buffs") and "The Green Howards."

The Yorkshire unit became best known by this name, even after their more official designation to Princess Alexandra and the display of her Danish cross in their cap-badge. The regiment fought in countless actions from the West Indies to the Crimea, and garrisoned Ceylon for half a century. It had always been able to keep its county character, until the demands of the Great War called for numbers of men far beyond that which the local population could supply. The regiment then began recruiting throughout Northern England so as to quickly make up enough manpower for its Kitchener battalions.

Among the rejected applicants had been many sturdy lead miners and coal miners. In early 1915, they and no less stalwart townsmen received a second chance to sign up when the call went out from the regimental depot at Richmond for men to join the 13th. (Bantam) Service Battalion. One volunteer was a young solicitor's clerk by the name of Edgar Robinson. Years later, he wrote 'A Teenager In The Great War,' a personal journal of his experiences which were typical of his battalion. The journal was not published, but quietly kept by Mr. Robinson as a private memoir. He contacted me during research for material about the Bantams, and generously allowed part of his story to be included here.

"Right up to Christmas 1914, long queues of men and boys waited daily to enlist, but afterwards things quietened down. I was impatient to get in and join my two brothers who had enlisted on the first day, but being under age, I had to think how I could do it. I realized it would be better to wait a few months until the recruiting office at Middlesbrough was left in sole charge of an old soldier sergeant, a type who lived for beer. The sergeant received one shilling (in those days equal to five pints of beer) for every recruit he swore in. One day during my lunch hour, I decided it was time for me to try to enlist. Walking boldly into the recruiting office, I said to the Sergeant, 'I've come to join up.'"

"He looked me up and down and said 'How old are you, son?' 'Sixteen,' I replied. He just shook his head. Seeing the disappointed look on my face, and probably thinking of the beer he was missing, he said, 'Tell you what to do, son. Take a walk round the Town Hall, see if you have got any older, then come back in.' I did just that. Walking into the office again, I said. 'I'm eighteen now, Sergeant.' 'Good.' he replied. 'I can swear you in now.' Taking a Bible in my right hand, I repeated the Oath after him. Giving me the 'Kings Shilling' and taking one himself, he shook hands and we parted. Looking back, I saw he was locking the office door prior to going to the pub opposite."

"Next day, I joined The Green Howards at Richmond, Yorks. When I told my mother later, she said that though proud of me, she would try to stop me going. I replied that I would only run away from home if she did, so she reluctantly gave in. On leaving the firm of solicitors where I was employed, they presented me with a silver wrist watch with my name on the back. I carried this watch right through the war, and still have it."

"After a few days at Richmond, getting my uniform, etc., I

was sent to Otley, where the 13th. Yorks was being formed. I was 5 ft. 4 in. at the time, and was one of the first members of the battalion. We stayed there for about two months until the battalion was made up to strength and did our training in the extensive grounds of a mansion. Part of our training was route marching about ten miles or so. During one I shall never forget, I was marching alongside an old soldier who had served in India, where it was a habit to chew plug pipe tobacco. He was chewing away and spitting the juice out as usual.

"Give me a chew,' I said. 'Righto,' he said and handed me his plug of tobacco. I bit off a good size piece and started chewing. Just as I was about to spit it out, he slapped me on the back saying, 'How are you doing?' I swallowed the whole lot and within seconds I felt proper poorly. I thought my tummy was on fire, and consequently had to fall out of the march, as sick as a pup."

"Later on. we proceeded to Skipton, 20 miles away over the Ilkley Moors, where we had another enjoyable two months with plenty of good food to build us up. Then on to Inkerman Barracks, Woking, where we finished our training before going to France."

"In those days, we were paid one shilling per day. If we made an allowance to our parents, we had sixpence a day stopped off; the government gave another sixpence and our parents received seven shillings a week. We received three shillings and sixpence, less sixpence a week to pay for our washing. This left us with three shillings, out of which we had to buy our own blanco, shoe polish, shaving soap, razor blades, etc."

"After saving up, three of us would have a weekend in London on about ten shillings, from Saturday after dinner until 9 p.m. Sunday night. We walked all over London seeing the sights, and slept the night at the YMCA, paying fourpence for a bed. During the time we were there all we had to eat was sausage and mashed potato at a cheap cafe, on Saturday night, Sunday morning, and tea-time, filling up with cold water. That was all we could afford and we were hungry growing lads."

"When at Woking, and after learning how to use our rifles properly, we had our firing course at the well known Bisley range nearby. I did very well at all ranges, especially the 1,000 yards, where I scored two bulls and three inners out of five shots. The total number of points I scored entitled me to be called a Marksman and to wear a crossed guns badge on my left tunic sleeve."

"Three weeks later, I passed as a qualified signaller, entitling me to wear a crossed flags badge as well. I also passed as a Scout, which entitled me to wear a badge of an "S" inside laurel leaves. I thought this was enough of qualifications, otherwise I would be walking one-sided !"

"When training at Otley, at the beginning, our company officer picked me out as suitable to be a lance-corporal. A corporal had to bear the brunt of all the mistakes made by those above him and could not be friendly with those below him. He had more or less a miserable life, isolated on his own, and so I refused to become one. I wanted to stay as one of the lads, with whom I got on very well. When our training was finished at Woking, we were inspected by King George V on Salisbury Plain. Men nearest to him said he was drunk. He appeared to me to be hanging round his horse's neck."

"Eventually, came news that we were off to France, causing great excitement. We received all our kit, tin hats, medical examination, the lot. Next morning, we were on the move at 4 a.m. entraining for Southampton and thence by an old fashioned paddle steamer, 'The Daffodil,' to Le Havre, France. We sailed after dark on account of the German submarines being busy in the Channel. The sea was very rough; we bounced all over and nearly everyone except me was seasick. Arriving next morning, we disembarked and marched through the town to the local station."

"Arriving at the station, we were put into dirty cattle wagons and proceeded slowly towards the Loos area of the Front. The train went so slowly that we used to get out and walk alongside to stretch our legs. It took twelve hours to do about thirty-five miles. After more training behind the lines we were ready for the Battle of the Somme. Being new troops, we were held in reserve to support the forward troops. What a din! Seven days and nights of non-stop bombardment of the German positions by our light and heavy artillery. We were billeted in broken-down villages near the Front.

We could hardly sleep for the noise. The ground trembled, we got headaches, and could hardly hear ourselves speak. Came the 1st. of July, the day to advance, tanks being used by us for the first time and really scaring the Germans. We followed up and occupied the ground our forward troops had gained. Very heavy casualties were suffered on both sides."

"After the battle died down and the thousands of German prisoners and the dead and wounded were removed, the troops dug and settled into trenches. We were moved to the south of Lens to occupy trenches there. Trenches which had previously been occupied by the French, who did not bother much about burying their dead and if they did, they only scooped soil over them, often leaving hands, feet, and heads exposed. Those not so buried were left to rot into skeletons."

"The horrible sickly smell of rotting flesh I hope never to experience again. It is like nothing on earth. We all soon became very calloused, even to placing army biscuits or a bunch of wild red poppies into a skeleton hand or a cigarette-end between the jaws. The millions of rats, some as big as cats, soon turned a dead man into a skeleton by eating the flesh. When they had nothing to eat, they often attacked us, and we in turn used to shoot, bayonet, and kill as many as we could."

"Entering the trenches for the first time, we were full of curiosity, while getting blown over and spattered with earth, stones, and shrapnel as German shells burst close by. Our sergeant-major led the way in, but it was not long before we passed him, lying dead with his head blown off. It made us realize that war was not a game, and we were rather shaken."

"Arriving at the stretch of trench we were to hold, we were assigned to our dug-outs. Dugouts were holes dug downwards into the sides of the trench nearest to the enemy. Steps went down about twenty feet deep and entered a corridor about thirty feet long, eight feet wide and six feet high, with an entrance at both ends. They were pitch dark, except for a candle burning here and there, and these were blown out by the blast whenever a shell or bomb burst close by. They were very damp."

"The first night as soon as it got dark, we were formed into working parties, repairing trenches and barbed wire. Another lad and myself were taken over the top between the lines by the sergeant. Stopping at a certain place he said, 'I want a hole dug here,' then he left us. In-between having a look round every time a Very rocket went up and with bullets whistling around us, we dug, and unearthed all sorts of things such as pieces of equipment, and tins of food."

"My shovel struck something which would not move, so I reached down in the dark to feel what is was, and what a shock I got. It was a cold clammy hand. I called my pal's attention to it, and we sat there very shaken until the sergeant returned. We told him about the hand and asked him what we were digging for. He said, 'Four men were buried alive there this morning when the trench was blown in and we want the bodies dug out again.' We were glad when he sent two men to relieve us."

"At other times, we used to help the Royal Engineers to dig 'saps,' which were holes shaped like dug-outs as close towards the German lines as possible, filled with explosive and then blown up. When blown up, troops from both sides rushed across to see who could occupy the crater first."

"Our rota of duty in the trenches was four days in the front line, four days in the support lines about 200 yards from the front and then four days rest in a broken-down French village about a mile further back. There we got shower baths, a change of underclothes, better food and caught up with our sleep."

"When in support, we had to carry barbed wire and Bangalore torpedoes up to the front line. Bangalore torpedoes were like drain pipe tubing, eight feet long, and four inches in diameter, closed at both ends and filled with high explosive. They were used for blowing up the German barbed wire when going on the nightly raids. We disliked carrying them, because if they were hit by a bullet or got a hard knock they would explode, and the two men carrying one of them would go up with it. Our worst times in the front line were at 'stand to' at dawn and dusk, when both sides threw everything they had at one another and when many a good pal went West. [Was killed.]"

"Our food in the front line, cooked and brought from the rest area consisted of: Breakfast, a small piece of cold-fried bacon on a dog-like biscuit four inches square by threequarters of an inch thick and one pint of lukewarm tea. Dinner at noon, about a pint of cold greasy stew with the same biscuit. Tea-time, one pint of lukewarm tea, jam and the same biscuits. All liquids tasted of the chloride of lime which was put in the water to sterilise it."

"We got these meals within two hours of the time due, provided they were not blown up or upset on the way. We had similar meals in the support lines, but when out on rest, the biscuits were replaced with bread, and the stew and tea were hot. In wet weather and winter months, a tot of rum was added to the morning tea to warm us up a bit."

"The trenches were from knee to thigh deep in liquid mud and water and, though we knew our legs were there, we could not feel them. We were supplied with whale oil to rub on but we often got trench-foot, anyway, for which medical treatment was given."

"In our spare time we used to 'chat up' body-lice. That meant taking off our shirts and killing, between our thumb nails, all the lice in the seams. They were up to an eighth of an inch long, grey and shaped like a crab, and boy could they bite! I remember the first time I saw a chap 'chatting up,' I thought, "the lousy beggar," and told him so. He replied, 'I bet you have some.' Slipping off to a quiet spot, I thought I would have a look and sure enough, I had. I could have cried when I saw them, hundreds of them complete with eggs, in the seams. They bit, sucked blood, and made one itch. To kill them, we squashed them and then ran a burning match or candle along the seams to get rid of the eggs. When I was first 'chatting up,' Lieutenant Simpkins came along, 'What are you doing, Robinson?' I showed him, and he was horrified, but shortly after, I saw him in a quiet corner 'chatting up,' too."

"What we had to put up with! Fighting the Germans, mud and dirt all over us, very little and poor food, no sleep, no relief of bowels for four days, lousy with lice, cold, wet and miserable, loss of pals, digging and repairing trenches and being shot at. It was hard to know which was the worst to bear. It was hell."

"While we were in the trenches at Loos, a new replacement officer came to our Battalion. It was Lt. Hodson, who lived next door to me at home. Before I had time to have a word with him, he was detailed for a night raid on the German trenches. Going over, he was shot in the knee, carried on, brought two German prisoners back, was taken to Base Hospital, awarded a Military Cross, and invalided back to England the same night. It was his first time in the trenches. In, out, and back home with a medal—all within two days! Lucky beggar."

"At this time I was an 'orderly runner,' that is, carrying messages. One night about midnight, I had to take a message to Brigade Headquarters about a mile away through communicating trenches. It was a showery night with the moon shining now and again. It was rumoured that German spies were about behind our lines, and that soldiers on their own after dark had been stabbed or strangled to death."

"On my return feeling somewhat nervous, rats scuttling in front and behind, duck boards clattering loudly when I stepped off them, I turned the corner of a trench just as the moon came out. There in front of me, placed on a board across the trench, was a grinning skull. I was scared to death, turned round and ran back so far, then climbed out of the trench. I went back over the top and risked being hit by stray bullets which were buzzing all over. Next day an order came out that we had to go about in twos."

"Daily rations used to come up to us after dark, in ration carts drawn by horses, and were left in sandbags in a shelter in Loos. Also left wrapped in sandbags in the shelter were men who had been killed that day, who were taken back by the ration carts for burial. One night, my pal and I, thinking the rations had come and feeling hungry, decided we would scrounge something to eat. Going into the pitch-dark shelter I felt around, and found a sandbag tied up just like the rations were. I put my hand in and pulled out what I thought was a piece of meat. My pal struck a match to see what I'd got. It was part of a human leg. It turned out to be the remains of a Lt. Lewis who had been carrying Mills bombs in his tunic pocket, and had been hit and blown to pieces. These were the pieces. My pal and I did not feel hungry any more."

"Altogether, Loos was a very unpleasant spot, and we were glad when we moved down to the Somme. The German trenches were high above us on the shale tips, near Loos coal mine. They could see nearly every movement of ours during the day and were sniping at us all the time."

"In 1916, when we got settled down to the Battle of the Somme, I being a marksman, was put into the sniping section. That meant going out before dawn, in front of our trenches, and finding a suitable ruined building or shell hole where one could see the German lines without being seen oneself. The first job was to smear dirt and mud over oneself to match the surroundings."

"I found a broken-down farmhouse, climbed into the false roof and got behind a broken wall, and sat down to wait for daylight. Our rifles had telescopic sights. After about three hours wait, I spotted something moving, and looking through my telescopic sights, I saw two German Staff Officers followed by a German orderly. (Staff officers had a white band round their hats). They were walking up a road towards the German trenches, side by side, with the orderly close behind."

"I waited until they were about one thousand yards distance, set my sights, and let them have it. The first officer started falling, then I shot the second officer and he fell. Reloading again, I aimed at the orderly, but did not fire, I thought, 'Poor devil, he is just an ordinary chap, like me.' When he saw the two officers fall, he turned and ran back hell-for-leather." For nearly half an hour, I watched to see if the officers moved. They did not, and I presumed them dead. Then the German guns opened up on my position. Time for me to move, and I dashed from shell hole to shell hole back to our trenches, wishing then that I had shot the orderly as well, and so stopped him from giving my position away. I reported it to our officer, he said, 'Well done, Robinson, well done. I wish I had been there to see it, then I could have recommended you for the D.C.M. However, I will see what I can do.' He did his best but nothing came of it, only a Mention In Dispatches. Gallantry awards like the DCM had to have a witness by an officer. But they all knew later that something important had happened because our position was heavily shelled by the Germans the rest of the day."

"When one of our lads was killed and others wounded by the retaliation fire, I was very upset about it. I felt like a murderer, killing the German officers in cold blood. I thought, 'Had they been shooting at me, and I had been shooting back, then that would have been fair." I still wonder, was it worth it—having one pal killed and others wounded through my killing two German Staff Officers?' I could not carry on sniping, and asked to be transferred to the signal section. I am not proud at what I did. Even to this day, I am upset when I think about it, but this is the first time I have let it be known."

Extreme youth of many Bantams volunteers shows in the faces of three Green Howards in the front row, and Edgar Robinson (standing, second from right) who was the only survivor of this group at war's end.

"Towards the end of 1916, when we were out for a fortnight's rest, I was summoned to see the Commanding Officer. 'How old are you, Robinson?' he asked. 'Nineteen, sir,' I replied. 'You're not, you know,' he said. 'I've just received a letter from the War Office to say you are under-age. While I admire your guts for coming out here, I'm afraid we have to send you back.' He shook hands and wished me luck."

"On this particular day, I was feeling pretty low, as my best pal had been killed two days before and I had not got over it. I confess that the news of being sent down the line cheered me up. I later found out that my mother, who was naturally very worried about me, had reported my correct age to the authorities."

"After saying goodbye to the lads, I was escorted by a sergeant to Domart-en-Ponthieu, 20 miles back, where I joined about a hundred other under-age soldiers who had been found out. We were called the Young Soldiers Battalion, and were mainly used for junior officers to practice training methods before they went up to the trenches. Being here meant having clean underwear every week, and good riddance to the lice."

"The young officer in charge of the platoon started a competition, the prize being a wrist watch for the smartest soldier picked out on guard parade the most times in two months. I was picked out sixteen times, won the wrist watch, and was transferred to be a waiter. The Officers' Mess was in a big French chateau, where I actually had a real bed instead of the ground I had slept on since going to France."

"We had quite a few Australian and New Zealand officers attached to us, and they decided to celebrate 'Anzac Day,' anniversary of the 1915 landing at Gallipoli. They fixed on a seven course dinner and dance in a local hall. The head waiter ordered the special food, with fifty ducks, and saw to the preparation of the food. I was in charge of six waiters and had to see to the setting of three long tables and the bar for drinks."

"About a hundred officers arrived, and by ten o'clock everyone was drunk, including myself. The officers kept falling down and rolling about when dancing and goodness knows what the ten-piece band was playing. Thinking to sober things up a bit, the other waiters and I got soda siphons and started squirting the dancers. The next thing I knew was that the officer in charge had me by the scruff of the neck and I was chucked out. What happened after that I neither knew nor cared, I do know that the officers were a sorry sight next day."

"I was with the Young Soldiers Battalion for about five months before I became nineteen and was to return to my unit. Saying goodbye to my pals, some of whom I later heard were killed soon after their return, I set off back to my unit, still on the Somme. It was good to get back to my old pals again but sad to see how many familiar faces were missing—wounded or dead. I soon settled down to the old routine of in and out of the trenches, with the discomforts and lice and the repeated cry of 'Roll on the end of the war!'"

"In the summer of 1917, seeing how exhausted and fed up we were, the powers-that-be decided to give us a short rest and sent us hay-making within a mile of the trenches. There was plenty of grass and there were hundreds of army horses to feed. It made a pleasant change for us, though one not without its dangers. When forking over the hay, we often disturbed live shells and Mills bombs that had been left around. One had only to catch the bomb release pin with the hay fork, pulling it out, and within ten seconds it exploded. It did not leave much time to throw oneself flat out of the way, and several lads were wounded. From their observation balloons, the Germans could see us working and often shelled us out of the fields, and of course the haystacks we built were just right for him to get the range."

"One day, two spotter planes flew overhead, circling one another, one British and the other German; only about two hundred feet high, we could see the pilots' faces. They were shooting at one another with revolvers, all that observation planes had in those days. They both must have hit one another at the same time. The planes crashed together, broke up, and the pilots fell to the ground, no parachutes, of course."

"They fell in the field in which we were haymaking and we went across to them. They took some finding, because they had sunk three feet into the ground. The German was on his side and the Britisher was spreadeagled, both dead in graves of their own making. Aside from these excitements, haymaking was a welcome break, but after two weeks, the rains came and we went back to the trenches."

"When I heard that after twenty months' service abroad, I was to go on leave for fourteen days at home, I was overjoyed. After a medical exam, two other lads and myself walked three miles back to Headquarters. We had a shower bath, were deloused, and fitted with a new set of clothes. It would not do for the civilians in England to see us in dirty, blood-spattered uniforms. We had another four miles to walk to the railhead where we got into cattle trucks for the all-night journey to Calais. Then by boat to Dover, train to London and home. England never looked so good to us, who thought we would never see it again."

"I thoroughly enjoyed every minute of my leave, fourteen days, less four days for travelling. I shall never forget the first day at home, in January 1918. I arrived at home unexpectedly at 8 a.m. My mother was ill in bed with the flu, which was very bad at that time all over Europe, but the shock of seeing me put her right straight away. Came bedtime, and how I looked forward to sleeping in a real bed again after over two years. But I found I could not get to sleep. I tossed and turned, got hot and sweated, it was agony. Eventually after an hour, I could stick it no longer. Putting a pillow on the floor under the wide-open window and wrapping a blanket around me, I lay down, fell asleep straight away and had a glorious night's rest."

"Came the last day of my leave and time to return. I did not want to go back, I wanted more time at home. But how? Then I remembered how a pal had extended his leave. He had reported sick to his local army doctor and had got a few days extra at home. Scabies was a skin disease, a bit like scurvy which every soldier overseas got off and on. So I scratched myself all over until blood showed and dried, and then set off to see the local army doctor. He was a young chap, just called up. I told him I was due to return to my unit in the trenches after the first leave for twenty months and thought I had got scabies."

"He examined me, then said, angrily, "You have like hell got scabies! What's the game?' I told him my story and that I was too young to have been out there anyway. He softened, then said, 'All right, I'll send you to the Skin Isolation Hospital on Redcar Racecourse for a few days. Will that do?' I thanked him and returned home with the good news. My family were delighted and off I went to Redcar."

"The hospital was in what had been the Stewards room on the racecourse, and there were twenty of us with beds to sleep on. We were well fed, and every morning we had to attend the slipper baths situated in the stables. A medical orderly filled the baths with very hot water in which he placed a generous supply of carbolic. Under his supervision, we had to scrub ourselves from head to toe. It was very sore and painful. After bathing, we were free to wander around the course and do what we liked, but were not allowed to go outside. Of course, we did. After dark, my pal and I climbed the eight foot stone wall into Aske Road. Away we went into Redcar, to the army canteen in Dene Grove and the canteen at the Coatham Convalescent Home, or to chat to girls on the promenade."

"Being a sniper when I first went out to France, it had become my habit to carry a spare clip of cartridges in my first-aid pocket, at the bottom of the left hand side of my tunic. One night, in jumping down from the wall into Aske Road, I stumbled and fell, the cartridges pressing hard into my groin. Angrily, I pulled them out and chucked them away into the darkness, although I had carried them all over France with me. (There were no houses built on Aske Road then, it was just a field. My clip of cartridges was found forty-six years later, in August, 1964, when a Mr. Beattie was digging in his garden. He reported his find to the local paper and was very interested when I told him all about it. For ten years, I had passed that way every day to Aske Road School where I taught from 1929 to 1940.")

"I was on the racecourse for a fortnight, 'swinging the lead.' and on the last day but one, I received a letter from my mother enclosing a ten shilling note. This was riches indeed. My pal suggested we go out that night for a drink at the Coatham Convalescent Home Canteen. Beer in those days was tuppence a pint, and when we got there he said, 'Let's see who can drink the most.' The result was a close draw, by the time we got to about the eighteenth pint we were both helpless, hanging on to the counter. At closing time, we set off back to the course. How we got there about two hours later, I do not know. Arm in arm we sang, staggered, and fell all over the place. Instead of going back in quietly over the wall, we went through the main gates and were caught by the sentry and reported."

"Next day, we were both sent off back to our units. I was escorted by a corporal to Middlesbrough station. He was supposed to see me off on the train to London. Wanting to slip back home again at Grove Hill, I said to the corporal, 'Look here, take this shilling, and when we get to Middlesbrough station, look the other way. He took the shilling, shook hands, wished me luck and off he went. I went home for another two days, then expecting the Military Police to call on me anytime, I decided I had to go back. After heartbreaking, tearful farewells, off I went, with a feeling that I would never see home again."

"Soon I was back in the 'mud, blood, and glory' of Bullecourt. I found that the farmhouse signalling post I'd been in before going on leave had been blown up by a shell, and my five pals plus the lad who replaced me had all been killed. I certainly had a guardian angel with me all the time. and realized it must be the spirit of my dear old Dad, who daily appeared in my thoughts and guided me to do the right thing when in danger."

"My brother Jack was on this front, about five miles away, and once spent a whole day trying to find me. He could not, as I was in the front line at the time. I am glad he did not meet up with me as it would have been heart-breaking to part after an hour or so together. It also might have meant the death of both of us, as one always had to keep alert and it did not do to be upset or worried about anything. Many a lad who came back off leave dispirited became so careless he was dead within a week of returning. You needed all your wits about you to survive."

"On the 21st March, 1918, I stepped out of our corrugated hut at dawn, to take a wet. I could not believe my eyes. German soldiers were coming into the sunken road about a quarter of a mile away. I dashed back into the hut, waking the others and we ran up the road. Although shot at, we got away and no one was hurt. Those Germans were rotten shots. It turned out to be the start of the big German Advance of 1918. Their entire army was able to concentrate on us, as the Russians had just packed it in."

"After retreating for two days, we made a stand near Armentieres. Here, I and two others in the signal section were sent to the Middlesex Regiment to learn how to use a new trench radio. We were issued with one of these instruments, a black box weighing about twenty pounds. We were told that it was the first of its kind in France and that whatever happened it was to be destroyed rather than allow it to fall into enemy hands."

"On the night of April 8, 1918, we in the signals section lay down in a ruined farmhouse, not knowing the Germans were beginning to send mustard gas shells across before starting to advance. We were awoken next morning by a corporal wearing a gas mask. 'Out quick!,' he shouted, 'Everyone has cleared off but us!' We could not stand up, and then started to vomit. We were helpless from breathing mustard gas which lies low on the ground. The corporal dragged us each into the open air, and after about three hours we had recovered sufficiently to move around."

"When shrapnel began flying near us, it dawned on me that we must try to save the wireless set. Leaving our rifles and packs, we set off for Headquarters, carrying the set between us. Unaware that we were surrounded by Germans, we wondered how the enemy could be shooting at us from nearby. Later we realized they had been shooting from very close range indeed, and were glad they were such rotten shots. We had gone about a half mile down the road when I was astounded to see a platoon of twenty Germans led by an officer march across. 'Quick, throw it in the ditch!' I said. In the radio went, and sank out of sight, but its splash halted the Germans. They turned and pointed their rifles at me. The officer waved us to come to them. During that twenty yards' walk, we expected to be filled with lead, but I acted as cool as a cucumber and cheekily said, 'Good morning, sir.'"

"The officer detailed an escort to take us back into their lines. On the way, we were halted and ordered to carry a wounded German to their first-aid station. He was slung in a groundsheet between two poles; a big heavy man who had been hit in the stomach and his insides were hanging out. We could not be at all careful with him, swinging him about as we struggled along, and everytime a shell burst close by, we just flung ourselves flat. He was moaning and groaning when we reached the aid-station a mile away; a sorry sight, blood all over and breathing his last. There were about fifty dead Germans at the aid post, neatly stacked on top of one another against a wall. Hundreds of German wounded lay about dressed with crepe paper bandages, as they had no cotton."

"During the next four days we were marched towards imprison-ment, were kept under heavy guard and given nothing to eat. When we reached Lille prison, we felt very sorry for ourselves, very thirsty and hungry. We were given thin soup similar to wallpaper glue, and a guard brought in a bin of water. There was such a rush that the bin and the guards were knocked flying, and fighting like animals we licked water from the dirty floor."

"We were counted off in hundreds, and placed in cells each designed to accommodate twenty people. One hundred men packed in each tiny room. At one end there was a barred window and at the other a latrine tub, always overflowing. I made straight for the window and stayed there. It was standing-room-only all day, and at night we all lay on our right side packed as tight as sardines. Each morning, two or three lads at the latrine end were carried out dead, suffocated by the foul air. Our only meal was at mid-day; watery soup, and one slice of black bread."

"After two weeks in this Hell-hole, we were taken to the rail-way station, locked into cattle trucks, and travelling all day standing up, we reached a proper PW camp in Germany. Now, I was Kriegsgefangener No. 89818. We were showered, fumigated, and our woollen underwear taken away and changed for a thin German type. I was able to share a seven pound Red Cross food parcel. What a good present for me—it was May 4th, my twentieth birthday. Then we went to the taps outside and for the next few days we were never away from those taps, drinking, drinking, drinking."

"Food was very poor from then on, and we were always hungry. The Germans very often punished us for any infraction of regulations by making us line up facing the sun for up to four hours, with brutal guards standing ready to use their rifle butts on us. After even half an hour of this 'stillestande,' we would sway like spinning tops. It was hellish, and for the rest of my life I have been unable to stand for long before starting to sway."

"We went to Hameln later, where we were worked very hard in stone quarries, mines, and sugar factories. Of these, the salt mines were most terrible, where we worked twelve hour shifts underground without food or water. One day while returning from the sugar factory, we saw a ragged party of German soldiers led by an officer on a very thin horse. We were dumbfounded at their looks. The factory boss then explained 'They are marching back from the front. The war is over!'"

In telling his story right to the end, Edgar Robinson has moved ahead of other chronological events. Before that glad day of peace dawned on November 11th, 1918, he and his comrades were to endure many more months of a war that also brought two new Bantam battalions from overseas.

British Columbia 143rd. BC (Bantams) Overseas Battalion recruiting unit included Lt. Robert Ely (centre), Cornish ex-miner Pte. Ben Barnes (front left) who was killed in action, and 46-year-old Welshman Pte. Joseph Daniel (far right, second row) a survivor.

Badge of Toronto 216th. Bantam Overseas Battalion featured an aggressive fighting rooster.

Marching song of the Canadian 216th. Bantam battalion
was composed by Captain Stanley Bennett (left), seen here
with members of the unit's band. Youth standing (centre)
would later become British millionaire Sir Billy Butlin MBE.

CHAPTER NINE

The Canadians

On Armistice Night, 1936, some two dozen tipsy but still dapper middle-aged businessmen in company with a large grey horse clattered into the elegant lobby of Toronto's King Edward Hotel. When asked to leave by the outraged but understandably nervous manager, the intruders solemnly assured him that all would be well, took long pulls from bottles in the brown paper bags they carried and burst into raucous song:

> "When the Bantam roosters crow,
> You'll find the enemy lying low,
> Though we're not much in height,
> Boy, how we can fight!
> Just count on the chickens
> To give them a licking . . .
> When we march into the line,
> That's when we show up mighty fine.
> Though we're not much in height,
> Boy, how we can fight . . .
> When the Bantam roosters crow!"

The group bowed to the amused applause of hotel patrons, boosted up one of their fellows astride the puzzled horse, and swayed out in its wake into the snowy night. For the bareback rider, Alex Batchelor, it was a fitting end to the 216th Old Comrades' Reunion and to a night of reliving memories which began when he had finally managed to enlist in the Canadian Army in 1916. Batchelor, whom we last saw two years earlier in this narrative, was among the first to enlist in the newly formed 216th (Toronto) Battalion.

Once more, a Bantam unit was born mainly through the efforts of a single forceful individual, who co-incidentally also dubbed it the "B.B.B." Major Frank Lindsay Burton was already a wounded veteran of France when he returned to his native Toronto in late 1915. Appointed to an administrative post in No. 2 Military District Headquarters, he began to chafe under his duties of helping to document the thousands of volunteer recruits who passed through the depot in the Canadian National Exhibition Grounds.

Long before the war, Burton had been involved in the Toronto Garrison Militia, a quasi-social group which nonetheless also managed to keep the martial spirit alive in peacetime. That there was more to the militia than the Garrison Ball and the annual 'drunk' at Camp Borden during summer manoeuvres was proved when it formed a cadre of trained men for the Canadian Army when war was declared. In the sudden crisis, the Toronto militia officers donated every last dollar in regimental treasuries to aid mobilization, and went $50,000 in debt before the National Recruiting League was formed.

While still attending Upper Canada College, Burton had been a private in the Simcoe Foresters. He took his reserve commission with the Toronto Light Horse, and later commanded the University Company of the Queen's Own Regiment. Early in the war, he had gone overseas as second in command, 75th. Battalion, Toronto Scottish Regiment, and had been invalided home after a year in France. Now, he wanted action again, and he wanted a command of his own. In January, 1916, he saw his opportunity for both.

Though for its part, Toronto had already sent 40,000 of its men overseas, and the entire country was doing its best to send more volunteers abroad, the Canadian army was experiencing a severe shortage of replacements.

Conscription was a serious political problem in Canada, preventing conscripts from being sent overseas involuntarily, so its military forces depended entirely on volunteers.

While recuperating in England, Burton had seen the 35th.

Division in training on Salisbury Plain, and subsequently wondered why Canada was not attempting to raise the same kind of units. While based in Divisional HQ at Exhibition Camp, Burton approached Colonel Mewburn about forming a Toronto unit of Bantams. He followed this up with a formally written detailed proposal that he be permitted to raise a battalion, and submitted it to the divisional commander, Brigadier General W. A. Logie. Major Burton signed himself as still "Second-In-Command, 75th Overseas Battalion,' his previous unit, to emphasize his practical experience.

This proposal seems to have sparked into action an idea which had been only talked about in Canadian military circles for some time. The following day, Brigadier Logie sent off his own letter to the Secretary of the Militia Council in Ottawa, requesting permission to organize a Bantam battalion in his division. Burton has suggested a minimum age of 19, and a minimum height of 4 ft. 10 ins. The General increased these to 22 years and 5 ft. He added that if the plan was approved, he would submit the name of an officer to command it.

Militia Headquarters contacted the Canadian Command in London, England, to check on the British army physical standards for their bantams. They reported that the minimum accepted height was 5 ft. 1 in., unaware of the actual elasticity of that rule in Britain. A mandarin in Ottawa leaped upon this one inch difference and Brigadier Logie was informed that as this British standard was "substantially different" from what he had suggested, he should offer another proposal. The General replied by asking that his original proposal stand, as any increase in height requirements might conflict with other existing battalions in Ontario.

In the meantime, Logie had told Major Burton that there was nothing new about the idea for bantams, and that Lt.-Col.R. A. Robertson, 13th Regiment—"who is himself a bantam"—was already being considered for the command. Bets were hedged by Colonel Newburn firing off a telegram to Robertson, urging him to take command and to catch General Logie while he was passing through Hamilton that same day. However, Robertson was still on sick-leave and was unable to accept the offer. Burton's name was submitted to Ottawa by Logie after all.

Two weeks later, February 17th, 1916, the Ministry of Militia authorized the formation of Number 216 Overseas Battalion, to be organized and commanded by Major Burton, recruiting only in the City of Toronto and County of York. The minimum height was set at 5 ft. ½ ins.; chest minimum 30 ins.; 22 years minimum age. Along with the job, Major Burton was promoted to the temporary rank of lieutenant-colonel.

Demonstrating the instinct for publicity he was to display throughout the whole of the recruiting campaign, Burton promptly called every newspaper in the Toronto region; explaining the new unit's formation. The result was a gratifying volume of press coverage, which helped draw 300 applicants within a matter of hours.

"I was feeling poorly that day and had taken the day off work," said Alex Batchelor. "Then I felt restless all of a sudden and got out of bed to walk across to Bay Street for a newspaper. The Bantams story hit me straight away and I realized I was only a few blocks from the recruiting address given, 16 Adelaide Street West. There were dozens of short chaps like me hurrying along the street towards a big cloth sign that said "Join Up Here—Burton's Bantam Battalion. "I went inside almost in a daze. Half an hour later I was in the army, walking down the street to quit my job, proud as a peacock of the white band on my arm that read 'BBB.'"

It was this proprietary use of initials which first raised the hackles of Burton's superiors. Lacking his sense of publicity, and not a little hostile to the entire enterprise, some of them resented his high-profile personal identification with the unit. The banners and armbands annoyed conventional officers who were further incensed by the new Lt. Colonel's use of bilious green stationery headed "BBB—Burton's Bantam Battalion."

On this letterhead, the new OC 216th. Battalion fired off a volume of memos and letters to press the unit's cause to Ottawa, military commanders, newspapers, and politicians. General Logie took offence at all these "unsoldierly flamboyances," and they were the source of continuous friction during the next twelve months.

Though recruiting for the 216th. moved with great smoothness during March, with a steady flow of recruits and repeatedly favourable press coverage, the Brigadier began to respond with increasing choler. He finally instructed Burton to "discontinue forthwith" use of any title other than the officially designated 216th. Overseas Battalion, C.E.F.

This problem had no sooner been resolved, when Burton was on the carpet again. His men were out on the streets of Toronto selling tickets for a unit concert, and he himself had outraged the chief recruiting officer of Hamilton by seeking men there for the Bantams. Logie was not sure which was the worse offence; soliciting money or soliciting recruits in another unit's territory. Burton was told off about both.

He cheerfully responded by once more applying for permission to have the Burton's Bantam Battalion unit name be retained, "as the slogan has become recognized by the public aleady." This received a one-sentence refusal, the sub-title "Bantams" was officially added to the unit designation.

Men were accepted at the average rate of fifteen a day, but this did not satisfy the impatient Lt. Colonel, who cast about for fresh attractions. In mid-March, a man fully uniformed as a German officer from pickel-haube to jackboots marched through the streets of Toronto to lure the curious to a recruiting drive. When the inevitable outraged telephone call came from Exhibition Camp, the 216th.'s Adjutant, Lt. Norman Williams, hastily assured HQ that the stunt would not be repeated.

By now, the unit had a full complement of officers, led by two acting majors, Lt. Stanley King Bennet, and Lt. Alexander Cameron Lewis, previously Secretary of the Toronto Harbour Commission. The Assistant Adjutant was Lt.-Col. McCallum, and the Quartermaster was Lt. H. A. Coach. These and other senior officers would receive promotions of two or three steps up the ladder before year's end. As well, the 216th. eventually took on strength a further 18 lieutenants who transferred from various other Canadian regiments.

Examination of the nominal roll of the 216th reveals that most of the recruits had been born in either Canada or Britain, but that ten other countries were also represented in the ranks. Americans and Russians, Italians and Anzacs, Poles and French, even a lone West Indian, had signed up. Among them was a 15-year-old youth named Billy Butlin who had recently arrived from England via Cape Town, South Africa.

He recalled his enthusiasm was fired by having seen photographs of motorcycle dispatch-riders. Instead, he was assigned to be a bugler and drummer-boy with the 170th Battalion. He wrote, "Though I was given the smallest uniform to be found, I was still lost inside it. The tunic hung down below below my knees, making me look like a Russian peasant, the trousers completely covered my feet, and the greatcoat was so long, I kept treading on it." When he arrived home in this state, and broke the news to his surprised mother he had joined up, she shed a few tears, then practically set to altering his uniform to fit. "My parents were not too upset, because neither dreamed the army would use a youngster like me. When eventually I was posted overseas, they tried to get me discharged, but by then it was too late."

Soon, Butlin was transferred to the 216 Bantam Battalion, in the regimental band. "I was a bugler and laboriously learned to play a few notes. Of course, I could not read music—and I suspect that the drum major couldn't, either. The band's main function was to take part in recruiting meetings, standing behind the recruiting officer while he painted a horrific picture of the beastly Germans destroying homes, raping girls, and torturing women. Listening to him, I felt very much an adult soldier about to go off and fight for civilization."

"The recruiting officer was a real-estate agent in peace time, and was the most bloodthirsty man I ever knew. His only enthusiasm, or so he vowed, was to get to France and kill Germans. His exhortations were so rousing, that he raised several battalions— though he never went to France himself."

The 216th. might have gained a more exotic quality if Lt.-Col. Burton had his way. He was approached in his office on Saturday morning March 11th, by a Japanese gentleman formally dressed in striped trousers, black cutaway coat, and a grey top hat.

The visitor stated he could bring in close to 100 Japanese young men if a place for them could be found in the unit. The understandable excitement with which Burton put forward the prospect of such good fighting material was dampened by General Logie. His frigid reply was that the proposal to raise a company of "Japs" had not received favourable consideration, and that Lt.-Col. Burton must confine his efforts to men of York County, with the unspoken implication they should be white.

By May, the battalion had reached a strength of 538, half the target goal, and Colonel Burton again pressed for more leeway in recruiting. He approached General Logie to allow the 216th. to recruit throughout the whole of the 2nd. Division area. He showed he had as usual been active before asking formal permission, by outlining a plan to recruit two platoons in Hamilton, one platoon each in St. Catharines, Niagara Falls and Brantford, and another entire company throughout the northern part of the Division, from Sault Ste. Marie on down.

He got permission to enlarge his recruiting mandate, but "only on the distinct understanding that he adhere to the age and height minimum in future." He was ordered to parade his men before a medical review board, which discharged six on physical grounds and questioned the age of thirty-three more. "Some of these appear to be somewhat younger than the minimum age of twenty-two years." Fortunately for the volunteers, this point was not pursued, as about one quarter of their number were really of such tender age they were eight years below the official minimum.

The Toronto Bantams' HQ staff was repeatedly confronted by overwrought mothers of boys in their early teens who had contrived to join up. "It was quite a sight to see a uniformed soldier being dragged off by the ear, taken home by his mother," says William Leyland, only sixteen years old himself at the time. "My father had managed to enlist in the Ordnance Corps by using his Boer War experience to offset his age of forty-six. I wanted my father to see me in uniform, too, before he left for overseas. Besides, I was looking forward to getting into the scrap myself. As I wasn't very tall, my best bet was the Bantams. They were suspicious about my real age—I'd told them I was nineteen—so they challenged my claim to be a bugler. I just played a few calls for the bandmaster, and I was in. No more questions asked."

Lt. Colonel Burton then came up with yet another recruiting gimmick. He had manufactured a miniature silver brooch engraved with a bantam rooster and the words, "I also serve." He organized a reception party and invited all wives and mothers of each man in the 216th. to meet the officers and be presented with a brooch. It was a good morale booster for the unit, but the ceremony was pointedly not attended by any of the invited District HQ staff.

Further irritation was communicated to 16 Adelaide Street West, when Burton inaugurated a canvas of the city for names of men of military age. Of the 18,500 men contacted in a house-to-house approach, only 1400 were found eligible as bantams. The direct telephone line from Exhibition Camp jangled irascibly again, and the aggressive door-step recruiting was halted.

However, by mid-summer, the battalion had reached its full strength of 1000 men. A late recruit was John Taylor, who travelled north with a final draft of one hundred men to join the 216th. in the desert-like sands of Camp Borden. "It was over 90 degrees at the Infantry School there," Taylor remembered. "We marched and drilled until we dropped from the heat. Then after a half-hour rest, we'd go off for firing practice. The Senior Musketry Officer at Borden told Colonel Burton that the Bantams' marksmanship had excelled any unit in camp, so we were given that Saturday off duty."

The battalion struck tents on October 23rd. and was entrained aboard fourteen Canadian Pacific Railway coaches back to Toronto. Never one to miss a chance for favourable exposure of his unit, Burton led the men on a parade up Bay Street to billets in Jesse Ketchum School. It was here the unit spent the winter, keeping up their musketry skill by shooting with .22 rifles at hordes of rats in the cellars. When they got to Flanders, they would find that this rodent-hunting practice was strangely prophetic.

Had it not been for administrative delays, the first Canadian Bantam battalion would have been formed in Victoria, British Columbia. Mobilization was authorized for the 143rd. B.C.

Overseas Battalion (Bantams) on November 29th, 1915, but recruiting work did not begin until February 20th, 1916. The driving force behind its formation was Lieutenant Colonel Bruce Powley, a front-line veteran who had been invalided home. Having enlisted in the pre-war Canadian army with the Prince of Wales Own Rifles, he was gradually promoted from private soldier to commissioned rank, served in the 88th Regiment, Victoria Fusiliers, and led the 7th. Battalion in France where he was twice wounded. He selected local officers who mostly already had combat experience, and recovered from wounds as he had. After he was appointed CO of the new 143rd. Battalion in December 15th, 1915, Powley found it difficult to find quarters for the 1000 men he hoped to sign up, and also ran into a certain amount of obstruction by people seeking recruits for other West Coast regiments.

Recruiting offices were set up at the corner of Fort and Government Streets in Victoria, headed by Lt. Robert Ely, who had newly transferred from the Rocky Mountain Rangers. Ely had been a national champion swimmer, and now put his energies to work to publicize the unit by staging parades each noon and erecting signage all across the city.

By February, Lt. Colonel Powley had been given part of Sidney Camp on Vancouver Island, along with enough tents and huts to house a battalion. From the outset, the 143rd. did not lack for applicants; civilians in the coalmining areas of British Columbia applied by the hundred, as did bantam-sized men already in other units of the army. The battalion did not have much luck in obtaining transfers of such troops from their present units, as warm bodies in Canadian uniform were then too prized to relinquish to elsehere.

At this stage of the war, Canada had 200,000 men under arms—all volunteers, as these was no conscription in Canada. The nation had been quick to send men soon after the outbreak of war. On October 3rd, 1914, the First Contingent sailed from Gaspe Basin in a convoy containing 1424 officers and 29,193 other ranks. Of them, 62 percent had been born in Britain, and another two

percent were from other British possessions. Over two thirds of
the officers were Canadian-born and had trained with the militia.
(Many more native-born Canucks without prior military training
also soon joined the parade. By war's end, 620,000 Canadians had
enlisted; 65,000 of whom were killed.)

By early 1916, Canada had sent three whole divisions to the
Western Front and a fourth division was training in England,
together making up the Canadian Corps. They had been the first
troops to experience poison gas in April, 1915, when the Germans
released the contents of 5730 cylinders of chlorine in the Ypres
Salient. That day, the Canucks had wrapped wet cloths around
their mouths and held the line despite appalling casualties. When
the flank-support Algerian troops fled from this horrible new
weapon, vomiting green foam as they ran, the Canadians had to
close the gap left in Allied lines. German troops braved their own
death-dealing vapour to attack the division's horse artillery. Lance
Corporal Frederick Fisher helped to successfully repel the enemy,
which gained him the award of Canada's first Victoria Cross of the
Great War. During the Great War, 70 Canadians earned a Victoria
Cross—the British Commonwealth's highest-ranking medal for
bravery.

A day later, the gas came again at St. Julien, where choking
soldiers of General Arthur Currie's Canadian 2nd. Brigade wept
from effects of the acrid fumes and the frustration of having their
notoriously flimsy Ross rifles jam during rapid fire. The Canadians
scavenged the battlefield for Lee Enfields from British dead to
continue to fight with, but in the end had to fall back from their
positions. Here, the 8th Battalion's CSM Frederick W. Hall earned
a VC after rescuing a wounded trooper under point-blank artillery
fire. By the time the battle was over next morning, two more VCs
had been awarded to Canadians—Lieutenant Edward Bellew and
Captain Alex C. Scrimger.

The British Commander in Chief, Sir John French, sent his
personal thanks to the Canadians for holding the Salient only 600
yards further back. The price for this foul yeast of mud and blood
was 6000, wounded, and missing. "These splendid troops averted

a disaster," said Sir John. The question was, how long could they endure without a constant flow of reinforcements?

The heavy fighting at St. Eloi had since butchered thousands more Canadians. Six giant mines had been exploded by the British, throwing up mountains of earth with a roar that was heard as far away as in Kent, in Southern England. Again it was Canadians who held against the German counter-attack, tussling for thirteen days to control the craters. One of these giant mudholes alone was the grave of 1373 soldiers. But how could enough young men be found to replace them?

Canada had no compulsory requirement for military service overseas, and throughout World War One, the Canadian army fighting in France depended entirely on volunteers for reinforcements. Even though patriotic support for the war remained strong in most parts of the country, the issue was strongly politicized in some areas. Most voters in Quebec province were absolutely opposed to sending its sons abroad to fight, and as they tended to vote *en bloc*, they managed to hold the balance of power in every Federal election. Without national conscription, maintaining the supply of suitable troop reinforcements to keep pace with casualties became a severe and permanent problem. [The French-Canadian "Van Doos" 22nd. Battalion fought with distinction on the Western Front, earning two Victoria Crosses and 340 other gallantry decorations.]

In such circumstances, Lt.-Col. Powley found that officers commanding other Overseas battalions containing bantam-sized men refused to transfer them, maintaining that the men did not want to leave. Despite his documenting lists of hundreds of such applicants, Powley was blocked in his attempts to take them into the 143rd. Battalion. "We only got fifty men from the 6th DCOR., and twenty from Colonel Vickers' 102nd. R.M.R. Kamloops," he complained to Ottawa, "The 11th. Irish in Vancouver railroaded their bantams into the 121st, notwithstanding many of them protesting. Other overseas regiments have Bantams, and one battalion after another went away with them."

The battalion's main hope lay in the direct entry of civilians, though this source had already been drained off to some degree by the recruiting efforts of other regiments. The sparsely-settled Province of British Columbia, which then held about a half-million people, had responded wholeheartedly early in the war. Intensely loyal, and with a high proportion of British immigrant stock, BC had virtually shot its bolt by early 1916 in its capacity for providing manpower for war. Now, the coal mining towns on Vancouver Island and on the BC mainland provided the likeliest source of strong bantams.

One of them was Benjamin Barnes, a red-haired Cornishman who volunteered from his well-paid job as fire-boss of Coal Creek Mine, Nanaimo. Another was Joseph Daniel, who had arrived recently in Victoria from his birthplace, Dingle, Bryn Mawr, Wales. He unhesitatingly joined the BC Bantams, despite being 44 years years of age and having a wife and three young children. After he reached France the following year, Daniel would began to keep a front-line diary that documents the appalling suffering he and his fellow Vancouver Islanders endured.

Peter Campbell, an office worker from Sidney, joined "B" Company in camp just down the road from his home. Allan Bell came over from Vancouver, on the same ferry that brought Humbert Campbell from his job on an Alberta ranch.

"It seemed the greatest adventure in the world," said Bell. "The sun shone on the water and the mountains stood out against the sky as we steamed across that day, and I felt my chest swell as if we were all setting out on a great crusade. My comrades proved to be such happy chaps, forever telling jokes, with never a cross word, and I never felt so happy in all my eighteen years."

Despite such enthusiastic recruits, Lt.-Col. Powley could not enlist enough suitable men at the pace he needed, He regretfully reported to Ottawa on October 15th, 1916, "We were finally forced to take in some larger men, with a view to later exchanging them for smaller men of other units. But exchanges in Canada are not easy, and the result is I have a battalion of over half Bantam and the balance of larger men, though their average is below 5 ft. 6 ins.

They are training very fast and I hope to proceed overseas with a smart battalion if not wholly a Bantam Battalion."

When the trained battalion returned to Victoria, it was so outspokenly impatient to be sent to France that they became known locally as "The Fire-eaters." Their attitude may be thought all the more remarkable in view of the high proportion of older, married men in the ranks. The 143rd. was a sober, well-behaved unit with few if any brushes with authority. Word spread about their high morale, which attracted a stream of volunteers towards the hoped-for total of 1,000 men, until Lt.-Col. Powley found it difficult to find accomodation for them all. The situation was solved by a grant of $9,000 by the city of Victoria, to secure building materials for a new camp at Beacon Hill Park. The recruits themselves quickly built wooden structures for sleeping barracks, cook-house, and headquarters. Withing a matter of days, they constructed an instant military village beneath clusters of spreading oaks, amidst a golden haze of flowering broom, overlooking spectacular ocean vistas. Having made themselves far more comfortable than the usual canvas tents, they still emphasised they expected the stay to be only temporary before going off to fight. The battalion drilled and practiced musketry daily, preparing for war with a serious competence, trying to befit themselves for frontline service.

Among those who chafed to go overseas, was Pte. Ben Barnes, whose skill as a cornet-player had placed him in the battalion band. In January, 1917, he wrote to his brother in immaculate penmanship from the Dominion Hotel, Victoria, "We are all classed as soldiers, and though bandsmen do not put in much time now with a rifle, we are all prepared for the firing-line. Each of us in the band has learned machine gun drill or signalling, first aid, and stretcher-bearing."

He wrote again in December, excited by rumours of embarkation, but depressed by feelings of foreboding. "I get a little downhearted when I dwell too much on my home, but I shake it off as best I can, and will be content when I get a little more excitement at the front. If I get a bullet to put me to sleep, I will only be beside my comrades, so should not worry."

Among men so keen, there was some disappointment when Ottawa announced the 143rd would be sent to France as a Railway Construction battalion, not as infantry. However, they were mollified by learning that trench railway duty was as vital as it was dangerous, a prime target of German artillery.

Three weeks later, they got orders for overseas at last. To celebrate the news and express their thanks to local civilians, the unit quickly produced a "Bantams Review" stage show at the Royal Theatre, which played to packed houses. Then on the bright morning of February 10, 1917, the 143rd Overseas Battalion (B.C. Bantams) marched proudly, four abreast, to tunes of their brass band, smiling at the cheering crowds that lined Humboldt Street. They were given a civic send-off by fellow townspeople with mixed emotions. After three years of what was known as the Great War, the notably patriotic city of Victoria had previously bade 'adieu' to seven other local units.—including the Canadian Scottish Regiment, Naval reservists, 5th. Canadian Field Artillery, and the Victoria Rifles. But now somehow, townsfolk expressed an especially fond farewell to these particularly high-spirited men who lustily sang,

> "Good-bye-ee,
> Don't cry-ee,
> Wipe that tear from your eye,
> Good-bye-eeee . . ."

News of their departure brought a tremendous turnout of Victoria residents, who cheered Bantams all along their march from Beacon Hill, past flag-draped balconies of St. Joseph's Hospital where patients and nurses gave rousing cheers. Banners proclaiming "Good Luck—God Speed" hung from buildings at the mouth of Courtney Street, and people leaned through open windows, adding their applause to those packing the downtown sidewalks.

By the time the soldiers reached the harbour, they had to break ranks and march in single file through the enveloping press of dense crowds. It gave opportunity for many emotional scenes, with time to snatch last-minute kisses from families, sweethearts, and admiring women. Quickly, the 32 officers and 667 other ranks boarded two Canadian Pacific ferries, *Princess Victoria* and *Princess Mary*. where many climbed the rigging for better views as the vessels pulled away. Cheers, cries, and shouted well-wishes mingled with a cacophony of horn-blowing from other ships in the harbour, while the Bantams' band played a last refrain of "Old Lang Syne" as they sailed over the horizon.

The 143rd. Battalion sailed from Halifax aboard *S.S. Southland,* on February 17th, 1917. Ten days later, they were in the Canadian Holding Depot at Purfleet Camp, Shorncliffe, England. "We felt like cattle, the way they treated us there," Allan Bell recalled. "The Canadian Corps needed more men in France in a hurry, and made no secret of the fact that we were viewed as potential cannon-fodder. One could not but notice that while ordinary soldiers were getting this treatment, there were over 500 young lieutenants lounging around camp, many of whom had been there idle since the previous summer. But that was the least of our irritations, because it didn't take long to figure out that the B.C. Bantams as a unit were going to be broken up forthwith."

Unaware of a similar disappointment ahead, the Toronto Bantams had received word of their imminent departure for Europe a few months earlier. The first signal it was coming was on November 27th, 1916, when the battalion paraded at the University Avenue Armouries. The ceremony packed the galleries and an estimated 4000 people were left outside, unable to gain admittance.

The Armouries were decorated with patriotic bunting, and clusters of Union Jacks adorned every wall. Promptly at 8 p.m., the battalion marched in behind their brass and bugle band, amid cheering crowds. The men formed up three sides of a square, gratified at the important civic worthies grouped in front of the unit's drums and colours.

Well-connected Lieutenant Colonel Burton was a member of the prestigious Timothy Eaton Memorial Church, and had already obtained it as the 216th's garrison church. He now further gained status for his battalion by having on hand Mrs. Timothy Eaton, one of the country's wealthiest women, to personally present the King's Colours to the unit.

Flanking her, was Major General Logie, who was probably gratified in more ways than one by the embarkation news, and a clutch of the city's establishment, the clergy, and the military. There was Hon. Colonel Sir John C. Eaton, Hon. Colonel Reverend Dr. Chown, Mr. W. C. Bolus, Secretary of the Board of Trustees, a bevy of Lieutenant Colonels and various society ladies.

When Mrs. Eaton had presented their Regimental King's Colours, consecrated by The Reverend Dr. James Henderson, the unassuming Bantam rankers were bemused to realize they somehow were now in a "social" battalion. Chests out, they marched away through cheering crowds, the words of the reverend gentleman ringing in their ears. "These colours send you off to assist in preserving the British Empire through what we feel is a holy war."

Their actual departure was all too ordinary a military event in that it was a complete foul-up. On April 13th, 1917, hundreds of friends and relatives of the embarking 216th. arrived as they had been told at Bayside Park Station to make their last farewells. At 3 o'clock, they were informed that the men were being entrained miles away at Exhibition Park Station, and a frantic rush of women and children surged across the city. They arrived at the last minute for tearful farewells, and the Grand Trunk train pulled out at sundown "with the Bantams singing lustily on their way to war."

When they disembarked from the S.S. Scandinavian on April 28th, 1917, the 216th. were sent to Dibgate for the same treatment received by the British Columbians. Lieutenant Colonel Burton found out that there was no intention to use his battalion as a whole. Despite his vigorous protests to Militia Headquarters in Ottawa, the 216th. was broken up within days of its arrival in England.

The Brigade Headquarters at West Sandling found that 660 men and 23 officers were in A.ii condition, but rejected 89 as below standard D.iii class. The medical report ended with this peculiarly mixed comment: "Although we have classified 666 OR's [other ranks] as fit, these men are short in stature, being of rather poor physique, and in my opinion they would be of more use in Railway Construction or Labour Units." This contradiction of recommending that men of so-called "poor physique" be transferred to heavy labouring duties evidently escaped the medical examiner.

On May 4th, 1917, Lieutenant Colonel Burton was given a copy of Divisional Orders which described procedures for winding up depleted units, and was told to act on them immediately. Thus without ceremony, the 216th. Overseas Battalion (Bantams) next day ceased to exist. The dazed men were sent off in small groups to various units being formed by the 1st. Canadian Reserve Brigade. Most of the Toronto men were separated and transferred into a number of artillery units, where their military identity as "Bantams" was lost. Bill Leyland spent the rest of the war as a camp bugler in England, and Billy Butlin went off to take up the dangerous job as stretcher-bearer in Flanders.

Butlin later wrote, "We finally arrived in France as reinforcements for the 4th. Canadian Mounted Rifles, in the 3rd. Canadian Division. "I was relieved to find we had no horses. In fact, we seemed to spend most of our time marching all over northern France, for we were a 'flying corps,' constantly being shuttled from one hard-pressed point to another. We took part in the battle of Vimy Ridge, and were at Ypres, Arras, and the second battle of Cambrai. Here, to our amazement, we saw tanks for the first time. One had lumbered over our trench during the night, but we were so exhausted we were not even aware of it amid the clamour of guns and exploding shells. Only next morning, did we notice its tracks which were within a foot from where I had been sleeping."

"During the two years I was at the front, I never fired a shot in anger," Butlin wrote, "But I vividly remember the horrors of trench warfare. There were times when I would have willingly parted with a leg just to escape from it all. But it was not to be and I slogged on as a stretcher-bearer, collecting the wounded, often under heavy shell-fire, and burying the dead. It was not so much the danger I remember, but the mud and the lice—our 'next of skin' as we wryly called them."

Lieutenant Colonel Powley was not even given the opportunity to say goodbye to the British Columbia unit he had formed despite many obstructions. Peter Campbell recalled how it was for the crestfallen Victoria battalion. "After spending a brief landing-leave in London, we were called before a medical board. The 143rd. Battalion was abruptly broken up, many going to the 47th. Regiment, some to the 2nd. Canadian Mounted Rifles, and many more, including me, to the 3rd. Battalion, Canadian Railway Troops."

Transportation was ever a big problem in France during the war, as roads were often impassable with mud and shellfire. Eventually, the Allies realized that the German secret of rapid movement of troops and supplies was the use of a network of light railways. Because of Canada's experience in building railroads, General Stewart was asked in late 1916 to organize the Canadian Railway Troops. Before long, there were 13 battalions of them, responsible for all railway construction throughout the British sector, and they proved to be vital to the conduct of the war.

Their work was to build light narrow-gauge railways beyond the standard gauge lines, right up to forward artillery batteries and reserve trenches. The Canadians' skill enabled troops and supplies to be quickly moved along the front, and revolutionized the Allied ability to wage war.

Campbell described how his fellow ex-Bantams were thrust into their new job in a matter of days. "We crossed the Channel in mid-March, and wound up at Poperinge in the Salient, in brand-new tents which Jerry enjoyed shelling. After a short time, we went to Three Trees Camp behind Messines, where we put in some light railways for the new operation. Then on to the south-east of Vimy Ridge, and we took over the maintenance of existing railways."

Pte. Joe Daniel was another BC Bantam who found himself abruptly transferred to the Canadian Railway Troops, in May 1916. Strictly against orders, he began writing a daily diary of his trench experiences, and his first entry read, "I don't think much of this outfit . . . working on the track at all hours. Rain, mud, gas attacks, shells falling all around." Work was hard, unrelenting; filling shellholes, repairing shattered tracks, digging trenches, loading supplies and ammunition. As well, there was constant guard duty. "On picket duty, 10 hours straight each time. Some outfit, this."

The Germans kept a vindictive eye on railroad movements, and shelled the construction gangs daily. Their shellfire was accurate, as usual, so that casualties were frequent, and repairs to broken lines had to be repeated as often as a dozen times every 24 hours. The 489 gallantry decorations awarded to Canadian Railway Troops throughout the war is some indication of the courage demanded of men like Daniel.

He soon discovered what deadly dangerous duty railway work was. Day after day, he recorded the same line, "Working up the line . . ." Just as often, he mentioned, "Heavy shelling all the time while we work. Old Fritz' visits us in his airplanes every night, bombing, and we don't get much sleep." Still, he learned that his Victoria comrades who became infantry were in even more harms way. "Told that our boys of the 143rd are losing a lot. The first night they went in, they lost 13 men killed."

Light railways found a new role when they began to be used in gas attacks. Many ex-Bantams were employed at this, which involved night-time building of rail lines parallel to front line trenches. Then carriages containing cylinders of poison gas were quietly brought up through the darkness, dragged by men using long ropes, as engine noises would draw artillery. The spectacle of hundreds of tiny men hauling their deadly juggernauts inevitably brings to mind Lilliputian imagery. Any instinct to grin at this picture fades at reading a report of how at Passchendaele on October 18th, German shells bracketed a gas train, moments after the nozzles were opened. Thirty-one British soldiers died there from enemy shrapnel or from the strangling fumes of their own cargo of chlorine.

Nearly all the Canadian Bantams who had been chosen as infantry replacements were shipped quickly to France. Alex Batchelor and John Taylor were among 225 "Bants" who joined various Canadian infantry units along the Vimy front. Giant trench rats were the first targets they fired at there with the newly issued Lee

Enfields which replaced their flimsy Ross rifles. Batchelor wrote, "It reminded us of those innocent early days when we potted at rats in that schoolhouse barracks in Toronto."

They and other newcomers arrived just in time to take part in the Canadian Corps' most historic assault. The modern pilgrim who follows in their trail leaves Arras and heads northeast over the gently sloping countryside. You have no sense that the ground has gradually risen until you reach the 475 foot summit of Vimy Ridge. Suddenly, the escarpment edge drops away, and a magnificent view opens wide in front of you. The horizon stretches across the Flanders Plain, clear to the Belgian border; but one's eye is drawn to the towns below, glowing redly in the sunset and their own sinister aura of tragic memories.

Just down there is Lens. Then there's Bethune, and Lille, and Armentieres of the oft-importuned mademoiselle. Messines lowers far off beside Mt. Kimmel, so grisly Passchendaele must be just beyond. They look strangely small and close together, to have been fought over for four years at the cost of millions of Allied and German lives. You avert your eyes, looking back the way you came, and realize then what a commanding position this gave the Germans. From here, the backslope of the ridge falls away, providing an uninterrupted view westward of what was once the British lines. You can see well beyond the towers of Arras, along the shining Scarpe River, and even survey the wrinkled *rideaux* of terraced hills to the southeast. From here, the German observation posts looked over the entire British sector, providing direct control of artillery fire against roads, railways, and troop movements. No wonder they fought hard and long to hold Vimy Ridge.

The wind rises chill and damp as the sun dips out of sight. The slope goes dark and you look down, half expecting in this ghost-ridden aerie to see thousands of gun flashes winking below as they did on the night of Easter Monday, 1917. For a whole week before, 377 heavy guns and 720 field guns ceaselessly pounded German positions on and behind the ridge. A rain of shells fell on fortified villages, supply points, and trenches, pulverizing defences which had been built up during the three years the Germans had held the position. Since 1914, the slopes of the hill had been the dying place of 200,000 men, most of them French. Recently, British troops had tried and failed to take the hill, suffering heavy losses. Now, the Canadian Corps had the job of storming up over their predecessors' graves.

The assault here was part of a wider move which pivoted on a massive French attack further south. The handsome young General Robert Nivelle had supplanted General "Papa" Joffre, and promised dynamic new methods of gaining quick victory. His plan for attack in the Champagne was soon known by the Germans, who countered it in advance by retreating to the Hindenberg Line.

They left behind them an area of complete destruction, laying waste everything in their wake, systematically destroying every town, village, and farmhouse. They slaughtered cattle, chopped down fruit-trees, and poisoned all wells. Thousands of booby-traps lay among the ruins to trap unwary souvenir hunters, and time-fused mines exploded and killed for weeks afterwards.

Nivelle's offensive into this desolation failed, but Field Marshal Sir Douglas Haig decided to plunge ahead anyway with the British support plan, despite the fact that its original purpose of drawing off enemy reserves from the French attack was no longer needed.

Three of his army corps were allotted to open the Battle of Arras along a twelve mile front. On the extreme left of the drive, stood Vimy Ridge, dominating the objective; a German Gibraltar swathed in barbed wire, honeycombed with deep machine gun posts and line after line of trenchworks. It was under the personal command of wily old General E. von Falkenhausen, who kept one Prussian and two Bavarian divisions in place to hold the bloodsoaked ridge.

His adversary was Lt. General Sir Julian Byng, a British practical soldier who alone amongst Imperial staff officers was able to hold the respect of his subordinates in the Canadian Corps. His demonstrated military commonsense along with his personal modesty was a refreshing change from the pompous ways of the General Staff, and he in turn respected the hell-for-leather fighting style of the Dominion troops. Since their arrival, Canadians had shown an aggressive spirit, tempered with a reluctance to be considered mere "Colonials." By early 1917, the Canadian Corps not only had a hard-earned reputation as shock-troops; they had been forged into what was in fact a National Army of Canada.

Their Canadian-born leaders were Major-General Sir Arthur Currie, 1st. Division; Major-General E.W. Turner, VC, 2nd. Division, and Major-General D. Watson, 4th. Division. The commander of the 3rd. Division, Major-General L. J. Lipsett, was British-born, though he had served with the Canadian Army for many years. These men were as determined to take their objective as they were to avoid the wasteful tactics of bad generalship imposed on them in earlier battles.

Among the 30,000 Canadians who started up the hill at 5.30 a.m. on April 9th, was at least a company of ex-members of the Victoria Bantams. One platoon was attached to the 7th. (B.C.) Battalion which picked its way through the forward trenches guided by stakes daubed with luminous paint.

"I remember the hundreds of dead horses which lay everywhere in front of our jump-off position," said Allan Bell. "There was heavy wet snow falling so we could not see well, and kept falling over the poor beasts' carcasses. We had practiced the attack time and again, and now we were doing the real thing it was hard to believe it. Then the German counter-fire started and there were no more doubts. We were not wearing our greatcoats, but the minute the shells began to fall, I felt actually hot all over and did not notice the cold all during the fight."

As Bell said, this was an attack which had been planned with a thoroughness rare in Great War battles. Aerial photography, trench models, and practiced assaults had prepared the Canadians well. Even more unusual, the attack itself was pressed forward with clockwork precision, and the men found themselves taking one objective after another exactly as planned. The hill was divided into Black Line, Red, Blue, and Brown Line, matching stages in the enemy trench systems.

A heavy blizzard of snow was falling, mixed with the smoke of explosions, so Bell's section saw nothing of the enemy until the

Red Line was reached. "We got rid of our bombs into some dug-outs there, when Heinie refused to surrender. None of our guys had ever fired a shot in anger before, yet there we were coolly shooting at men as if it was a gallery in a fairground."

The 7th. Battalion rolled past the Kiegel Stellung, leaving a party of sharpshooters to watch tunnel-mouths. Too many Canadians had died before in battle from eagerness in over-running enemy machine-gun crews who arose to shoot them in the back. By 6.45, the 1st. Division had got in amongst the Bavarians, driving them back beyond La Folie Farm. All along the line it was the same, a relentless, steady advance that rolled the Germans off the hogback ridge like a flayed skin.

The Bantams tried to stay together, watching each other's fortunes. When one machine gun ripped through their ranks, the dead and wounded received prompt attention from comrades, while others fanned out for vengeance. "We went after that gun with our blood up," said Allan Bell. "We fired and fired our rifles in a volley so they had to keep their heads down. A lucky bomb killed two of the crew and the third one stood up to surrender. It didn't do him much good. We left the crew all dead. Funny thing was, each one of them was an officer."

By 7.30, the 3rd. Division had reached Brown Line, the crest of Hill 145, and the entire ridge was in Canadian hands by 9 o'clock. For the battalion including the Bantams, the fight went on for hours more, as they helped mop up groups of Germans who held out until killed or captured.

"The idea was to re-fortify the trenches at the top," recalled Allan Bell. "So when we finally got up there, I was handed a shovel and told to lower the parapet's back wall, to face it the other way, in Heinie's direction. The sun came out late that afternoon and you could see far down, where the enemy were running away below. Some of our men tried pitching grenades onto them, but mostly the bombs went off before they could do any damage." As reinforcements settled in to the splendidly-built fortifications, German dominance of the Douai Plain was ended.

More significantly, the victory that day gave the Dominion its final step towards nationhood. So it was on April 9th, 1917, while 3598 men of the Maple Leaf died, the proud national consciousness of a truly independent Canada was born on Vimy Ridge. A few years after the war, the crest of Hill 145 was ceded in perpetuity by France to Canada, a shrine to more than valour. In 1936, 200 ex-Bantams were among the 6000 Canadian veterans who returned to witness the dedication of the soaring Vimy Memorial, unveiled by King Edward VIII.

Meanwhile, the remaining Victorian troops in Britain were sent for toughening up at a battle school prior to service as infantry in France.

In early May, Ben Barnes wrote of the "quite hard training they put us through here at Shorncliffe. But we all have been picked for different drafts and are having final inspections, so we shall be going at any time. We are not sorry, as we came over here to do our bit, and cannot stand this hanging around. We all feel very good, and expect to make a name out there."

Barnes was among a draft of 667 men from the B.C. Bantam Battalion which went to the 24th Canadian Reserve Battalion in France on May 11th, 1917. Barnes' group was joined by Alex Batchelor and other Toronto Bantams who were immediately thrown into the hideous meat-grinder that was the Battle of Lens.

This affair was yet another brain-wave of Field Marshal Haig, who despite having earned a nickname of "The Butcher" for his costly mass-attacks policy was still kept on as British Commander-in-Chief. The more impatient French had thrown out the briefly-hailed Nivelle and replaced him with General Petain, fresh from the bloodbath of Verdun. Haig did not like his new opposite number, and expected scant aid from the now-demoralized French Army, so he decided to increase British pressure on the Flanders front. As part of this grand strategy, he threw the Canadian Corps against Lens as their first objective.

The Canadians surveyed the black slag heaps, the broken, churned graveyard of so many troops before them and were not inspired. "If we have to fight there at all," said General Currie who now commanded the Corps, "Let us fight for something worth having." His eyes were on the country beyond. He wondered, why not try to sidetrack Lens and Hill 70 and burst into open mobile warfare instead? But Haig was adamant. Lens had to be taken by assault.

On August 15th, the Canadians took Hill 70; nothing more than a low mound, really, but riddled with concrete pillboxes and concealed artillery. In a single morning, they captured the hill which had defeated the British Guards' Division in 1915, and pushed on through the smoke and poison gas and shrapnel into the mining hamlets on the outskirts of Lens itself. The ruined suburbs, called 'cites'—St. Emilie, St. Pierre, Calonne—were made up of clumps of miners' cottages and pithead workings, which had been fortified in an interlocking maze of German defences over the past two years.

All Lens was like that—street after street of rubbled buildings that hid blockhouses and m.g. posts, and interconnected by miles of passageways knocked through cellar walls. Alex Batchelor recalls an officer telling him, "Fix your bayonet soldier, we're going to have to winkle them out, room by room."

Batchelor found his small size to be an advantage during the next ten endless days and nights. "I could pop through those tunnels easy as could be, you see. We left our packs off, stripped down to undershirts, and went crawling around with a bagful of bombs and a revolver. Find a hole, bung a bomb through, and then nip through after it before the dust settled. After a while, I could tell if no bomb was needed in the next cellar. The smell would tell me when the Heinies had been dead in there for a time."

Allan Bell fought here too, attaching himself to some Nova Scotian machine-gunners to keep them supplied with ammunition. He would make repeated trips back through the hellish streets, casually employing his Lee Enfield on stray Prussians who tried to stop him. On one such journey, he stopped to aid the wounded Humbert Campbell, the English clergyman's son he first met an age ago on a British Columbian ferry.

Street by street, the 4th. Prussian Guards were forced back, dying hard for every cellar and crossroad. On the third day, reinforcements came in; two more Guards' Divisions, the 11th. Reserve, and the Saxon Brigade, until there were 46 German battalions battling to keep the Canadians from capturing the battered compost-heap that used to be Lens.

Ben Barnes mentioned this carnage to the folks back home. "Had a busy time of it," he wrote in his flawless copperplate on Y.M.C.A. stationery, "But we all went forward and accomplished our objective. It was mostly all street fighting and we worked hard for protection from gunfire. When we got settled in our new ground, Fritz did not give us much rest, as he had our range down pretty fair."

"He tried to come back but we were always ready. We had quite a few casualties but not so bad. We are all very thankful to God for his protection, as we had no time to think what would come next. I had a very close shave with his heavy high explosives. They nearly split your head when they came anywhere near your trench. There were three of our old band boys wounded and sent back to Blighty."

"I saw some of my old chums fall, and it only gave me more grit to dash ahead, and believe me there was not a man but who was anxious to get a score. We took quite a few prisoners and they told us that the Canadians were a hard class of men to fight. Little do they think that the majority of us here in my outfit are Englishmen, though proud to live in Canada."

"We are resting for a short time after some hot streetfighting in the ruins. We even went quite ahead of our objective to make sure we had cleared them up good. Our officers acted well and we got pretty fair treatment. It was one of the biggest affairs that has been pulled off by us."

"The Bantams certainly made a name for themselves this time. We are all of British stock here and fight with British spirit, and the Canadian Bantams are not going back without a name worthy of being set down in history for future generations to take notice."

He was never to know the eventual futility of those words he wrote on the battlefield, minutes after being in close combat. The belief that his comrades' courage would be remembered in Canada ever after sustained this modest, dedicated soldier, whose letters were filled with loving messages for nephews and nieces he had met only for a few precious days. Though he had already seen so many friends cut down 6000 miles from homes they left in beautiful British Columbia, he retained his generation's simple faith in posterity's appreciation. Perhaps it's as well they never lived to see how quickly their sacrifice was forgotten by future Canadians, most of whom are now largely ignorant of their own nation's military history. Yet in 1917, this faith sustained many men through that last bitter winter of the Great War. But for Barnes, and for most of his comrades in the platoon, time was running out.

During the next few months, they were in constant action—a wild-eyed crew of trained killers whose steady drain of casualties only served to hone the survivors' skill at their dreadful trade. From the letters written home, it seems they seldom knew exactly where they were, dully accepting higher authority's orders which flung them here and there along the desperate front line.

In October, the Canadians went north to Flanders again, summoned there to help break the deadlock on a vile, mad place called Passchendaele. Though the General Staff's neat, colourful maps of this region in the Ypres Salient showed green patches of woodlands surrounding a quaint village, all that existed now was a desolate swamp of shellpocked mud, stinking with high explosives and the ripe putrefaction of 400,000 dead. For four months, British and Australian and New Zealand regiments had been plunged into this foul mire, losing whole battalions in a matter of days.

Now it was the Canadians' turn. Torrential rain mingled with the sleet of steel and lead from German guns when the Canucks went forward on October 26th. There was no cover available. No trenches could be dug there, and to lie down was to invite suffocation in minutes, so they waded forward at a painfully slow walk. "We just chucked everything away but rifles and ammunition," said John Taylor. "It was a hard job to even walk fast, let alone run, so we lost a lot of men from the shelling and snipers on the way across. But when we finally got to grips with Heinie, we paid them back in kind."

The site of what had once been the village of Passchendaele was on top of a low ridge, and the key to its capture was the Belleview slope. All along it, was a string of concrete block-houses which had directed machine-gun fire to cut down every previous attack. The Canadians concentrated here, knocking out the pill-boxes one by one, and by late afternoon they had a toehold. At dusk they set about reforming, sending down their wounded and even sending troops to relieve the New Zealanders nearby.

George Marr was an infantryman with the 4th. Battalion of the New Zealand Division that held Abraham Heights since taking it by storm three weeks before. "We were successful in taking the strongpoint, after some fierce fighting and losing a good number of killed and wounded on both sides," he wrote. "After digging in just down from the top of the ridge, we held out for days. One night at dusk, our relief arrived, and at first glance I honestly thought that they were just young boys. When I got a better look, I marvelled that they were really some of the small Bantam soldiers we'd heard of."

"One of them was sent to take over my possie in a shellhole. I said in a joking way, 'Those fellows out in front of us are a pretty tough lot, Tommy.' His reply was simple and to the point. 'We'll fix the bastards, don't worry, chum!'"

After four days of desperate fighting, the Canadian 3rd. and 4th. Divisions managed to cross the Ravelbeekstream, storm the ruins of Meetscheele village, and take the high ground at Crest Farm. They held on there and opened the way for the final assault by the 1st. and 2nd. Divisions to attack during a violent gale and rainstorm, capturing Passchendaele at last on November 6th, 1917.

The day after the battle ended, Sir Launcelot Kiggell, Haig's chief of staff, arrived to take his first look at the battle zone. When his limousine motor car began to lurch through the cloying mud, the general stared out unbelievingly at the endless quagmire. He is said to have burst into tears. "My God!" he moaned. "Did we send men to fight in this?"

One of the men who had fought there was Benjamin Barnes. On October 29th, during a lull, he wrote home in near despair.

"Moved to another area after quite a long journey. Had a busy time of it for eight straight days and nights. "Not many of the originals are left now. I am sorry to say that my pal Alf Patterson got napooed [killed] yesterday. He got hit with one of Heinie's high-explosives. He was on an M.G. and 3 of his 5-man crew were hit. I had many narrow escapes myself. Two men were in a dug-out and a heavy came over and killed the man by my side. Another time, one burst outside the dug-out, buried 3 of us—one blinded, one wounded, and all I got was shock. When I came out and heard about Alf, it brought tears to my eyes. I have the painful duty of writing to his aunt in Cumberland. Kindly excuse scribble as I am quite upset. Au-re-voir."

Because of Ottawa's political refusal to send conscripts overseas, fresh replacements were getting scarcer every month for the embattled Canadian Army. So, veteran troops of any kind were kept in the line until death released them, or a lucky "Blighty wound" got them evacuated to hospital. Barnes managed to get letters home past the indulgent light censorship of his officers. On January 22nd, 1918, he wrote, "In trenches. If we did not get our rum ration, we would be laid up sick very often, as we are subject to wet feet and chills all through our system. Disappointed at no leave. Anxiously awaiting a square deal, as we can't see why we have not had it yet. There are quite a few of the boys had their leave who have not been in the line so long as your humble servant."

There were only a couple of more letters from Ben Barnes that spring, in which he made no further mention of warfare, other than the address, "In trenches." He poured out a stream of suggestions about how to make his nieces and nephew happy, and sent them what small amounts of money he could afford. His last letter from the front was devoted to this same theme, "Whenever you feel like making up a parcel for me, fix things fine, then let the children have a party of their own instead and enjoy its contents. I know you are kindhearted, but rationed in England, and I would be the last one to see those dear little ones go short for my sake. Not much time to write. Continually on the alert. We last Bantams are in a Battle Platoon, so we are not here as ornaments."

A week later, he heard his C.O. read out a commendation for his gallantry in rescuing a wounded comrade. The same day, August 11th, 1918, Ben Barnes' luck finally ran out, and he was killed in an obscure skirmish near Amiens, just two months before the end of hostilities—the last BC Bantam to die in the Great War.

CHAPTER TEN

Along Death Way

The wet streets of Amiens teemed with British and Dominion soldiers as they roamed in search of diversion from thoughts of what they must soon face under the guns which boomed less than 15 kilometres away. A shilling a day paid by a grateful British government did not buy much, and Tommies enviously noted the greater number of dollar-a-day Canadians and Anzacs who had girls on their arms. But there was not much to spend their meagre pay on while in the line, so survivors arrived at rear areas with pockets relatively full after the enforced savings, eager for a few hours of relaxation.

Two years later, the Germans would push back the Allies and occupy this area; but in mid-1916, Amiens was a boom-town, the nearest that most non-commissioned men ever got to the storied fleshpots of "Gay Paree." Even junior officers seldom reached the French capital, but took their leave in Amiens, where their sexual appetites could be served by certain "officers' houses"—also known as "knocking shops"—identified by discreet blue lamps. Safer entertainment was available at elegant cafes such as Godbert's Restaurant, which prospered so well that it stayed in business for another 40 years.

The only places open to the troops were either drab canteens serving "char and wads"—weak tea and tasteless buns—or a score of drinking establishments. One of these, known as Estaminet Caze's, was popular with the 35th Division Bantams who had recently moved to this sector. The place provided a variety of rough entertainments; boozing, sing-songs, and gambling on 'Housey-

Housy'. At the side door, a red lamp advertised the services of women available upstairs, and cast a warm glow on the pale faces of soldiers who stood in a long line to shuffle slowly forward in turn. However, from all accounts, the majority of soldiers did not frequent the "poules" (prostitutes.) Most of the youths and men in khaki were only a few months away from their own largely respectable homes, where their Edwardian upbringing instilled a morality which shrank from harlots, even after the brutalization of trench life. For them, a night of getting drunk was desperate enough. They jammed the bar downstairs, to swill beer or "van rooge" and blot out hideous images of trench warfare.

Singing and drunken laughter filled the smoke-laden barroom of Caze's one memorable night in July. Standing at the zinc counter then was Victor Lill. Near him was Second Lieutenant William "Titch" Cook, of the Lancashire Fusiliers, who had donned an other-ranks' tunic so as to be able to drink with his troops.

Two years before, Lieutenant Cook had been selling newspapers aboard a Mersey ferry. He had walked off the boat at Liverpool with a group of would-be volunteers and successfully enlisted in the Bantams, despite a cherubic choirboy look and an actual age of sixteen. After reaching the rank of sergeant, his repeated bravery gained him a battlefield commission. Despite this, he remained unaffected and had a democratic way with his men which horrified more haughty superiors.

A buxom barmaid peered at his shoulder-flash of a red rooster, expertly identified the 35th. Division, and overheard his men address him as "Sir."

"La!" she remarked, "Your officers are very small."

"Yes, Madam," Titch replied gravely, "But we have big privates."

His riposte brought down the house in a bellow of laughter and became the Bantams' favourite joke forever after. "It might seem like a corny old tale now," said Mr. Lill, "But at that time we had precious little to laugh about, and an officer who would crack any kind of a joke with us was rare indeed."

After assembly at Doullens, the Division had been moved to a new sector of the line, running north from the riverbank at Moulin

Fargny, up through Maricourt Wood to the edge of German-held
Guillemont. This was the lower end of the bloodiest ground in
British Army experience, where 60,000 of its men had fallen in a
single morning on July 1st, 1916—opening day of the Battle of
the Somme.

Throughout history, the River Somme has provided a military
defence line. A map of northern France shows that it is one of a
number of rivers which slice the landscape inwards from the
seacoast, protecting Artois and Picardy. At the apex of these natural
barriers, lies the ancient fortified town of Doullens, said to trace
its name from *vallum dolens*, "vale of sorrow," because of its long-
suffering guardianship of the Authie defence line. Germanic tribes,
Roman legions, and the Spaniards rampaged here, and the Somme
also had an eerily repeated link with British armies over the
centuries. In 1346, the English victory at Crecy was as much
credited to King Edward III's cunning deployment of his forces in
Maye Ravine near the Somme as to the skill of his archers.

Seventy years later, Henry V led another invasion, and again it
was the Somme that acted as the French defence line, which had
to be forded before the English could win at Agincourt. Now, in
1916, the river formed the British main defence bastion. The much-
vaunted "breakthrough" of early July had withered under German
machine-guns and settled down to a series of wasteful attacks which
would last until late autumn.

The 35th. (Bantam) Division had inherited French trenches
which were in bad repair and contained fearsome momentos of
battle. One officer wrote in the war diary, "Trenches full of liquid
mud. Smell horrible. Floors and walls contain many dead
Frenchmen, too bad to touch. Our men quite nauseated." Other
battalion diaries tell the same story, "Clay, muck, and mud rather
bad here. Men have to pull each other along to walk. If you stand
still, you sink, and have to be hauled free with horrible sucking
noises. To be wounded, is certain to die in the mire."

Having to struggle to even walk through such cloying mud
made the crushing load of standard issue equipment bad enough
when piled on soldiers of average height. When carried by Bantams,

it became almost grotesque, making them look like moving mounds
of luggage. Before the 15th. Cheshires left for France, Lt. Colonel
Harrison Johnston recorded, "Paraded with everybody in full kit
with all our Christmas Tree decorations on. As we officers are only
allowed to take one valise weighing 35 pounds, we all took as
much as possible on our persons. Luckily, being mounted, my
pack was on my horse. The men's total weight of stuff including
packs, clothing, rifle, and 120 rounds of ammunition each, averaged
70 pounds. Each man's weight, stripped, averaged 126 pounds.
Yesterday, we weighed several as a test."

Though such a load bore heavily on any men who had joined
straight from school or from sedentary occupations, it was generally
accepted that all Bantams should be treated the same as other
troops. J. J. Hutchinson maintains, "Our equipment and Lee
Enfield rifles were no trouble to us at all, and we carried the same
weight of pack as any other regiment on the Western Front."

"Today, a lot of people seem to think that the Bantams
were a bunch of little Boy Scouts. Well, we had miners, shipyard
men, men who worked in the lead works carrying heavy metal
all day, and bakery workers used to carrying two-hundred-
weight sacks of flour, and we also had some pretty sturdy dock
workers from Liverpool and Birkenhead. None of these men
were exactly weak."

It is difficult today to trace the adventures of Bantam units
during the summer of 1916, because the 35th. Division was seldom
used as a complete unit during its service on the Somme. Brigades,
battalions, even companies and platoons were broken up in penny
packets for work anywhere they were needed along the front sector.

Two such units were the 15th. Sherwood Foresters and the
16th. Cheshires, who were sent to a sector northeast of Maricourt.
Moving up at night, they made their way through the maze of
trenches which straggled in all directions to no particular plan.
Hastily dug in minutes for dire convenience, the trenches would
be later reinforced and finished until they became permanent. As
thoroughfares, some trenches bore names which commemorated
their original inhabitants, like Scottish Trench and Cornish Alley.

Others echoed past tragedies like Deadman's Ditch, and Machine Gun Alley, while more flippant others were Beer, Hops, and Pint Alleys.

The Sherwoods took over Maltz Horn Trench, relieving a badly-punished regiment. "On July 14th, we are rushed to the front line," wrote J. E. Taylor, who had just that day returned from sick-leave in England. "Some of Y Company are in Trones Wood and Z Company is in the chalk trenches. Just outside the wood, 16 Platoon of Z Company join up with the French soldiers who are on our right. In a short communications trench are the Signals Officer, Mr. Dexter, and three signallers, including myself. On entering the trench at dawn, my eyes are gazing into those of a dead soldier, his body leaning over the top of the trench. On his tunic shoulderplate is the name Buffs, the battalion here before we took over."

A new draft of Cheshire Bantams arrived in time for the battle. One of them was Nelson Spencer. "Silently that night we followed our guide into the trenches, unaware we were about to be baptized by fire. Indeed this night soon proved to be a horror. No sooner had I spoken to my new platoon officer, the darkness was split by the multiple explosions of Hun rapid fire. One shell burst on the left of this officer, with me to his right. Both of us were blown over a sunken road into a field. The officer was found dead and I was taken unconscious to a field hospital for ten days. Later, I realized that the officer killed had been a business acquaintance of mine in civilian life."

The Cheshires travelled along Chimpanzee Trench in chaotic conditions. Somehow, the unit managed to arrive at dawn more or less intact. Two platoons which had scattered down side trenches during a bombardment were reunited with the rest of their comrades in time for stand-to around four o'clock in the morning.

As the darkness faded, the Bantams looked across the short desolation of No-Mans-Land towards their objectives. Straight ahead was a low mound of bricks and rubble which marked the site of Waterlot Farm, a strongpoint which had repeatedly changed hands. Far to the left lay the pulverized village of Guillemont,

which the Germans had stubbornly held against a score of attacks
to dislodge them. A sunken road called "Death Way" led to the
village through the stumps of shattered trees—daring more British
troops to join the numberless others who had been slaughtered
there.

Death Way was now no more than a churned mud track, pitted
with countless shellholes, and flanked by limbless poles which
once had been luxuriant trees. The wrecks of wheeled transport
were strewn along the road, attesting to the accurate ranging of
the Germans. Wafting along the track was the stench of unburied
men, and dead horses and mules, hundreds of whose bloated, stiff-
legged carcasses lay beside the wagons.

This was the hazardous route taken by "W" Company of the
16th Cheshires when they advanced to relieve the Cameron
Highlanders at Waterlot Farm. The position was a pulverized heap
of bricks which once had been a historic old building typical of
fortified farmhouses in the area. Now it was flat and pitted with
muddy shellholes that it made an ideal defensive site for infantry
wanting a commanding view of the German trenches between
Delville Wood and Guillemont.

The company moved out shortly after midnight on July 17th,
1916, groping their way through flame-stabbed darkness. At dawn,
the men were able to begin shoring up the broken trench walls
and prepare for visitors. Their commanding officer, Lieutenant H.
D. Ryalls, set out with 2nd. Lt. R. MacLaren to see if the Camerons
could be somehow withdrawn despite the bombardment. In
minutes, Lt. MacLaren was mortally wounded and the isolated
Camerons lay pinned down under intensified shellfire. The
Cheshires' own position was in danger also as shellfire boxed them
in and strong parties of the enemy were spotted darting forward
along the deep railway cutting leading from Guillemont Station.

Ryalls sent Private Hoare back to Battalion H.Q. with an urgent
request for reinforcements. Lt. Colonel Johnston explained why
they could not be sent. "We got a request from our brother Battalion
(the 16th) to send them two companies as reinforcements, but as
they were in one brigade and we in another, this was impossible.

Furthermore, we were each holding a wood, they run parallel, with instructions to hold it to the last man. If we sent two companies, we could not be sure of doing our job. In fact, we couldn't risk it."

"The wires were all cut and we could not contact Brigade except by messages carried along a heavily shelled road by runners. Requests came from the same source for ammunition and bombs. The large dump had been cleared during the afternoon and we had little to spare, but we fished round and sent them all we could—about 20,000 small-arms ammo and some bombs."

The hard-pressed Ryalls sent a Lewis gun team to a brick wall south of the farm, to hold off the advancing German infantry. A hand-to-hand fight raged here until the enemy was thrown back. They were observed to join up with about three hundred other Germans who came forward pulling two Maxims on sleds. The plucky Private Hoare went off with another request for help, while the Cheshires attacked as best they could. Private Harry Barlow was the sole survivor of a six-man Lewis gun team. He picked up the weapon, which had a shattered butt, and two magazine pans. As the forward slope was under direct fire from the enemy, he crawled on hands and knees across it until he reached the crest. A methodical man, Barlow tapped out three-shot bursts at each of an enemy rifle squad in turn. He had knocked over all but four of the Germans when a sniper killed him with a shot between his shoulder blades.

This time, Colonel Browne-Clayton was able to send help. It arrived in the form of a Vickers gun team led by Lieutenant G. Frazer of the Machine Gun Corps. The team set up in a shellhole west of the farm and began to drop harrassing fire among the attackers. The Germans fell back, and made no more advances from the south.

Then, right in front of the farm, an entire battalion of the enemy suddenly rose up from a trench whence they had infiltrated from Delville Wood. The Germans charged in six rows, over 900 determined opponents against the 100-odd Cheshires. It was high time for the company to spring their one ace in the hole.

An apparently wrecked trench had been secretly occupied by two platoons against this very eventuality. They were commanded by 2nd. Lieutenant R. B. Schofield, who waited until the last minute before he ordered his riflemen and two concealed Lewis gunners to open fire at almost point-blank range.

The fat Lewis barrels spat .303 bullets at 550 r.p.m. into the packed target, and this time miraculously did not jam at the crucial moment, as they were prone to do. The l.m.g fire was so devastating against the close-packed attackers that the survivors fled, leaving many casualties.

The fight for Waterlot Farm was costly to the Cheshire Bantams, too. At the moment of triumph, 2nd. Lt. Schofield was fatally wounded, and Lieutenants MacLaren and A. C. Styles were already dead, along with 32 other ranks. Other casualties were 134 wounded and seven missing presumed dead. Before the survivors went into rest, Colonel Clayton called Lieutenant Ryalls in front of the battalion, thanked him, and announced his immediate award of the Distinguished Service Order.

Next, it was the Notts & Derby's turn. General Pinney travelled forward to Brigade Headquarters in Stanley's Hole, "an evil-smelling dug-out" only four hundred yards from Maricourt. He arrived at 8.30 p.m. on July 18, to personally order that units of the brigade must go forward immediately to capture 1000 yards of German trenches between Arrowhead Copse and Maltz Horn Farm. The attack was scheduled for dawn next morning, July 19th, and the job was handed to the 15th Sherwood Foresters who occupied trenches right opposite Pinney's objective. They had only a few hours to prepare, so things rapidly began to go wrong. There was no clear observation available for accurate artillery support, and storming parties would have to go out in two separate groups. This split attack was dictated by the 1000-yard wide target which was really too extended for assault by a single battalion. The rushed plan was to lay down the best artillery support possible under blind conditions and have the infantry attack the far ends of the enemy trench, then bomb their way towards each other.

Shaky as these arrangements were, matters worsened shortly after midnight, when battalion commander Lt.-Col. Gordon sent brigade headquarters an urgent message. He reported his battalion was badly shaken after being under shellfire and gas attack for four hours—only two companies remained fit to attack. Hastily, troops of the 23/Manchester were sent as replacements, struggling forward through the mud and darkness. The Mancunians arrived in position at 3 a.m., physically exhausted even before they were due to go over the top.

The attack went ahead at 5.00 a.m., June 19th, and the Bantams didn't have a chance. Sunrise limned the troops, perfect targets for Spandaus, and many fell before they got across No Man's Land. The Manchesters did penetrate the enemy line but were quickly driven out into shell-swept open ground. What was left of them straggled back to their own trenches.

The right hook of the attack went in anyway, launched at the strangely late hour of 10.45 a.m. Manchesters and Sherwood Foresters rose from their parapets into the steel teeth of German machine-guns which had been waiting expectantly. One entire company of Mancunian late-arrivals literally ran down the communication trenches and carried on straight over the top into the attack. Their zeal stopped short at the empty fireswept line which the Germans had prudently abandoned. An avalanche of explosives came down and the newcomers ran for their lives. Somehow, they managed to stand firm in their own trenches and the expected German counter-attack fizzled out. Later that day, what was left of the two battalions staggered out of the line.

The 23rd. Manchesters left behind nine dead officers, including Lt.-Colonel E. L. Maxwell, and 162 slaughtered Bantams. The 15th. Sherwood Foresters, which had been shelled and gassed for four days, lost ten dead officers and 39 soldiers, and carried in 146 wounded. Another 36 were missing, presumed dead.

General Pinney received a letter next day from General Magnan of the French 153rd. Division. He congratulated the courage of the 23/Manchesters whom he had witnessed advancing "as if on parade" against heavy fire. It was a panache the 35th. could ill-afford. There were frighteningly fewer Bantams every hour and their reservoir of fit replacements was drying up fast.

That bloody day, a 40-year-old NCO of the 15/Sherwood Foresters, Cpl. Jesse Wilton, was placed in charge of ten men in a forward dug-out facing Arrow Head Copse. He was told by Lt. McIntosh it was a die-hard position that "must be held at all costs for forty-eight hours or until relieved." The post was repeatedly under fire from machine-guns and artillery for the next 43 hours, until Cpl. Wilton told his men, "We had better go now. I think the Germans are coming on." Without contacting superiors, he ordered his men to abandon the position and led them back to safety in the front-line trenches. A Pte. Hughes who saw them come in later testified that Cpl. Wilton warned him, "Look out— the Germans are coming!"

Wilton reported to his company commander that he had on his own initiative evacuated the position six hours before he had been ordered to. His timing was unfortunate, as Lt.-Col. Gordon had just been humiliated by his battalion's inability to go back into combat. A scapegoat was needed in a hurry, as a grim example of the consequences of failure to lead. No delinquent officer being handy, an NCO would have to do, and Cpl. Wilton was immediately charged with quitting his post in face of the enemy. He did not contest the charge but made a statement about the intensity of the gunfire to explain his actions, saying, "My nerves and those of my men were very much shaken." The court was unmoved. found him guilty as charged, and sentenced him to death, but with a recommendation for mercy.

What probably finished him though, was the unusually critical opinion written by Lt.-Col. Gordon on the trial papers. "As an NCO he is a failure, being too familiar with his subordinates, and surly to his superiors . . . There was nothing to prevent him sendidng a message to his company commander, a comparitively easy matter for him to do. I see no favoring cause as regards his actions, which in my opinion were deliberate." Cpl. Wilton was executed by firing squad on 17 August, 1916.

The 104th. Brigade had remained intact as a unit and found much to occupy its Lancashire grit, any deviance from which received short shrift from officers. "I found myself sharing a shellhole at Guillemont with several lads," said Frank Heath. "We were all afraid, but that youngster the French girls had called their favorite *"Piccanini"* completely lost his nerve. Sergeant Pregnall brought over Captain Crooks who said, 'What's the matter with you, Felton?' The boy lay in the bottom of the hole and sobbed, 'I have heart failure, sir.' The Captain said, 'If you don't stand up, my boot will give you arse-failure!' It had the desired effect immediately."

This happened at dawn on July 22nd, when the 18th. Lancashire Fusiliers were withdrawing from an ill-planned attack which had begun at 1.30 a.m. Brigade Headquarters was then in the process of moving its position, which may account for the last-minute dispatch of orders from Brigadier Sandilands for a strong raid to go forward within six hours. The 18th. Lancs were to destroy wire across a 500-yard front to open the way for an advance against Guillemont by another regiment.

Detailed orders were not ready until midnight, with the result that the raiding parties were only in position ten minutes before the attack was set to begin. They were forced to huddle in open ground in front of the parapet, instead of in a gully as was originally intended. Their movements alerted the Germans, who sent up dozens of Very lights and star shells to illuminate their wire. Just as the Bantams began to advance, the enemy sent up red signal rockets. Their artillery responded in seconds.

"I recall thinking what a bloody silly business this was," said Ronald Marsden. "Here we were walking along as if it was broad daylight on the Promenade at Blackpool, while the Gerries were plastering us with every gun they had!"

The raiders went forward in two columns, 500 yards apart, hoping to destroy wire across as wide a front as possible. The right-hand column was under heavy fire from the start, and suffered their first setback when the Bangalore torpedo was touched off. This long explosives-filled pipe had been intended to blow a gap in the wire, now it was gone, along with the two soldiers carrying it. Soon, the column was forced to retire.

Marsden was with the left-hand column, which got into the German front line and bombed its way back into the support trenches. They settled down to hold the position, hoping to aid the expected follow-up attack, though in fact this did not arrive. Although wounded, Lieutenant M. R. Wood retained active leadership and kept his platoon together as a fighting unit. They set up two Lewis guns on each side of a shellhole and continuously engaged the enemy for five hours.

After inflicting numerous casualties and breaking up a counter-attack, Lt. Wood and Corporal A. Pattie began to collect their wounded. They fought their way out through a ring of enemies and returned to their own lines in midmorning. Their losses were ten killed and ten wounded. Cpl. Pattie received the Distinguished Conduct Medal for his bravery in dressing wounded men under shellfire and carrying six of them to safety. Lieutenant Wood was awarded the Military Cross for his leadership.

All three Lancashire Bantam battalions endured heavy shellfire during the next week, with scant opportunity to hit back. Then on July 25th, they sent up companies to prolong the line at the Eastern end of Trones Wood, under the command of Captain R. A. S. Coke.

"When we went to help at Trones Wood, we found the front line was just a jumble of shell holes under heavy German gunfire," recalled Fusilier Heath: "What a sight! Mangled bodies, arms and legs and bits and pieces everywhere, and about a hundred and fifty Royal West Kents lying dead in No-Mans-Land. While coming along the wrecked communications trench, we passed an officer carrying a soldier on his back. The soldier's leg was hanging almost severed at the knee. Somebody said, 'The poor devil!' The wounded man said, 'There are dozens up there worse off than me.' We tried, but the fire was so heavy it was impossible to bring in the dead and wounded lying beyond the front line."

The enemy saw this activity as being the prelude to an attack and laid down a heavy bombardment of high explosive and gas.

"You could always tell a gas shell by the funny 'gobble-gobble' noise it made," recalled Ronald Marsden. The troops had to dig their own new trenches as the perfectly-registered German artillery destroyed the front line within an hour. Not for the first time, the miner's skill of many Bantams was the difference between life and death, and freshly-dug earth flew to give them sanctuary.

"At Trones Wood, I did a foolish thing," explained Fusilier Heath. "We had been without water for twenty-four hours, and I spotted that a few yards from our position was an iron lattice gantry with a round tank on top. Hoping there might be some rain water in it, I climbed up the girders. Right away, bullets whizzed around me and punched loudly through the tank. I didn't climb down, I fell down, trembling at my lucky escape."

Captain Coke was unearthed from a destroyed trench which had temporarily buried him, and he proceeded to organize rescue parties to dig out the other men. He devotedly dressed wounds of his troops, and occasionally noted down the last messages of dying men. When his company was relieved 30 hours later, he had been awake at his post the entire time although badly wounded by a shell-splinter. His men heartily approved of his subsequent award of the Military Cross.

The 104th. Brigade was thankfully ordered into rest on August 1st, a suitably appropriate date. They paraded in the miscalled "Happy Valley" near Bray-sur-Somme with other units of the Lancashire Fusiliers for a combined Minden Day Parade. This goes back to 1759, when the regiment marched forward at beat of drum across Minden Heath to Hanover, against massed French artillery and cavalry. As they passed among the wild rose briars that day, Lancashiremen snatched up blossoms and stuck them in their hats. Thus bedecked, they plodded forward, delivering musket volleys that cleared their way to victory. Ever since, the regiment has celebrated the event wherever they are stationed.

Someone at HQ saw to it that enough roses were available to enable three battalions to wear them on their steel helmets for Minden Day, 1916. The troops were reviewed by Brigadier J. W. Sandilands, who read a message to the 35th. (Bantam) Division from Major General Shea, G.O.C. 30th. Division. "In the name of my division, I wish to thank you and yours most sincerely for all you did for us. You gave us all help you could, and it is our earnest hope that someday we may be able to repay you. We much deplore your losses, but will always remember the gallantry of your men."

The troops took more comfort in being given a real rest behind the lines at last without the expectation of carrying supplies up the line each night. They were moved to Corbie, a quiet spot untouched by war, at a junction of the Somme and Ancre Rivers. A latter-day visitor to the now peaceful village can only imagine what a haven it must have seemed to those battle-shocked Bantams who snatched a brief respite there, long ago.

Glorious hot weather encouraged the men to enjoy bathing naked in the river below the beautiful old town, under the giggling appreciative gaze of local women. "We all went a bit mad that month. Lads who'd been too tongue-tied to say so much as 'hello' to a girl before, now were dragging them off into the woods after a few minutes acquaintance," Ronald Marsden smiled dreamily. "From all the threshing in the bushes, I'd say there must be a fair number of people with English blood in their veins around Corbie to this day!"

While the 104th. Brigade unwound, the 106th. was suffering a dangerous and unglamourous time along the Montauban front. The West Yorkshires, Durhams, and two Scottish battalions supplied carrying and road-building parties under heavy shellfire without being able to fight back. Some idea of their martyrdom can be gained from the brigade's fatal casualties; two officers and 183 other ranks dead between the 15th. and 20th. July.

The 19th. Durham Light Infantry took no part in these attacks, being occupied with trench-building and the escort of prisoners-of-war, yet they lost 12 officers and 250 men during the last two weeks of July. It was the same for the 17th. Royal Scots and 18th. HLI—hard labour with all the danger and none of the stimulus of actual combat. "Lost seven men this morning to shellfire," wrote a Royal Scots officer. "We buried them within ten minutes of their death and went back to digging trenches."

The 17th. West Yorkshires had a particularly bad time at Bernafay Wood. While working as burial parties and ammunition carriers, they lost seventy-one NCOs. One company paid a toll of three out of four sergeants dead in an hour. One entire platoon was reduced to one officer, a lance-corporal, and six men.

The casualties of the battalion since the 13th. of July was ten officers and 304 other ranks, a remarkably high percentage, considering their so-called "purely support role." In one operation on July 30th, it received this commendation from Brigadier H. O'Donnell: "I consider that the O.C. of the 17th West Yorks did well in firstly proceeding himself to the front line trench at Zero Hour and, secondly, in pushing his battalion through the troops ahead of them, and occupying the front line at a time when it would otherwise have been left vacant; more especially as his battalion had, during the early hours of the morning, suffered from the effects of gas shells."

When the battered remnants of the battalion marched back for a "rest" in a wrecked trench less than one mile behind the line, they still wore the canvas hoods that passed for gasmasks but were heard to be singing in muffled tones the Yorkshire anthem, "On Ilkley Moor, Bar T'at." This was the valiant battalion a Leeds Ph.D. in military history would in1978 sneeringly dismiss as "a total failure, no more than a recruiting gimmick."

The Bantams persevered, gallantly fighting on, but the drain of casualties and strain of service was beginning to wear down the division as a whole. A shock rippled through the ranks when two more members of the 18th. Highland Light Infantry were court martialed on charges of desertion. Five-foot tall Pte. Hugh Flynn had disappeared while his unit was moving back into the trenches at Mariecourt on July 26th. He was soon apprehended miles behind the lines and brought back to face trial in mid-September. His commanding officer said Flynn was a "useless soldier," then opined that the accused did not deliberately run away to avoid duty, but his nerves simply could not stand the heavy shelling. Despite this understanding, the commander of the Bantam Division recommended execution. At the same time, VI Corps Commander Lieut-Gen. Sir Aylmer Haldane wrote a stiff note of criticism of Flynn's battalion commanding officer: "It would appear that this officer has been aware for some time of the man's [Flynn] constitutional weakness regarding shell fire, and should have taken steps either for him to be withdrawn from the line or such disciplinary action as was neccessary." Compassion did not help Flynn in the end, though, and he was shot at dawn on 15 November, 1916.

Lieut.-Gen. Haldane wrote in his diary of his personal disquiet over these executions. "I can only feel sorry for the poor beggars, as there are so many shirkers at home and conscientious objectors it is doubly hard on men here to suffer."

Another HLI man went absent on 31 August. Pte. John McQuaid fell out of the line of march while his battalion was moving to Sus St. Leger. Having already been court martialled once before for going absent and handed a suspended sentence for that, McQuaig's second desertion made the death sentence almost a foregone conclusion. His commanding officer noted that "both crimes of desertion were deliberate to avoid service." The court martial papers went all the way up to FM Haig, who signed his approval for sentence to be carried out. McQuaig was executed at Harbacq on 6 November, 1916.

Between the Draconian threat of executions and the constant hell of battle, it is small wonder that some soldiers considered it the height of good luck to "catch a Blighty one"— a wound serious enough to send the soldier back to hospital in England. Once a wounded man was seen to be in no danger of dying, the bloody recipient of a 'Blighty' would be congratulated by his comrades and watched enviously as he was carried away. John Hutchinson of the Cheshires laconically told about his. "We went out on a big raid one night. I had a spot of bother with a Jerry. I got him with my bayonet and he got me with his rifle butt on the head. I was sent home to hospital, and when I came out I was given a medical discharge and sent back to the shipyard as I was an apprentice rivetter, and that's how I ended my days with the Bantams."

A self-inflicted wound—deliberately shooting oneself—was tempting to men to whom even maiming or loss of limbs was preferable to having to endure any more torment in the front line. Pain and mutilation was less of a fear than the knowledge that, if detected, an "S.I.W." was a capital court-martial offence

"Not everyone was able to stand up to the conditions without cracking," points out HLI Bantam survivor George Cunningham. "As the war went on and on, with a few of your mates dying every day, life in the filthy trenches seemed a purgatory, so good men would do anything to escape. One of our young officers walked around one morning saying, 'I've got to get out of this.' A bit later on he was found dead with his revolver still in his hand."

"Another time, we were bringing up supplies at night to a stores inside a big factory. The Engineers had carefully blacked out the doors and windows, but somehow forgot to cover the glass roof. A Jerry aeroplane came over and dropped a bomb right through the roof and killed a lot of horses and men. Some of us got behind a nearby wall when the raid happened. Next thing I knew, one of my pals was moaning, holding his leg and saying he's been hit."

"You couldn't have been," I said. We were safe behind the wall. But I pulled up his leg and found a ragged hole right through his calf. I knew right away what he'd done. He'd fired through a sandbag into his own leg. "You crafty bugger," I said. "You've finally given yourself a Blighty one."

"We got him away to an Aid Station and I kept my mouth shut about it when he was sent home as wounded. But that same night, I threw away the special bullet he'd asked me to keep for him a few days before. He had made a 'Blighty-round,' by taking out the bullet and sticking pieces of shrapnel into the cartridge. I didn't want to be caught with it, as having a doctored round was a court-martial offence."

For ordinary soldiers serving in the line, there was not much prospect of home leave. They stayed there continuously for months on end, even years, in a grinding routine of six or eight days in the trenches, a week in reserve, and another week of rear-line labour. The unofficial period between leaves for the troops was about twelve months, but as the average life expectancy was six months at the most for front-line troops, the only relief to look forward to was a a disabling wound or serious illness or death itself. No relief based on consideration for length of active service was given to soldiers, even after being sent back wounded. As soon as they recovered, they were sent back into battle again, reducing their statistical odds of survival even more.

Canadian Bantam Joe Daniel served well over a year close to the front line before being granted 14 days leave in London. After enjoying a visit with his mother, Daniel wrote in his diary, "Gee, but they do monkey with a man when he is going on leave and returning. When I was going from here, I had to go and get my pass at 7.30 at night, then wait around until 8 o'clock next morning before we started in a lorry for the station. Got there at 9.30 then waited around again until one o'clock for a train. We were on it nine hours to go 60 miles. Then they marched us up a big hill to the rest camp. We were in tents covered with ice and snow until next morning at 5 o'clock to get the boat, which we got at 2.30 in the afternoon. They done the same thing to us coming back. They seem to try to make men as uncomfortable as they can."

  One Gloster Bantam tells of the fear-laden atmosphere aboard the boat trains carrying once-wounded troops back to France. "It was all smiles and laughter during family goodbies at the railway station in London, as men wanted to keep loved ones from feeling too bad," recalls Graham Ormsby. "But once the kisses stopped being blown and the train pulled out, a terrible quiet fell over the carriage I was in. You could tell from the songs and skylarking where the first-time soldiers were sitting. We old sweats—I was all of twenty at the time—knew what we were going back to, and we were scared to death. The best song we could raise was:

> "Send out the Army and the Navy;
> Send out the rank and file
> Send out the brave old Territorial,
> They face all danger with a smile,
> Send out my Mother and my Father,
> my brother and my sister,
> But for Christ sake, don't send me!"

In Ormsby's case at least, he was saved from repeating his ordeal by what seemed a miraculous whim that suddenly whisked him into an atmosphere of glittering luxury far from the filthy realities of the common soldier's experience. "When I was getting off the boat at Boulogne, I was all spiffed up with shiny boots and a beautifully pressed new uniform. My mother and sisters had even tailored the jacket and trousers so they actually fitted me, instead of looking like potato sacks. Anyway, I was marching along the docks, saluting like an idiot every few seconds because there were so many officers there. One of them stopped me, asked my name, and complimented me on my appearance. Then he turned and called out to another, 'Major, here's a smart-looking little chap. Just the ticket for the mess!' Next thing I knew, I was in the back of a motor lorry on my way to base headquarters to start work as a waiter. I just couldn't believe my luck!"

Ormsby's delight at being saved from returning to the front line was tinged with fear that the sudden transfer would be countermanded by his regiment. "I daren't mention it to anybody, in case they changed their minds. But I needn't have worried, because when I arrived at HQ, I found out that staff-officers could get away with anything they wanted, including taking squaddies off front line drafts!"

"I'll never forget how different it all was there in the senior officers' mess, like one of those smart West End clubs you saw pictures of. All lights and chandeliers and music and officers laughing and drinking, even French waitresses in white aprons, and silverware on snowy tablecloths. No wonder the General Staff never understood what the war in the trenches was really like. It was like paradise after what I'd expected to go back to. I thought about my mates on the draft who'd be settling in at that very minute to face mud and rats and shelling, and I felt a bit guilty to be missing it. But not much!" Few of his comrades would have begrudged his luck of avoiding being returned to the front line.

The Bantams' problem of sub-standard new recruits was again brought out following an abortive attack by the 16th. Cheshires on August 21st, 1916. They had been ordered to go forward that

morning to capture a German strong point on the outskirts of
Guillemont after heavy artillery had bombarded the objective.
However, a few minutes before zero hour at 9 a.m., Lt.-Col. Clayton,
the Cheshire's commander, reported the British artillery was still
firing, shells falling dangerously short among his own men. He
considered it was impossible for him to attack, as their their forward
trenches had been blown in and most of the Stokes mortar
ammunition buried. Though zero hour was advanced to 10 o'clock,
he was ordered that his battalion must then advance regardless.

But instead, the commanding general received an astounding
note from Lt.-Col. Clayton: "I am ashamed to say, the Battalion is
quite demoralized. I do not think they would stand up to anything,
and I honestly think it would be safer to get them relieved if
possible." One can read between the lines Clayton's grinding
embarrassment, the second battalion commander of the brigade
to admit his men were unable to carry on. They were replaced by
the 14th. Gloucesters which sent out a strong patrol next day to
reconnoitre the strong point, but encountered barbed wire
entanglements and heavy machine gun fire that forced them to
retreat.

Clayton's humiliated note along with failure of the attack
sparked a furious top-level inquiry. The Brigade Commander
concluded that three factors were involved: the artillery barrage
firing beyond the specified time disorganized the attack, the short-
falling British artillery had killed some troops and demoralized
the rest, and that the class of new recruits were no longer proper
Bantams, but were "either half-grown lads or degenerates."

There is no question that the 35th. (Bantam) Division was at
this stage in trouble so far as replacements were concerned. In
addition to casualties, endless bombardment by artillery, fragmented
employment as infantry shocktroops and gruelling physical work
at trench-building and carrying parties had worn out many of the
surviving Bantams.

There seems to have been an ambivalent attitude of "Work the
little buggers harder!"—as expressed by one Royal Engineers colonel
at Montauban—and at the same time, an expectation that such

outwardly cheerful troops had no need for rest out of the line. The result was steady attrition of the original men with scant ability to provide suitable replacements.

Lt.-Col. Davson wrote in the unit's history, "The original Bantams had done all that were expected of them, and, indeed, until the end of the war, the survivors manfully played their parts and earned a large share of the military awards which were from time to time gained by members of the 35th. Division. But when losses occurred, the men who were sent out to take their places were, in most cases, not "Bantams" at all, as the term was originally understood, but were undeveloped men, who had been previously rejected by the commanders, and who were unfitted, both mentally and physically, to take their places in the fighting ranks of the British army. This was recognized at a later date, and the unfit among them were withdrawn. Their retention appeared likely to endager the morale of the whole division."

The three brigades had each suffered a high turnover of men from casualties and illness throughout their first nine months of service. This was, of course, a common-enough experience for all front-line units during the First World War, when an average of 4000 men died every single day. But the problem was worsened for Bantam battalions in that their replacements were required to conform to set physical standards of height and chest measurement.

Divisional medical officers were by now so concerned at the low quality of replacements that they recommended the division should return back to the depots every man of poor phyisique who had arrived in recent drafts. It was decided by GHQ that though rejecting sub-standard men was a good idea, the division should wait until they had left Fourth Army and moved to their new sector.

The brigades were sent by train and bus north to the VI Corps, Sixth Army, and began to arrive at Arras during the first week of September. Here, they found they would be fighting a different style of warfare. At their back was the ancient city, resting on a system of catacombs hollowed out in medieval times and which now provided safe, dry quarters during rest periods. The trenches also promised to be a great improvement over the wet ditches and precarious above-ground embrasures of the Somme. Miner-like, the Bantams set to digging, shoring, and revetting their lines, while sending reconnaissence patrols to get to know the territory.

Not much was seen of the Germans, despite the closeness of their lines. The opposing troops were believed to also be recent veterans of the fierce fighting on the Somme. The German veterans contented themselves with continual trench-mortar fire, but showed a marked preference for a quiet life. The Bantams' commanders resolved to change this condition as soon as possible.

CHAPTER ELEVEN

The Bells Of Hell

The troops of those days were fond of singing, and what they lacked in technique they made up volume. Born in a less sophisticated time than today, they had few entertainments other than those they provided themselves. This may be the main reason why they now seem to later generations to have been so relentlessly cheerful; marching into battle with songs on their lips.

Even those of people in the 21st. Century who are barely aware that the Great War occurred at all have sometime heard old song lyrics like "It"s A Long Way To Tipperary" or "Pack Up Your Troubles." These and a dozen other popular melodies were sung with heart-breaking buoyancy by troops under the most trying of circumstances. Less familiar to modern ears may be one doggerel verse which the Tommies would sing repeatedly over and over in a mind-numbing mantra against the fearful reality they endured.

> "The bells of Hell go ting-a-ling-a-ling,
> For you but not for me.
> The angels they all sing-a-ling-a-ling,
> They hold the goods for me.
> O death, where is they sting-a-ling-a-ling,
> O grave, thy victory?
> The bells of Hell go ting-a-ling-a-ling,
> For you but not for me . . ."

In early September, 1916, Lancashire Bantams were heard chanting it as the 104th. Brigade swung along the slate-tinted road to Blangy, entering the trenches which would be the division's graveyard in more sense than one.

The village of Blangy was a suburb of Arras, the nodal point of their new front which stretched from Faubourg St. Sauveur below the Cambrai Road and northward to Roclincourt. The area was criss-crossed with trenches notable for being well organized in a system of named streets and avenues.

The 104th. Brigade took over "I" Sector which ran up from the banks of the Scarpe and included trenches named Iceland Street, Iron, Imperial, Infantry, and Ivory Streets. Next to them, the 105th.

Brigade got "J" Sector with trenches named after months, centred on January Avenue. At the far north of their turf were three mine craters named Claude, Cuthbert, and Clarence. The 106th. Brigade flanked them in "K" Sector, fronted by Kick, Kent, and Kate Craters, and backed by a maze of derelict trenches known as The Gridiron.

While the trench improvements had been underway, there was also a number of other activities to occupy the division. In the face of more complaints about the poor quality of Bantam replacements, a series of medical inspections began to examine new men and veterans alike. These resulted in several hundred recent arrivals being sent back to Amiens as unsuitable. The rejects included men with "both physical and morale defects," who should never have been sent up the line in the first place. Less fortunate escapees from front line duty were those combat veterans whom authority decided "were in need of some battle training and a general smartening up." They were sent to the Bull Ring.

In those days, a series of training camps had been built along the French coast south of Boulogne. The worst of them was Infantry Base Depot Number One, situated near the fishing town of Etaples, just across the bay from the fashionable resort of Le Touquet-Paris Plage. Now, Etaples is the site of one of the largest of British war cemeteries, where 11,000 men lie buried amidst lonely sandhills in a silence broken only by the scream of seagulls and the Atlantic wind.

Most of them died in nearby military hospitals once so busy trying to patch up gassed and mutilated bodies brought an agonizing distance from the front lines. Also buried here are the uncounted hundreds of accidental victims of the most notorious training camp in the British Army—the "Bull Ring."

Every soldier who passed through this hellish travesty of a training camp looks back on "Eat-apples" as being among his worst experience of the whole war. God only knows what rationale was behind its brutal ill-treatment of soldiers, many of whom were after all volunteers. Etaples Camp was staffed by screaming, bullying sadists who pounced on fresh-faced youths and bronzed old sweats alike the moment they arrived, and subjected them to two weeks of unrelieved humiliation, abuse, exhaustion, and outright torture. The camp staff, dignified by the title of instructors, were senior NCOs who wore yellow armbands and have thus ever after been hated for their nickname, "Canaries."

Harry Hurst said of them, "All that you may have heard is true about the horrors of the Bull Ring. Those base-wallahs were absolute sadists in their treatment of the front line troops. Their hatred for us was only equalled by our contempt for them."

The hard-bitten louts in charge were evidently terrified that they would be transferred to the front line at the first sign of showing humane treatment of troops. The cold-eyed officers in charge often threatened the Canaries with this fate so as to encourage deliberately brutal methods of training, and seem to have turned over the running of the Infantry Base Depot to the NCOs. Most of the officers, like their Commandant, Brigadier General Andrew G. Thomson, lived in fastidious isolation inside the Commissioned Officers' Compound.

Thomson would only be dismissed in September, 1917, after the I.B.C. finally erupted in a mutiny by 100,000 troops. The mutiny was put down with the utmost severity and hushed up so successfully that not much is known of it in England to this day. Unfortunately, these events occurred too late to help men of the 35th. (Bantam) Division sent to sample the Bull Ring.

Cyril Wright remembered Etaples with clarity after sixty years. "Every minute of the day, instructors shouting at us. 'Nip to it, short-arse! At the double! Move! Move!' The Canary points a long, ringed pole at me. I'm supposed to stick my bayonet through it while we both run. Then us squaddies lie down in the mud and crawl while they fire live rounds from a Lewis gun just over our heads. One man gets shot in the foot and is sworn at all the way to the first aid post. We polish our boots like mirrors every night, then right after inspection next morning we are marched into ankle-deep mud again. And all the time, the Canaries shouting filthy names at us, bullying us, abusing us, and even hitting us with their canes when they feel like."

The cruel "training" never varied at Etaples. Awoken before dawn, given a quarter of an hour to bolt down sausages and tea, new arrivals from various regiments were paraded on the barrack square. A careful inspection of brasses, boots, and rifles brought the inevitable flurry of men being "put on a charge" for later trial and punishment at various types of hard labour. Then, the troops were marched off behind a small pipe band, bound for the distant sand hills.

It was a routine the soldiers would be subjected to for the next 14 days. Laden with 60 pounds of full equipment, rifles stiffly at slope arms, they were marched at double-time up and down towering sandhills. When exhausted by hours of marching, they would then be put through every imaginable type of battle-drill—and every humiliation—the instructors could devise. The loathed Canaries drove the men with frantic savagery. Assault courses, trench digging, bayonet charges, went on by the hour, to the obscene screaming orders of the instructors.

The brutalizing two-week course was supposedly intended to prepare men for what they must soon face at the front. Live ammunition was used during training exercise. This along with high explosives and shellfire gave the men a taste of the danger to come, but also caused frequent accidental deaths and injuries. At the merciful conclusion of training, they were grudgingly told they were as ready as they'd ever be, and sent off to join their regiments.

Drafts of the 15th. Sherwood Foresters had an equally hard time in the Bull Ring, as J. E. Taylor wrote. "It was a very tough camp. Talk about jumping to it! Bayonet fixed, you run at stuffed sacks, screaming as you stab them. Then, 'On the hands, down! Knees bend! Arms out—in—out!' On and on, with no letup. I could have wept. How I wanted to get away. I actually wanted to be back in the line with my little Don Three telephone, shellfire and all. When our time is up at Etaples, almost happily away I go to fight the foe."

There would have been plenty of need for Taylor's skill as a signaller on his return to Arras. The Germans had brought up a strong concentration of heavy trench mortars against the British lines. These monsters hurled fat shells known as "rum jars" with enough explosive power to wreck 25 yards of trench at a time. As well, the Germans fired off salvos of smaller mortars and thousands of rifle-grenades. To avoid insupportable casualties, the front lines had to be cleared of all but suicide-squads of holding troops for days at a time.

Such constant damage required endless hard labour to dig out trenches and repair the parapets. Harry Hurst was guiding a fatigue-party bringing duckboards from the rear up to the front line at Arras. "Leading the way, I happened to glance backward, and saw a lot of lengths of duckboard sticking up well above the parapet. The Germans had seen them too, for as I expected I noticed a flock of 'toffee apples' [trench mortar bombs] coming through the air. I evacuated hurriedly, and I'm sure the survivors of that fatigue party didn't carry duckboards in that give-away manner again."

The casual finger of death could tap a man at any time. Lancashire Fusilier Frank Harris tells of his narrow escape while working behind the lines. "Our party of twenty men was coming back after a trip up the line with a load of empty sandbags and concertina wire. We were just jogging along (amazing how fast one can travel on the way back) when swish-bang! a mortar shell dropped just behind us. After going another hundred yards or so, we all pulled up. I was shocked to find that instead of having five men behind me I now was the last in line."

"We went back and found only two of the five still alive, and they badly wounded. I never will forget passing the same place the next morning. Although the bodies were gone, I saw three steel helmets lying there, and knew from the stencil badge they had belonged to my pals."

The infantry troops found themselves mainly employed as mortar artillerymen, their only way of hitting back at an enemy they scarcely ever saw. The Stokes mortar was a simple tube which lobbed a shell at high trajectory into the German trenches as close as fifty yards away. The 104th. Brigade tested their skill at this when a sniper shot an enemy and some of his comrades came out to his assistance. A Stokes bomb was dropped neatly right into the centre of the luckless group.

More effective counter-batteries had been set up by the Divisional Artillery guns in the ruined hamlets ringing the town, to try to silence German mortars which threatened to soon destroy the entire front line faster than it could be rebuilt. The artillery began to be able to at least discourage the enemy when Heavy Trench Mortar Batteries arrived on September 12th. The Bantams grinned appreciatively even though half-deafened when the four 9.45 mortars of V/35 HTM opened up to give "Fritz" a taste of his own medicine.

On the night of September 10th, the Germans came across the Gridiron to raid what they hoped was a thinly held sector. However, the Durhams were expecting them, and manned the rim of Kate Crater. A salvo of Lewis gunfire and grenades fought off the Germans that time but it was the first of a series of probing moves by the enemy all along the front. They had been alerted either by aircraft or espionage agents that large shipments of poison gas were arriving at Arras and were not unnaturally curious to learn where the cylinders would be placed.

About 960 deadly containers arrived, their red nozzles soldered tight, and were brought forward by nervous carrier parties of the Cheshire Regiment.

Colonel Johnston recorded, "Our men had an important job at night, carrying gas cylinders for the Brigade on our left. The gas is worked by a special battalion who go about for the job. Most of the men are chemists, generally over military age, and most wear spectacles. They are a very intelligent lot of men, and do nothing but look after our various forms of frightfulness. It may interest you to know that the British have made 122 gas attacks this year, and the Germans.have made four. It is nice to feel that the Boche, having invented these pretty things, is getting some himself, beaten at his own game."

The gas cylinders were lined up in specially dug pits and aimed towards the German positions. Several times, elaborate plans were made for their employment, then cancelled at the last minute. The cylinders lay in their pits for weeks, unused, pregnant with

death, and an ever-present threat to the British troops stationed
nearby.

Two weeks of trench-digging and dodging mortar shells began
to tell on the Bantams' nerves. They impatiently asked when they
might get a chance to pay a visit to the German lines. It was an
aggressive attitude which needed the outlet of raiding. The 15th.
Cheshires were the first to go over, on the night of September
14th.

Their target was the enemy line between Claude and Kate
Craters, where three smaller holes were known as Three Craters
Salient. It was a badly shelled area which would be difficult to
cross even during daylight. "The salient looked devastated," said
Nelson Spencer, "Water, mules, and dead men covered in foam
caused by gas could be seen everywhere."

A well-planned support programme involved rehearsals at
Duisans against replica trenches, and a co-ordinated attack by
artillery and diversionary mines being fired between Cuthbert and
Clarence Craters to distract the defenders. The guns opened up at
8 p.m., their shells forming a box-barrage to fence off the point of
entry in the German front line. Sixteen minutes later, four large
camouflets were touched off with such force that they shook Arras.
By then, the Bantams had reached the enemy trench and suffered
a dozen casualties from shells of their own artillery that fell short.

Despite the 1400 rounds fired by the 159th Artillery Brigade,
the German defenders showed their typical bravery under fire by
popping up along the parapet to shoot at the bayonet-waving
Cheshires. But hot work at point-blank range enabled the raiders
to get into the trench, and they began to bomb their way along in
both directions.

One of their purposes was to enable a party of New Zealand
miners to search for a suspected mine shaft, so there was even more
need for speed. The Germans resisted so vigorously that Captain
Bertie LeMesurier led his men up outside the trench to bomb it
from above. They fought in this way for about 40 minutes, then
sounded the recall at 9 pm., and retired with a loss of five men
dead and 27 wounded. Whey they reached their own trenches, it

was found that one New Zealand officer and his sergeant were missing.

Three search parties went out for them without success. The mystery of their fate was probably solved at 9.45 p.m. when a huge crimson flame, which looked like a charge of ammonal, shot up in the German trenches. The determined Kiwi officer had found his target after all, and its destruction formed his own funeral pyre, for he was never seen again.

The enraged Germans intensified their mortar fire, to discourage further invasions. In this they were disappointed, as the Bantams began to send over raiders virtually every night all along the Arras front. Manchesters, Scots, and Lancashire men took their turn at commando-style raids. They suffered relatively few casualties beyond the wire but paid a steady toll inside their own trenches.

One night, three men were killed and six wounded by one rifle grenade which landed among a party of 20th Lancashire Fusiliers. Moments later, another grenade dropped into Iodine Sap and killed two men of the 18th Lancs. They were revenged the following dawn when Sergeant Tinsley shot five Germans at a range of seven hundred and fifty yards.

Sniping was a constant danger to men on both sides throughout the war. A moment's carelessness in passing an open space or in raising one's head over the parapet could bring a bullet from marksmen who lay patiently waiting for just that opportunity. Aside from the casualties, the very threat of snipers wore down men's nerves, adding to the terror of trench life.

Early in the war, the Germans enjoyed superiority in this mode of killing. From 1914 on, their snipers were specially equipped with Mannlicher hunting rifles and Leitz telescope sights which gave them a murderous accuracy. However, when British snipers were finally equipped with Ross telescope sights tapped onto standard-issue Lee Enfields, it was found they had a weapon every bit as good as the enemy's, and the menace of snipers was balanced. Men with good marksmanship scores, patient dispositions, and the required implacable temperament were given special instruction in how to kill selectively. The Bantam Division trained their snipers at ranges along the French coast near Le Havre and at First Army' School of Scouting, Observation & Sniping, near Arras. There, Major Hesketh-Pritchard had gathered a team of experts to show troops the arts of concealment, the needs for patience, watchfulness, and ruthlessness, then send them back to units to ply their lonely trade of killing at long range.

Young Pte. David Hammond, 17th. Royal Scots began sniping enemies in revenge for death of a friend, and considered it a "rotten business," but became a skilled man-hunter for the rest of the war,

By no means all snipers were formally trained. One official war diary records that a sniper of the 106th Brigade killed a German staff officer who was accompanying his general around the line. This officer's death was a personal act of vengeance by a young Bantam. Private David Hammond of the 17th Royal Scots was a stores clerk who, because of his job seldom had to stay in the forward trenches. For weeks, he spent a dangerous enough time dodging shells as he would bring up supplies to his fellows in the front lines. "I had a particular chum," he said, "A Cornishman called Jamie Smith, who was a proper fire-eater of a lad. Forever going on raids, he was. But he was a happy-go-lucky sort of fellow, too, and many's the night he would sit singing and cracking jokes with us all down in the trench as Jamie would give us a song."

"I had just said 'so long' to him one morning and turned away along the trench when I heard a 'crack!', and heard his mates cry out. I turned back, and there was Jamie with a little hole through the side of his head. He had stood up once too often and had been sniped by a German.

"I don't mind saying I cried that day," said Hammond. "I picked up his rifle after a while and climbed up on the bank behind some wagon limbers. I waited there for a long time, watching Jerry's trenches. A bit later on another one of the lads was sniped, but this time I saw a puff of smoke and knew where the killer was. I put ten rounds rapid into a pile of wreckage where I thought the man was, though I never did know whether I had hit him."

"The trench mortar retaliation was close enough to warn me to never fire more than one shot in future, but this experience started me off. Every day after duty either in the morning or twilight I would go off to near where Jamie had been shot, and I would watch for a Jerry. The very first morning I got down to being a sniper, I bagged a senior German officer and a sergeant, one after the other."

"After a while, my officer got to hear of this and called me into the dug-out. 'You're not supposed to be a sniper,' he said. 'What are you doing this for?' I told about what happened to my mate, and how I used to shoot a lot on the farm. 'Good luck to you, then,' said the officer, and gave me permission to take time off from my regular duties every second day, just to hunt Jerries."

"Soon it was my full-time job, and I put paid to over forty Jerries in the next two years by sniping. It was a rotten business, but they started it and by God, I wanted to help finish it."

The Germans also developed special camouflaged equipment for their Jaeger [hunters], including flash-eliminators, false tree-trunks made of concrete, and porthole shields. One innovation was discovered by HLI Private Peter Cassidy, "While on patrol in No-Mans-Land, we learned of one dangerous trick of Jerry when we found a dead cow which had been hollowed out and steel plate put in for use as a sniper's post."

The discovery of another well-concealed sniper's post on September 20th, earned the personal congratulations of the new Divisional Commander. Major General A. J. S. Landon that day replaced the popular General Pinney, who left to command the 33rd Division. Sergeant H. C. Bolton of the 20th Lancashire Fusiliers became suspicious of an old chimney in No-Man's-Land. Carefully carrying a small pack of guncotton explosive, he went out in daylight to examine the ruins and came under frequent sniper fire.

Dodging bullets, he finally managed to enter the brickpile and found a ladder placed below a shellhole in the wall about twenty feet up. Iron spikes had been set aside the chimney to enable a sniper to climb up to the top. Noting traces of fresh mud on the ladder, Sergeant Bolton decided to use the guncotton he had thoughtfully brought along. Blowing up the chimney, sniper and all, earned him the Military Medal.

There were many opportunities for acts of individual bravery during the next couple of months while the 35th Bantam Division held the line at Arras. Daily bombardments and nightly raids took away a few more familiar faces each week and the survivors hardened into professional soldiers ready to follow a good leader anywhere.

There was a strong bond of comradeship among officers and men in the front lines, where death was always so close that caste and position were rendered meaningless. Many who were there spoke of how this levelling influence would be quickly felt soon after experiencing the continual shelling and trench raids. This was particularly marked with good-quality troops who had served together for a long time, among whom mutual confidence reduced the need for rigid differences in rank. However, officers and NCOs in charge of less familiar replacement troops felt greater need to keep an iron discipline.

Whatever posturings were fashionable at Officer Cadet Training Units, any wise front-line officer learned how to adopt a friendlier and more easy-going manner with the rankers under his command—men whom he would have to order to follow him into deadly danger; men whom he might need to rely on to save his life; and men calloused to killing, whom he would have to present his back to when he led them over the top. A harshly unpopular officer could risk grievances being settled permanently by a bullet during the handy confusion of battle.

"Our officers were gentlemen in all things," maintained George Palmer, of the 14th Gloucesters. "We all understood that there was the Book of Army Regulations to be followed, and we would do anything for a leader who was fair to us. But the officer or NCO who was a real bastard to us never tried his Vernon [nastiness] twice, as many a bad one was shot in the back during battle."

Though British troops usually endured much hard discipline without taking reprisals, it would be surprising if they did not occasionally turn on their tormentors. Brutalized in battle and constantly exhorted during training to "Kill the Boche, even prisoners!" the Bantams frequently became creatures of their hideous environment.

Sgt. H. T. Crook was an instructor in musketry and sniping. In 1916, he went overseas and found himself with the Birkenhead Bantams. "A more blood-thirsty lot I never met," Sgt. Crook would long recall. "They were of course embittered by six months of unrelieved fighting service in the front line, and when I arrived, I was seen as someone who had been skulking behind in England. They were so hostile to me and behaved so badly towards me that I had to fully explain my position before I even dared go up into the line with them."

"I observed they killed everyone they did not like—and took very few prisoners. It took some time to convince the Bantams that I was worthy of being followed and obeyed. Once accepted by them, I couldn't have had better troops to lead."

"They had seen so much bloody fighting, that many were quite deranged, just like some soldiers of other regiments. The result was that once they were in the line, killing was the order of the day, and woe betide the German who faced the Bantams, and woe betide any NCO or officer who did not act towards them in a way that they approved of."

Going by a number of reports, though, it seems most Bantams managed to retain some form of civilized conduct, despite the brutalization of combat. But the "trench-happy" minority who did become unhinged by their experiences, displayed a somewhat fearsome attitude. Moved constantly from one regiment to another, continuously thrown into trench raids and suicidal assaults, some became so battle-hardened they fought ruthlessly and fearlessly with no expectation of surviving.

Asked how smaller Bantams would fare in personal combat against larger enemy soldiers, George Palmer replied simply, "The bigger the German, the bigger the target. You could always spin your helmet into his teeth, or put the butt in, or a knee in the groin. One thing we were taught was to spit in his face and when he shut his eyes, which most people will, then was the time to give him clobber. In, out, and away! We always kept a .303 up the spout for such times, too, in case you had to shoot your bayonet free of Jerry's ribs. Not very sporting tricks, but I came back."

"Many of our officers were Regular Army types, kind if stern," George Palmer continued. "Some of the taller fellows in charge were inclined to say us small chaps suffered from 'duck's disease'—our backsides too close to the ground. Be that as it may, I never regretted my lack of height since the time a sniper's bullet hit the tree just above my head while I was making water. Any taller, and I'd have been dead. I was soon down in the latrine pit, clean boots and all!"

Nelson Spencer had the same sentiments. "One time whilst leaning against the trench-wall, a whizbang exploded right above me, burying a lump of hot shrapnel in the wall not three inches above my head. My short stature saved me, as it must have done on many occasions unknown to me."

Their views on this were not always shared by taller troops. Captain Richard Peirson was commanding a company of the Northumberland Fusiliers when they went into the line to relieve a battalion of Bantams. "A little while after the relief operation was completed, my company sergeant major came to me in a great state and said, "Sir, them bloody little dwarfs have built up the fire steps so they could see over. Now when my lads stand up, half their bodies are above the parapet." Soon afterwards, standing orders on trench relief procedures were read aloud to the 104th Brigade. 'Two sandbags per man for filling and placing on the firestep are provided. Parapets are not to be lowered."

These orders were doubly important by early November when a combination of very heavy rain and bombing kept trenches and parapets in an almost permanent state of damage. It became dangerous to sleep in the funk-holes dug in trench walls which could suddenly collapse to bury the unwary. This happened in "I" Sector where most of the gas cylinders had been moved, and gave troops the ticklish job of digging out the containers by hand for fear that spades broke the seals.

"J" and "K" sectors received a heavy bombardment just as a raiding party of the 17th West Yorkshires set out on November 9th. Despite the mortar bombs, they reached the enemy, killed six Germans, and brought back identification of the 89th Grenadier Regiment. Later that night, a patrol of the 15th Cheshires captured a German near Clarence Crater. He was wearing a gas mask. The Cheshires eyed the red-tipped cylinders squatting near them. Jerry was definitely up to something.

At dawn that day, firing was heard overhead and a British aircraft crashed into the wire south of the Cambrai Road in "I" Sector. Several Germans fatally exposed themselves to division snipers when they curiously peered over the parapet to watch the wounded pilot crawl to safety in the British line.

Another of his squadron was not so fortunate, as Nelson Spencer witnessed. "My officer looked upwards and said, 'What is that?' I looked up, and there was something like a large cross dropping from the sky. As it came nearer, one could define it to be a man with outstretched arms, turning and turning head over heels, and I heard my officer quietly say, 'Poor man.' The body dropped some distance in front of our trench, but we could not bring him in then because of enemy fire. That night, we recovered the body of a young British airman who we concluded had been in an aerial dogfight and lost."

Officers and men alike began to increasingly sense that an enemy attack was in the offing. It was little things, like a German calling across to a Royal Scots sentry of No. 1 Sap in "K" Sector, 'It's cold tonight, Jock.' Though they had not raided for identification, the Germans knew already exactly which regiment was stationed there. Signs that the enemy was preparing a major attack was perceived when they began to bombard the division's front in massive strikes. Aerial torpedoes, rum jars, and petrol shells pulverized February Avenue, "K" Sector, and the Pope's Nose in "I" Sector. More fighting patrols came out along the enemy front, and a German officer was even discovered in an empty British listening post. Perhaps it was because the British Command was planning to loose a major gas attack at last, that these signs of German preparation were mainly ignored.

On the night of 25-26 November, 1916, the front line of the 104th Brigade in "I" Sector was ordered cleared as a gas discharge was to be released. The men had been battered by very heavy mortar fire all afternoon and thankfully retired down Iceland Street, leaving only a few Lewis gun parties in forward saps. Using a confusing series of codewords—Duncan and Jack, and Rubber and Gravel— the gas was alternately ordered used or not to be used in a manner which Brigadier Sandilands later called "a perfect nightmare." The gas was ordered released at 11.45 p.m., cancelled for an hour, then cancelled again. Finally it was ordered to be released at 2.35 a.m., although the scattered defenders knew nothing of this and had been wearing masks for over four hours.

"The first type of gasmask was just a bag saturated with chemicals," said George Palmer. "By then, we had better ones, with two eyeglasses, a nose-clip, and a rubber spout like a duck's bill. You could only blow out and suck in a little air, so the glasses steamed up. All you could do was breathe shallowly and hope for the best. Not very useful during a raid, though."

A three-pronged German raid hit the divisional line around 2 a.m. Large parties of the enemy had advanced under cover of a massive artillery duel and arrived at exactly the weakest section of trenches before the gas had been released. General Sandilands had ordered Lt. Colonel Mills of the 17th Lancashire Fusiliers to take special precautions to defend a number of bombarded trenches just vacated by men of the 12th Division further along, and this move further depleted the defenders. The pleased Germans jumped into the trench gap unopposed and purposefully fanned out, hefting stick-grenades.

The second enemy party encountered a Lewis gun section at the top of Hulluch Street, which emptied four 47-round pans of ammunition into them and then withdrew. Two Lewis gunners at 16 Street were shot before they could go into action. This firing alerted a lone Stokes gunner in his emplacement near 19 Street. This spirited man, whose name we regretfully don't know, fired off all his ammunition and had one bomb still in the breech when called on to surrender. "You voss my prisoner," a German shouted. "Oh, voss I ?" the Bantam replied, and pulled the lever. The German went up with the bomb and the Bantam escaped with his gun.

Not all the troops were as valiant. Most of the Tommies at 16 Street had fled without firing a shot. One of them was fortunate in that he reached a rear first-aid post commanded by a sympathetic Canadian doctor, Captain W. O. Whitman. Medical orderly Ernest Quickenden was there and describes what happened.

"Down the dug-out steps staggered a terrified trembling teenager, poor kid. Witty asked him, 'What's up, lad?' The boy said, 'We have run away.'

'Who from?' the captain asked, 'Your mother?' Shaking, the kid answered, 'No sir, we were in the front line and the Prussian Guards came over, so we ran away.' The captain said to me, 'Hell, if they are sending these kids up here, what hope have we got? Give him a red ticket.' That was a four-by-three card with large, red letters NYD, meaning 'not yet diagnosed.' I tied a card to his tunic, and Witty made sure the boy would be passed straight down to base, away from the firing line. No questions asked. That way, he'd escape a court-martial."

Some other Bantams were not so lucky.

The third German raiding party met no resistance when they came into "K Crater" sector that night. By chance, they hit the line just where the usual sentry groups holding King Crater had been withdrawn in expectation of retaliation shelling after a raiding party of the 19th DLI went across. The Durhams reached the German wire only to be hit by short-falling British shells, which wounded Lt. Welbourne and killed two privates. Pinned down by their own barrage, the patrol did not encounter the German raiders, and returned after they had left.

The opposing front lines were very close at this sector, the outer lip of King Crater being only 50 yards from German trenches. Normally, two groups of six men each stood guard at the northern and southern edge of the crater, but as the DLI was about to launch a raid, the sentries were reduced to a minimum to avoid casualties from enemy retaliation fire. So the two posts were held by two men and three men respectively. Two other men were on sentry-go at a post nearby in Cecil trench, plus four others in a dugout.

At about 2.15 a.m., German heavy mortars renewed bombardment of the crater edges, just as Lieutenant Mandy and Lance Sergeant Willie Stones ventured out to check on the sentry positions. The pair was Duty Officer and Duty NCO of the sector that night. After visiting Post 'A', Mandy led Stones along the edge of King Crater towards the northern Post 'B'. In the darkness, they met 12 German raiders, who shot Lt. Mandy and he fell mortally wounded. According to Stones' later testimony, "Lt. Mandy cried out, 'My God, I'm shot. For God's sake, sergeant, go for help!'"

Stones claimed later that though his rifle was loaded, he was unable to fire at the Germans as the canvas cover was over the breech, "because I never had any orders to take it off." That explanation by a front-line soldier would have sounded improbable to the experienced infantry officers who judged his actions afterwards. Covers were often used to protect the mechanism from mud, but every trench-wise combat veteran patrolling beyond the front line carried his weapon ready to fire immediately.

Odder still, the sergeant claimed he had jammed his Lee-Enfield across the trench to slow down his pursuers. Whatever the reason, Stones somehow lost his rifle—an act that would damn him—and scrambled away with the attackers in hot pursuit along the forward trench. Yelling something about the Germans being in, he kept on running about a thousand yards to the rear until he was stopped by battle police at the junction of Wednesday and Bogey Avenues.

Lance Corporals John McDonald and Peter Goggins and three private soldiers manning the northern positions followed his example, fleeing down Cecil Avenue, shouting "Run—the Germans are on you!" until stopped by a sentry of 18/HLI.

Meantime, Corporal Stevenson from Post 'A' had rescued the dying Lt. Mandy and bombed the pit free of Germans. However, survivors of this raiding party encountered Lt. Harding and Sergeant Napier, and shot them both before retreating. By this time, it was realized through the din of bombardment and the chaotic flow of troops moving up for counter-raids that a large force of Germans had broken into the line. Grenades were heard exploding amongst the front trenches and troops in the reserve trenches began hurrying forward despite the shellfire. By the time they arrived, two more Bantams had been killed and six were wounded, and the Germans had gone, taking with them about 20 to 25 prisoners.

Other attempted raids were beaten off later that night, which resulted in a congratulatory after-battle report. The action of defending parties in the trenches was described as prompt and effective, and the valiant behaviour of the 35 Div., troops despite being subjected to a more than usually heavy bombardment for several hours was praised.

Several of the men swore they had only pulled back when they heard blasts of an officer's whistle and shouted orders in English to withdraw. Their statements were accepted by Brigadier Sandilands who remarked that, "As bad luck would have it, the enemy finished up their bombardment by raiding the line at exactly the same zero-hour as our own gas was discharged lower down the line. On account of this gas discharge, orders had been issued to vacate most of the front line, which made it all the more easy for the enemy to get in. The raiding party was composed entirely of English-speaking men; this added to the general confusion and resulted in some of our men being taken off as prisoners." Loss of so many prisoners to the enemy shook the British commanders, and an inquiry was convened before dawn.

The Bantams' general steadfastness contrasted with the two dozen men who'd been arrested for running away from key positions. It was not unheard of for soldiers to take to their heels when outnumbered, and many did so that fateful night. Yet, the mass death sentences of 26 Bantams for quitting their posts seems an act of almost hysterically vengeful fury by commanders determined to make examples "to encourage the rest." Some commonsense did prevail in the end, however, and just three of the executions were actually carried out. The 23 other convicted men had their sentences commuted to savagely-long terms of 10 years' penal servitude.

DLI Lance-Sergeant Willie Stones was executed for desertion in the face of the enemy, and his death became a *cause celebré* eighty years later.

Judging by his previous military record, one of the accused in particular was unlikly to be derelict of duty. Lance Sergeant Willie Stones had served in France for eleven months and performed his duties well enough to be promoted to the rank of Lance Sergeant. Yet on the night of the raid, he had deserted a wounded officer, dropped his weapon, and run far behind the lines. The Military Police who arrested him that night on the outskirts of Roclincourt village reported Stones "was in a pitiable state of terror."

His court martial trial was held hurriedly at Ricametz on Christmas Eve, 1916. He stood accused of, "When on active service shamefully casting away his arms in the presence of the enemy in that he when an NCO of the watch and attacked by the enemy shamefully cast away his rifle and left the front line and ran away." Sitting to judge him was a panel comprised of a lieutenant-colonel and three captains, one of whom was a medical officer. Against them, Stones was defended by Captain Warmington, who had been a lawyer in civilian life. Warmington kept up an assertive defence throughout the trial. He argued that Stones had been acting on the last orders of Lt. Mundy when he left to get help, and that he placed his rifle as a barrier to delay pursuing Germans. Stones swore to the same circumstances when he testified about his actions during the raid. The CM panel considered this defence position briefly in private, but then insisted the trial continue.

A dozen witnesses told of seeing Stones, unarmed, running along trenches away from the front line, calling out warnings to retreat, being finally halted at the end of Bogey Avenue, then later declaring that muscular pain in his legs made it impossible for him to return to the front. A medical officer who had examined Stones three days after the raid spoke for the defence, but let drop his opinion the sergeant's rheumatic condition was not acute.

Despite the serious accusations, L/Sgt. Stones' previous good military behaviour caused five officers and senior NCOs to testify favorably on his behalf. Company Sergeant Major Holroyd stated, "He was the last man I would have thought capable of any cowardly action." Lieutenant Howes said, "He behaved very well during the Somme and has always been a good soldier." Lt. Rider testified,

"Stones has done good work on patrols and when in charge of wiring parties. I have personally been out with him in no man's land and always found him keen and bold. For the trenches, he never showed the least sign of funk."

But no amount of this praise did him any good. That he, a senior NCO, had apparently panicked, left his wounded officer to die, fled the front line, and "shamefully cast away" his rifle doomed him. Despite his previous good record, and the skilled defence of Capt. Warmington, L/Sgt. Stones was sentenced to death.

He and the five other men who abandoned Posts "A" and "B" were convicted after unusually short trial hearings. Soon afterwards, the three private soldiers' death sentences were commuted to long terms of imprisonment instead. But it was decided the three non-commissioned-officers must be held accountable for their responsibilities of leadership and shot. The real reason for this unusual triple execution is clearly indicated in Brig. Gen. H. O'Donnell's notation on their court martial papers. After stating he did not think the evidence against them was sufficient for a conviction, he still wrote, "I am reluctantly compelled to recommend that should the finding be confirmed, the sentence be carried out for the purpose of example and to show that cowardice in the presence of the enemy will not be tolerated in the British Army."

Private Albert Rochester, himself in detention under arrest at the time, witnessed their execution at 7.35 a.m., 18 January, 1917, near Roellecourt, France. He later wrote an account of it. "A crowd of brass hats, the medical officer and three firing parties. Three stakes a few yards apart and a ring of sentries around the woodland to keep the curious away. A motor ambulance arrives carrying the doomed men. Manacled and blindfolded, they are helped out and tied up to the stakes. Over each man's heart is placed an envelope. At the sign of command, the firing parties, 12 for each, align their rifles on the envelopes. The officer in charge holds his stick aloft and, as it falls, 36 bullets usher the souls of three of Kitchener's men to the great unknown. As a military prisoner, I helped clear the traces of the triple murder. I took the posts down. I helped carry those bodies towards their last resting place."

"I collected all the blood-soaked straw and burnt it. Acting upon instruction, I took the belongings from the dead men's tunics, discarded before being shot. A few letters, a pipe, some fags, a photo. I could tell you of the silence of the military police after reading one letter from a little girl to 'Dear Daddy,' of the blood-stained snow that horrified the French peasants, of the chaplain's confession that braver men he had never met than those three men he prayed with just before the fatal dawn."

L/Sgt. Stones was buried alongside L/Cpl. McDonald and L/Cpl. Goggins at the St. Pol Community Cemetery Extension. Remarkably, Willie Stones' execution was to become the focus of national attention in Britain 80 years later. Much of public attitudes had changed by then, when a new cult of 'political correctness' rejected the old virtues of patriotism and military valour in favour of victimhood. Modern civilian peacetime attitudes disparaged the past when the death penalty was universal and psychiatry scarcely existed. A "Shot At Dawn" [SAD] protest movement emerged in the 1990s, and one of its leading spokesmen was Tom Stones, a great-nephew of L/Sgt. Stones. SAD campaigned for a Royal blanket pardon for all British soldiers executed for cowardice during the Great War.

Two British Prime Ministers had the matter looked into, then both in turn gave the opinion that while the deaths were tragic, a retroactive blanket pardon was unwarranted and it would be impossible after such a long time to evaluate the circumstances of each individual execution. Nevertheless, in June, 2001, SAD organizers arranged with the National Memorial Arboretum in Alrewas, Staffordshire, for 306 stakes to be erected in memory of those executed. The posts symbolize the ones to which men were tied before being shot, and each bears a metal plaque giving the deserter's name, rank, age, and date of his execution.

Such goings-on would have likely seemed incomprehensible to the embattled troops at Arras. Back then, Brigade commanders felt obliged to demand a drastic evaluation of the 35th Division's ability to continue to hold the line. Immediate action was ordered for a review of all personnel on the Arras front, and hurried

conferences about reorganization were held at Divisional
Headquarters. On December 6th, Lt.-Col.Johnston wrote, "A
circular letter had just come round which states that we are not to
be known as the Bantam Division any more, and that our
reinforcements in future will be normal-sized men. I'm sorry, as
the little men have done so well, but I suppose there are no more
to be had by us, as all regiments now take small men."

There was a certain amount of reluctance by regimental officers
to lose men who were for the most part good soldiers, even though
the physique of some was not up to regular standards. Too,
experienced troops of any quality were in such short supply in the
front line that officers were more concerned with keeping whatever
men they had for day-to-day fighting. Soon though, the final knell
for the Bantams as a distinct unit was sounded by Lt. General Sir
Aylmer Haldane, VI Corps Commander.

He was something of a rarity, a senior officer who often
personally visited his front line trenches to inspect conditions first-
hand. He had served previously in several colonial wars, and fought
beside Winston Churchill before they were captured aboard an
armoured train during the Anglo-Boer War. Haldane presented a
fierce and demanding manner in front of subordinates, but privately
wrote sympathetically about the Bantams in his diary, "I am sorry
for the poor little devils, for it is positively cruel to put them against
the sturdy Germans." He had already sent two directives aimed at
"weeding out undesirables" without much response, when he arrived
at a special parade near his headquarters on December 21st, 1916.

Seizing the opportunity, General Haldane began to stride
through the ranks, followed by red-tabbed aides jotting in
notebooks. Prodding his leather-covered swaggerstick at the most
undersized, deformed, or sickly-looking troops, he barked, "Take
his name—out! . . . You can go . . . you can go! Out ! Out!"

While rejecting unfit tiny men, the general suddenly came
upon Sergeant Benjamin Peirson among them. He stared up at the
6 ft. 5 in. NCO for a long moment, then exploded to an aide,
"Ridiculous! Send this man away, too." He moved on down the
line in search of other rejects.

Far from feeling humiliated, Peirson gleefully looked forward to being sent behind the lines. With any luck, it would be weeks before he was transferred to another unit in action. He began to make farewells to his friends in anticipation of the reprieve. That night, he and part of his battalion was sent into the reserve trenches on yet another fatigue party. Many of the officially rejected troops were included in the job, as the paperwork had not yet been completed for their release. The supply-laden Bantams were caught in a heavy counter-barrage, suffered casualties, and scattered for cover.

Sergeant Peirson found an empty dug-out and crawled to the back, followed by a dozen of his platoon. Even above the barrage, he heard one of them jokingly shout, "Get out, Peirson. We can get six in where you are!" He remembers nothing more until rescuers reached him with their shovels the next morning. Only two of the twelve others buried in the dug-out with him survived what had been a direct hit by a Jack Johnson shell. He was dragged out of the charnel hole, and confessed that his main concern was the fact he had been wounded in the hand. He was terrified of being accused of causing a self-inflicted wound.

Thankfully unaccused and alive, he walked to the light railway for evacuation with 2784 of his rejected comrades.

As the open train pulled away, one of the rejected Bantams looked back at the smoke-wreathed battlefield of Arras and said to Peirson, "I wouldn't have minded staying, you know. I must be daft."

The three Lancashire Fusilier battalions were least affected by these arbitrary dismissals or medical inspections. The 17th battalion lost 170 NCOs and men, the 18th had about 190 rejected, and the 20th Bttn., sent away 135 men. Though the units were then still essentially composed of undersized men, orders were received that "the Bantam standard must be disregarded for good and all." New drafts were of regular-sized men and the units gradually became a mixed bag of no particularly uniform level of stature.

Brigadier Sandilands paid them tribute in his memoirs after the war. "It is a matter of common knowledge within the division that until the Armistice in 1918, we never attacked without one of the old original Bantams distinguishing himself, and there had never been a medal parade in this brigade without at least one of them being present."

However gallant their motivation, the very uniqueness of the Bantams had all along contained the seeds of inevitable problems. Lt.-Col.H. M. Davson, who later wrote a superb unit history of the 35th Division, commented "Those who had knowledge of the Division when first formed unite in describing the original drafts as a fine body of men, whose shortness of stature was compensated for by breadth of chest and physical condition. If the supply of such could have been continued, the arguments of those in favour of the employment of small men would have been proved."

"As it happened, it was found no more possible to continually support a Bantam Division consisting of well-developed men below the average height of the nation than it was to fill up the ranks of the Household Cavalry with men above it. The result in the former case was that the type of recruit deteriorated. Many who joined were immature and with the laudible intention of serving their country when enlisting become somewhat hazy about the actual date of their birth."

"Others who were conscripted later, were weaklings who would never be fit for the strain of active service, and who were passed to the Division as the supply of men of the original Bantam standard had failed. These later men had not the fortitude to endure fatigue and hardship, and although possibly a long period of training might have given them the discipline which would have to some extent counter-balanced the failing, this was denied them. The complaints of battalion commanders became frequent, and the efforts of the Division Commander to have the weaklings removed were only partially successful."

Davson concluded, "Whilst in training at Masham, a certain number was withdrawn, but the recruiting authorities refused to have them discharged and instead sent them to the depots and kept them there. The result was that, but half-trained and as yet unsubordinated to habits of automatic obedience, they rejoined at a critical period of the war and took their places in a series of battles which tested the courage and endurance of the most highly trained soldiers of the three nations. This was not only disastrous to these men themselves, but harmful to those who fought alongside them."

The Bantams lasted until losses in battle had decimated their ranks, and the Bantam Division continued to exist for another six months. By then, it was recognized that there was not a sufficient number of small fit men in Britain to supply so large a unit. So in the spring of 1917, the 35th (Bantam) Division passed away. The 35th Division took its place, and the rooster divisional sign was replaced with seven fives in a circle.

It was a period of regret, for great expectations had been entertained in the success of the enterprise. The ultimate result was not the fault of the officers and men of the original battalions, who all went into battle with high hopes and desire for action. As one of their officers once remarked, "They were little men, but had big hearts."

But war is no respecter of hopes or theories, and it was to war, and war alone, that the settlement of their case was entrusted. The project failed, but the failure was not due to the men who gave their lives in early battles, or to their comrades who survived and took an honourable part in the succeeding years of warfare. For them, the bells of Hell kept ringing.

CHAPTER TWELVE

Butchery At Bourlon

Joy-bells rang all across Britain at noon on November 23rd, 1917. For hours before the stroke of twelve, huge crowds had gathered on the steps and in the churchyard of St. Paul's Cathedral in London. When the clock struck noon, one of the small bells in the campanille rang out, followed in slow time by others. Then there came a loud crash as the carillon began tolling in great chords. At the first note, the thousands of pigeons feeding on the pavement in front of Queen Anne's statue rose fluttering up in a silvery cloud and circled high above. There was a burst of applause from the listeners, and a white-haired man with a powerful voice began to sing the National Anthem. The crowd joined in the words. For the first time since the end of the South African War, the bells of St. Paul's were ringing a joyous victory-peal.

The Cathedral chimes signalled the whistles of steamships along the Thames to join in, as did bells of other London churches. The cheerful sounds spread across the country, echoing from belfries in towns and villages amid England and Wales, and reaching to dioceses in the far north of Scotland. The idea had been suggested by 'The Times' newspaper, taken up by the Bishop of London, and arranged by Canon Holmes, Archdeacon of St. Paul's. That day, the whole country gave itself up to tintinnabulant triumph over the announcement of a great victory at Cambrai, which seemed to herald the end of the war within weeks.

As events of the next few days proved, the celebration was bitterly premature. The initial British success at Cambrai was reversed by the German counter-attack which actually gained them seven square miles of new territory. However, though it could not be then seen, the new open-warfare tactics with massed armoured vehicles which the British employed did eventually pave the way to ultimate victory one year later. But in the meantime, the nation nursed its sheepish disappointment over Cambrai and the War Office sent letters of condolence to many soldiers' next-of-kin, including those of 4000 Bantams who had been butchered there.

Exactly a year before, the 40th (Bantam) Division had left the Loos Salient. It was then employed continuously in the Somme country, putting in a winter of almost unendurable cold in trenches between Rancourt and Bouchavesnes.

"Our division finally reached the Somme battlefields at their worst climate-wise, in the deadly 1916-17 winter when both sides were completely immobilized," reminisced Andrew Gilmour of the 14th Argylls. "We suffered cruelly unnecessary losses, manning trenches up to the waist in mud. Judging from our own casualties from trench-foot, frostbite, pleurisy, nephritis and so on, I should imagine that the Bantams must have lost up to thirty percent of their effectives. This is where I myself finally dropped out from frostbite, twenty-three degrees below zero in trenches on the slopes before Peronne." Another casualty from frostbite there was the diminutive New Yorker, Cpl. Henry Thridgould, whose hands were afterwards crippled for life.

The troops had to hold the line in these appalling conditions against a very aggressive enemy, the 104th Infantry Regiment. In one of their attacks, a large party came across to raid a listening-post manned by six Green Howards. After a heavy barrage of mortar bombs and tear-gas shells, 25 Germans arrived, led by a "powerful and loud-tongued non-commissioned officer." He was one of the first to be wounded in the hand-to-hand fight, which may be why the enemy began to lose heart despite their superiority of numbers.

The pugnacious Yorkshiremen flailed away with sharpened entrenching spades—a favourite weapon of theirs for close combat—while the wounded German leader kept shouting orders even as he lay dying at their feet. His opposite number, Lance Corporal Smith, was killed, as were two more Britons, while another ran away.

The surviving two Green Howards fought on desperately back to back in the dark. They were saved when the man who had left returned well-armed. Private W. Cooke had braved the barrage to grab a satchel of Mills grenades from an adjacent trench, then bombed his way back into the listening-post.

When the raiders retreated, leaving four dead comrades, the wounded *feldwebel* gamely refused to tell his captors anything more than that he was with the 20th Company of his regiment. Though Private Cooke and Evans carried him to an aid-station, the man died soon after. For this act of valour, Private Cooke received the DCM, but he was killed at Villers Plouich in May, 1917.

Because of constant rumours that the enemy was about to withdraw, British troops went out on nightly raids to test his strength and obtain prisoners. Bill Parkes ascribed the Bantams' success at raiding to their short stature being an advantage at night. "Us little guys could hide much better in No Man's Land than the tall guys. Some of our taller officers got knocked off the very first time they went across on a recconnoitre."

Sniping became a vicious game on both sides, their task made easier by the slower reaction and dulled alertness of miserable, half-frozen men. Every day, two or three would die this way in the division's trenches, plus the steady trickle of victims from shellfire and periodic volleys from fixed rifles clamped to cover vulnerable open spots in the support lines.

The carnage in the line tore at all men's minds, though most were unable to express it so well as could Private Isaac Rosenberg of the King's Own. He left a scene of horror clearly illuminated as if by Very lights in his poem, "Dead Man's Dump:"

> "A man's brains splattered on
> A stretcher-bearer's face;
> His shook shoulders slipped their load,
> But when they bent to look again
> The drowning soul was sunk too deep
> For human tenderness.

They left this dead with the older dead,
Stretched at the crossroads.

Burnt black by strange decay
Their sinister faces lie,
The grass and coloured clay
More motion have than they,
Joined to the great sunk silences.

Here is one not long dead;
His dark hearing caught our far wheels,
And the choked soul stretched weak hands
To reach the living world the far wheels said,
The blood-dazed intelligence beating for light,
Crying through the suspense of the far torturing wheels

Swift for the end to break
Or the wheels to break,
Cried as the tide of the world broke over his sight.

Will they come? Will they ever come? ven as the mixed
hoofs of the mules,
The quivering-bellied mules,
And the rushing wheels all mixed
With his tortured upturned sight.
So we crashed around the bend,
We heard his weak scream,
We heard his very last sound,
And our wheels grazed his dead face."

His stark prose added to Rosenberg's increasing reputation as a war poet. On May 27, 1917, he wrote to one reviewer: "My Dear Mr. Marsh. I liked your criticism of 'Dead Mans Dump'. Mr. Binyon has often sermonized lengthily over my working on two different principles in the same thing and I know how it spoils the unity of a poem. But if I couldn't before, I can now, I am sure, plead the absolute necessity of fixing an idea before it is lost, because of the situation it's conceived in . . . I have written a much finer poem which I've asked my sister to send you. Don't think from this I've time to write. This last poem is only about 70 lines and I started it about October. It is only when we get a bit of rest and the others might be gambling or squabbling I add a line or two, and continue this way."

"The weather is gorgeous now and we are bivouacked in the fields. The other night I awoke to find myself floating about with the water half over me. I took my shirt off and curled myself up on a little mound that the water hadn't touched and slept stark naked that night. But that was not all of the fun. The chap next to me was suddenly taken with Diarrhea and kept on lifting the sheet of the Bivouac, and as I lay at the end, the rain came beating on my nakedness all night. Next morning, I noticed the poor chap's discoloured pants hanging on a bough near by, and I thought after all I had the best of it."

Famed poet Isaac Rosenberg returned from South Africa to serve in the King's Own Bantams. Killed in 1918, his work has steadily gained in popularity in years since.

Few surviving veterans of the 11th King's Own were aware of Rosenberg's reputation as a war poet, yet they still remembered him as a comrade. A few spoke of him as an untidy, polite, but painfully reserved man. "I remember one morning sitting on a step in the support trench trying to talk with Private Rosenberg," said Corporal Harry Stansfield. "He always was a shy sort of fella, very quiet and seemed to keep to himself. He was writing and paid no attention to me. I wanted to show friendship because I think he thought he was often shunned because he was Jewish. Believe me, we didn't think much about a person's background one way or the other. When you were in the trenches, all we wanted to know was if you were a reliable comrade or if you weren't. Religion or race had nothing to do with it."

When reminded that Isaac Rosenberg was killed by a German raiding party on April 1st, 1918, Harry Stansfield said. "I also well remember the other Jewish member of our platoon, Lt. Sternberg. He was from Manchester, where his parents had a large business. He was a very good and heroic officer, well-liked by us all. Unfortunately, he was killed while meeting a raiding party. That night we were out on the raid cutting wire, and things were going well, when suddenly a Very light gave an enemy sniper the chance to shoot. Lt. Sternberg was shot in the spine, and we abandoned the raid right then but we dragged his body back to our trenches."

"That same night, it was my duty to take the rations up the line and collect Mr. Sternberg's body to take it back on the same limber cart for burial at Marizincourte Cemetery. I found it a difficult task," said ex-Corporal Stansfield. "It was hard to hold the body on the limber, because of the rocky roads and his rubber ground-sheet got in the way. Each man was issued with a rubber cape. This was first a raincoat, second a ground-sheet, and finally your coffin, should it be needed for such. The ground-sheet had lace holes all round, and laces to tie up the corpse for burial. Somehow, I managed to shove the limber back through the darkness, and felt very sad the whole time as he was such a good officer."

Just as the weather began to slightly improve in mid-March, 1917, the division found it could leave the icy mire of their trenches and advance across a suddenly deserted No-Mans-Land. The Germans had decided to shorten their front by withdrawing to the immensely strong Hindenburg Line. They left behind a systematically destroyed wasteland of ruins, ingeniously strewn with booby-traps that took a steady toll of deaths and injuries among the advancing Bantams. Troops of the 40th Division moved gingerly forward to occupy a still-burning Peronne and the dozens of brick mounds which once had been villages. Just as they were beginning to enjoy themselves with mobile warfare, they were withdrawn from the advance across open ground and put to work as labourers on road-building.

"This was a heart-breaking and back-breaking job for raw-boned youths of eighteen years," a Bantam newcomer wrote. "I rather think we were not particularly sorry when the time came for us to join our company for a spell in the trenches."

His first sight beyond the division's new front line at Gouzeaucourt was the spires of a city eight miles away across the open plain. It was Cambrai, headquarters of the German Second Army. Over to the left, rose a low ridge covered with oak trees—Bourlon Wood—unattainable until six months later, and then be associated ever after with the 40th (Bantam) Division. First, they had to fight their way through the ravines and fortified villages west of the Canal du Nord.

All three brigades tested themselves in battle by successfully taking all of their three designated objectives. First was Fifteen Ravine, a shallow depression named after a row of pine trees that had provided useful ranging points for British artillery until the Germans sensibly felled them. Decades later, ex-Sergeant Bill Parkes still vividly recalled an eery experience during the bloody work of clearing the ravine. While crouching in a shell crater, he found himself lying beside the frozen corpse of a German soldier. "A funny feeling came over me," he said. "I don't know why I did it, but I brushed the snow off the dead Jerry's face. What I saw was shocking, as he looked so exactly like my eldest brother, he could have been his twin. It upset me so much, I jumped up and ran off like hell towards the enemy." Before the day was out, all his officers were dead, and he ended up commanding the company throughout the rest of the action.

Soon afterwards, Parkes was badly wounded in the leg by shell splinters. More irritated than anything else, he told a medical orderly to bind his wound tightly so he could hurry to catch up with his men. However, when he attempted to stand, he simply fell over. After evacuation to England, he started training for a commission, but found his lack of education made him unsuitable. Declaring himself, "almost relieved to return to the Front," Parkes soldiered on as an n.c.o. until war's end.

The next obstacles facing the 40th Division were the reinforced villages of Villers Plouich and Beaucamp. The 13th East Surreys and 14th HLI were given the main responsibility for taking Villers Plouich. They assembled at 2 a.m. on the night of April 24th, every man carrying two sandbags and two hand-grenades, and some also equipped with shovels and picks. A heavy artillery barrage signalled Zero Hour at 4.15 a.m. and the East Surreys went forward in four waves towards the enemy wire. Most got through unscathed, but 14 HLI bringing up the rear had worse luck. The "overs" and "short-falls" of British shells dropping where they should not killed eight Scotsmen immediately. Still the rest carried on to take their target trenches, and soon telephoned their commander with reports they had penetrated Villers Plouich.

A fierce battle flared, the scene of much unknown bravery on both sides, but one act of particular gallantry was recorded. When two German machine guns held up the East Surreys' advance, Corporal E. Foster and Lance Corporal J.W. Reed decided to do something about it. They used Lewis guns to attack the enemy weapons, putting them out of action, and capturing the surviving MG teams. For this feat, Cpl. Foster was awarded a Victoria Cross and a *Médaille Militaire*, while L/Cpl. Reed received a Distinguished Conduct Medal.

Villers Plouich was captured shortly afterwards. However, the Germans aimed a very heavy and continuous counter-bombardment on the position, making it almost untenable. The East Surreys had taken the brunt of things, and suffered 200 casualties, including 29 dead, requiring the HLI to take over defence of the village.

After much hard fighting, the village of Beaucamp was also captured. This grim work cost 964 casualties, a quarter of which were fatal. If the price was high, the lessons of open warfare had been well learned, and the division settled down for a long summer of raiding the Hindenburg Line.

Edgar Robinson was with the 13th Green Howards when his battalion occupied Villers Plouich. They were heavily bombarded often and lost a steady trickle of men killed, but Robinson still declined an offer of alternative employment. "About this time, we were asked if any of us would like to transfer to the new Royal Tank Corps. They specially wanted small men like we were. I was expecting to get my fortnight's leave at home any day, otherwise I might have transferred. Had I done so, I would not be alive here now."

Small stature was a useful factor in manning the newest weapon of war, the tank. This British invention had been introduced during the Battle of the Somme but had not performed successfully, because of being used in too few numbers. Now the Tank Corps was being rapidly expanded and crews were at a premium. The limited space inside the first primitive armoured fighting vehicles left scant room for their wretched crews jammed in the hot, noisy, fume-filled interior amidst driving controls, weapons, and all manner of ill-designed sharp corners. Small men were seen as logical crew members to function in this cramped hellish environment.

The Mark IV tank was a steel rhomboid in which was crammed a crew of eight men, one of whom was an officer. He and the driver sat on raised seats in the nose of the tank. The rest of the crew huddled in two narrow gangways, just two foot wide by eight feet long, which ran the whole length of the vehicle on either side of the engine. These narrow corridors were only five feet high, making it even more difficult for average sized men to move about.

The 100 h.p. engine reached to the roof, and behind it was a small platform with a starting-handle which required four men's strength to turn. Two gearsmen squatted here in deafening closeness to the motor; their job being to manipulate two secondary gears to steer each track.

Between the officer and gearsmen on one side and between the driver and gearsmen on the other, were the gunners, two in each gangway. A "male" tank had two 6-pounder guns, cut-down naval cannon in sponsons, with a gun-layer and gun-loader for each. The "female" tank was armed with machine-guns only, usually five or six Hotchkiss .303s. Both types of tank also had forward-firing Lewis machine-guns operated by the officer. Crewmen were armed with Webley revolvers for use through pistol-ports against enemy infantry who might climb aboard. Even entering the cramped interiors was difficult. Door hatches were only two feet by three feet; vertical in the male tank and horizontal in the female version, so that crews had to wriggle inside on their backs.

While smaller men found it easier to function inside the hulls, they were by no means the only types to appy for tank training at Bovington Camp in Dorset. Soldiers of all shapes and sizes volunteered from infantry and cavalry units and the Service Corps, as did men from the Royal Navy and Royal Flying Corps. Though volunteers were preferred, the need for personnel was so great that drafts of veteran soldiers were transferred and sent for compulsory tank training.

One of those chosen for this new role was Private Len Marks of the Middlesex Regiment, when about to board a troop transport at Folkestone. "There were two of us London lads picked out that morning," he recalls. "Sam Pearlman and me had grown up together in the East End, and joined up on the same day in 1915. We were among six Jewish boys from the same neighbourhood who volunteered together for the Bantams. A year later, Sam and I were the only two left alive."

"I'd been wounded just seriously enough to get sent back to Blighty for three months. Sam had been in hospital for trench-feet, and we weren't feeling too good about trying our luck in the mud again. Then out of the blue, this officer comes along and tells us to report for special training. He signed us off the regimental rolls, there and then, and gave us railway warrants to report to Bovington Camp. When we found it was the tanks for us, we couldn't think why we'd been chosen for the job. Neither one of us had ever so much as ridden a bicycle."

Alan McKenzie was a volunteer with a group of Manchester Bantams who became tankers when the 35th Division was reorganized. "After being trained at Bovington in driving and machine guns, I did 6-pounder gun training at Chatham Naval Barracks. Our gunnery practice was at sea in the English Channel on naval gunboats; the motion of ships being supposedly similar to that of a tank on rough terrain. We were classed thus—Lewis-gun 1st Class, Hotchkiss 1st. Class, 6-pounder 1st Class, Tank driving 2nd. Class, also trained in revolver-shooting, signalling and pigeon-handling. For all this, we got paid a few more pence a day."

Following training, crews were sent to France for collective tactical exercises at Tank Corps HQ, Bermicourt, near St. Pol. Unknowingly, they were intended to lead one of the most ambitious attacks yet devised by the British High Command. But the enterprise had not begun any way near that ambitiously. On August 4th, 1917, Colonel J. F. C. Fuller presented a plan to the General Staff for a large tank raid south of Cambrai. He was an enthusiastic proponent of tank weapons, but was maddened at their being mis-employed at Ypres, where they all too often sank in the mud and became sitting targets for German artillery.

Fuller believed that armored vehicles could be used better on the Cambrai front where there was firm earth on open ground with room for tanks to manoeuvre to best advantage. His plan called for a local raid "to destroy the enemy's personnel and guns, to demoralize and disorganize him, and not to capture ground." The covering letter stated, 'The duration of the raid must be short, eight to twelve hours, so that little concentration of the enemy may be effected for counter-attack.' If these original objectives and time restraints had been kept, the joy-bells which ran in November may not have been as premature.

Haig's staff were intrigued. Here might lie the chance for that elusive master-stroke, the massive breakthrough that could take

Cambrai, and even keep rolling all the way to Berlin. Excitedly, they began to revamp and enlarge Fuller's plan, which had only proposed a raid by two tank battalions across an 8000-yard front. General Sir Julian Byng of the Third Army went to see Field Marshal Haig and suggested a major surprise attack to capture Cambrai. A large success was needed by the Commander-in-Chief. Any kind of success would be welcome to erase criticism of the costly failure at Passchendaele which was still grinding whole divisions into the mud. His staff set to devising an ambitious new campaign, based on Fuller's tank raid plan.

By mid-October, Haig had approved General Byng's proposal for a major offensive against Cambrai, with a target date of November 20th. The project had grown to a massive effort involving 380 fighting tanks, a thousand guns, two Army Corps, three infantry divisions and three Cavalry Corps. There was no longer any thought of Fuller's preliminary vision of a few score tanks setting off to "advance, hit, and retire." However, by the time the attack had been finally approved, nor was there enough volume of manpower readily on hand to sustain it. Most of them lay dead where they had been expended recently in the Ypres Salient. Just whatever troops as were available would have to be used to take Byng's grander objectives.

These were threefold: to penetrate the Hindenburg Line between Canal de l'Escaut and the Canal du Nord, to capture Bourlon Wood and Cambrai, and to cut off the enemy south of the Sensee River. As students of ancient military history knew, the Germans around Cambrai were well protected on all sides, being in the naturally fortified quadrilaterial known through centuries of warfare as Caesar's Camp.

On three sides, they were moated by the Scheldt and Sensee Rivers and the Canal du Nord, and on the fourth side lay the wooded heights of Bourlon. This dominating feature not only commanded the surrounding plain and the Agache Valley carrying the Canal du Nord, it also overlooked the Scheldt and territory as far as Bouchain. If Bourlon Ridge could be taken, the Germans would have to pull back from their carefully prepared defence systems for a considerable distance to the north of it.

English, Scottish, and Welsh Bantam battalions sacrificed
themselves when they fought to capture the crucial Bourlon
Wood objective during the epic Battle of Cambrai in 1917.

This vital objective was later earmarked for the 40th (Bantam) Division, one of the thirteen support groups which would follow the mere six divisions put at Third Army's disposal for the initial attack. When General Franchet d'Espery arrived at British Headquarters in Albert, he was puzzled to learn that offers of French army support had been refused. "But where are your reserves?" he asked. He was languidly told, "My dear General, we have none." The Frenchman turned on his heel to leave with a disgusted *"Mon Dieu!"*

Code-named 'Operation GY,' the assault remained a close secret while troops were quietly assembled behind Bois d'Havrincourt. The tanks' noisy engines posed the biggest problem to security, so several old Mark I's were kept running up and down just behind the lines to obscure from the Germans any tell-tale indications of an unusual build-up of the machines.

All the tanks in the first wave had been specially modified to be able to bridge the wide trenches and canal ditches they would encounter. Huge fascines made of about seventy-five bundles of brushwood compressed by steel chains were hoisted onto the nose of each vehicle. A simple releasing gear would enable tank commanders to drop their fascines into a trench to fill it when required, and so allow them to roll forward over the obstacle.

Each bundle weighed a ton and a half, and required twenty Chinese labourers to roll on to its tank. Many of the workers at the Central Repair Workshops at Teneur belonged to the 51st Chinese Labour Company. Their skill and capacity for hard work which they brought from the other side of the world was taxed to the utmost during early November.

One thousand Chinamen managed to make and fit over 350 fascines within three weeks, often working 20 hours at a stretch. They laboured also at engine maintenance, gun-fitting, and hull modifications to help prepare the tanks for the assault. In mid-November, the tireless Chinese began "tank fills," the final touches to their clanking charges. Each vehicle was loaded with 60 gallons of water, ten pounds of grease, and either 10,000 rounds of s.a.a., or two hundred 6-pounder shells. When the British tank crews swung aboard, they found Chinese good wishes chalked inside the doors.

"We drove away with all the coolies smiling and waving," recalled Len Marks. "We shouted back the only words in their language we knew—'Shi-Shi,' which, as far as I could make out, means everything from 'yes' to 'good luck.' We certainly needed lots of the latter."

Early on the morning of November 20th, 1917, Marks' tank was one of hundreds which waited, engines ticking over, at their point of assembly near Beaucamp. Somewhere among them too, was Alan McKenzie, in the right-hand gun sponson of the tank 'Blair Athol.' Soon after 6 a.m., the sky began to lighten and it was possible to see the rolling expanse of greyish dead grass that offered such a promising arena for the armoured attackers. Low clouds dipped curtains of mist and rippling rain-squalls across the sea of grass. It was uncannily quiet for a few minutes, then precisely at 6.30 a.m., a single gun roared. Far to the right, came an answering roar and a flicker of flame, then link by link, the whole line broke into a chain of explosions.

Through the grey half light, the German lines were seen to erupt in shell bursts, signal rockets, and fountains of golden sparks from smoke-shells. Machine-guns began yammering from each side but were drowned in the roar of hundreds of tank engines at full throttle as the armoured giants slowly moved off like monsters into the mist. The infantry followed them in waves, fixed bayonets glowing coldly in the dawn, while squadrons of British, Australian, and Canadian fighter-planes flew low above them to strafe the opposing trenches. The Battle of Cambrai had begun—and the unknowingly-doomed 40th (Bantam) Division had not much time longer to exist.

The German Second Army of General von der Marwitz was taken by complete surprise, and was further thrown off balance by being in mid-transfer of front line units to two divisions which had just arrived from Russia. In the first few hours, his 54th Division was destroyed; the 107th Division and Pomeranian Grenadiers being particularly hard-hit. Only their artillery was able to enjoy any success. For the German guns, it was like target practice, being able to "brew up" British tanks as fast as gunners could pull their lanyards. Soon, the battlefield was strewn with the hulks of wrecked tanks, but the others kept driving forward regardless of their vulnerability.

Tank commanders exposed themselves with reckless bravery to press home the attack, as Alan McKenzie attested. "We were ordered to patrol a ridge to draw fire so that the Cavalry could ride over and get the German gunners, which they did. During this, we received a direct hit on the left sponson, disabling the tank. The order came, "Abandon tank." The other right-hand gunner was a Bantam named Clapton. He threw open the door and jumped out into direct fire, shouting, "Follow me!" I was a bit dazed, but managed to get out. Clapton saw a shell land and make a big hole, so he headed for it, dragging me with him, saying, "A shell doesn't land in the same place twice."

"There we stayed until the barrage lifted, and went back to the tank which was now riddled. The other Bants were dead or wounded. Murray had taken a direct hit and the man behind him did not live long. Taylor, the driver, had a foot missing. Clapton had saved my life for sure."

When the Germans recovered from the first shock of the tank attack, they began to fight back with characteristic courage and ingenuity. Many of them remembered they had been recently issued with a 5-round clip of new "K" bullets—high velocity rounds with a tungsten-carbide core specially able to pierce armour plate. Tank crews began to feel their effects, and one nearly ended Len Marks' life.

"The heat inside our tank must have reached a hundred degrees by mid-day," he said. "Shrapnel and small-arms fire rattled on the walls like rain, and two or three times we had to poke revolvers through portholes to shoot Germans who'd climbed onto the hull with grenades. We were all pretty badly cut about from bullet-splash coming in through the ports and from being thrown against sharp edges of equipment. We were issued with padded leather clothing and steel-mesh face-visors against this, but nobody wore them because of the heat. The only man who always did wear a visor was our driver, whose name I can't recall."

"The moment we rolled over a high bank, there was a noise like Big Ben striking one o'clock, then metal buzzed around my head like a swarm of bees. An armour-piercing bullet had punched through the raised tank nose, hit our driver underneath, passed all the way up through his body, and went ricocheting around inside the tank."

There were 65 tanks destroyed or disabled during the first day of fighting, with another 114 out of action with mechanical troubles. The vehicles had helped win the first phase however, and the infantry had thrown back the hard-fighting Germans all along the line. The British 6th and 12th Divisions had secured their objectives, then let the 20th Division pass through to capture Masinieres and Marcoing. This was the picture all along the front from Gonnelieu to west of the Canal du Nord, which had been cut by tough Northern Irishmen of the 36th (Ulster) Brigade. The British Army had advanced four and a half miles in a day. It was the receipt of such news in Britain which called for celebrations.

The field commanders were less exultant, for half the objectives still lay in enemy hands, the most important of which was Bourlon Wood, a roughly diamond-shaped small forest. On the second day, the entire thrust of the British attack began to focus on the all-important Bourlon Hill which guarded the door to Caesar's Camp. Repeated assaults by the 51st Division were broken against the bottom of these heights; and regrouping there was impossible with the Germans firing down upon them from the slopes and the village of Fontaine Notre Dame. The exhausted 51st were pulled back after three days of vainly fighting here, and the 40th (Bantam) Division was brought forward from reserve to take their turn at storming Bourlon Wood.

The division was now part of IV Corps, and had a new commander, Major General J. Ponsonby. After six months continuous service in the line, they had been relieved in October and sent far back to Doullens. They entered camps in the Forest de Lucheux and were given training in woodland fighting, a fortuitous preparation for what then lay just a month ahead.

Now, rushed orders had brought the 40th back to the Cambrai battlefront, and on November 22nd, the brigades were grouped around Havrincourt awaiting final instructions for their first major battle. General Ponsonby's written orders arrived at Brigade

Headquarters in the catacombs below Graincourt Church at midnight. The 119th Brigade would send in the 12th South Wales Borderers and the 19th Royal Welsh Fusiliers to assault Bourlon Wood across the Cambrai Road, between Anneux Chapel and Fontaine. The 17th Welch Regiment were to act as support from positions along a sunken road leading from the cemetery at Anneux, while the 18th Welch waited in reserve south of the Sugar Factory on the Cambrai Road.

This factory has since been rebuilt in the same place, so that the visitor today can stand in the exact vantage point of 1917 and see across the open fields bordering the wood, with the edge of Bourlon village beyond. These buildings mark where the 13th Battalion, Green Howards, formed the 121st Brigade's left flank. The 20th Middlesex were assigned to the section east of there, next to the Welsh Brigade. The 21st Middlesex and 12th Suffolks would provide support from trenches behind the Sugar Factory. For a while, the entire 120th Brigade was held in reserve at Havrincourt.

Bloody Bourlon: Artillery signals officer crouches amidst shattered remains of Bourlon village after the savage battle that virtually annihilated the 40th. Bantam Division.

Zero-hour was set for 10.30 a.m., so the two assault brigades had to move into position overnight. They marched up through the darkness, along tracks reserved for them past Flesquieres and Graincourt. The commanding officer of the 13th Green Howards recalled, "The morning of 23rd November came in with a blustering north-east wind, sending cloud shadows chasing over the undulating ground. An occasional scud of sleet made way for spells of sunshine in which Bourlon Wood to the east glowed in ragged autumn finery."

Their objective was formidable; 600 acres of dense forest, fir, oak, and ash trees choked with thick underbrush which hid machine-gun nests and snipers. The ridges and paths were under constant shellfire, drenched with poison gas, and garrisoned by the Germans' crack 3rd Guard Division.

At 10.30 a.m., Saturday, November 23rd, 1917, the Welsh Bantams went forward behind sixteen tanks, while just ahead of them the barrage crept up the wooded slopes, splintering trees, setting fire to the undergrowth, and wreathing the hill in smoke. On their left, the Londoners and Yorkshiremen loped towards Bourlon village, straining to arrive before the Germans had time to recover from the bombardment.

The South Wales Borderers drove into the forest and spread out through the trees as they had been taught. One group made the mistake of following along the pathway, and ran into machine-gun fire immediately. The Welshmen faded into the trees and began to creep forward "like a bloody pack of Red Indians," as Jack Jones put it. They sniped the gun-crew and pushed on until they reached a sunken road and encountered more Germans face-to-face. These were tackled with the bayonet and the survivors forced back into the woods. "Nothing could stop us," said Jones. "We were laughing and yelling and firing at anything that moved. When a Jerry popped up, a half-dozen of us would run at him with bayonets and jab him to tatters."

This exultant mood swept through the men. Private Plummer single-handedly attacked a strongpoint, killed several Guardsmen and took eight prisoners. He ran on to repeat the performance twice again, capturing a machinegun, an officer and fifteen more prisoners.

Battle-fury was no protection against shells, machineguns, and poison gas, however, and casualties began to mount as the Borderers got deeper into the forest. The Prussian Guard were as tough a group of soldiers as any on the Western Front and adapted themselves to the rushing tactics of the Welshmen who popped out of the trees on all sides.

"Soon, we dropped any resemblance to platoon advance," said Jones. "It was every man for himself, and we scattered to go hunting Jerries, just as they were doing to us. Now and then, you would hear some poor wounded devil scream as he was caught by the blazing underbrush, but you just had to ignore him and go on regardless."

The 19th Royal Welsh Fusiliers moved north-east, fighting their way across difficult broken ground and under constant shellfire from guns along the railway embankment at Fontaine. The stubborn German defence of that village eventually proved to be a key factor in the outcome of the battle. In the meantime, it caused many casualties among the Welsh.

"The Jerries started to lob fire-shells over about midmorning," observed Trevor Jones. "These caused the Christmas trees to burst into flames in a moment and made it so dangerous that many of my oppos were so busy watching the treetops, they missed seeing snipers and got shot instead."

Despite this enfilade, the Royal Welch drove their opponents back, and by 11.40 am. had reached the road from Fontaine to Bourlon which ran through the wood. To their left, the rattle of Lewis guns and crish-crash of grenades signalled the presence of the South Wales Borderers, who were still moving ahead despite the fact that many of their officers had become casualties. After only an hour of fighting, the 119th Brigade was halfway through the wood that had defied the previous British attacks for three days.

Things did not go as well for the 121st Brigade. They had moved across open ground with orders for the 20th Middlesex to capture a long wooded spur north of Anneux Chapel while the 13th Green Howards kept pace with the 36th Division on their left and attacked Bourlon village. The 21st Middlesex were to advance in support of the Yorkshiremen and cover their left flank where the enemy was known to be strongly entrenched. Even before they advanced, the Green Howards began to suffer heavy casualties from enfilade fire from guns in Quarry Wood to the north, when Second Lieutenants Stanford and Walton were killed along with 19 other ranks. The battalion was glad to leave their death-trap when at 10.30 am. whistles blew for them to advance.

"At that time, I was a signaller," Edgar Robinson recounts. "I was in the second wave to go over, with a portable set on my back and a revolving spool of thin telephone wire in my hand. It was my job to run out the wire and when we got to our objective, to report our progress to base. All went well when we began to advance. The Germans were taken by surprise at first. When they did open up, lads were killed all around me and I was spattered with mud and blood."

Casualties worsened when progress of the 36th Division on the left was halted, and the 13th Yorkshires walked into a hail of machine-gun fire from their unprotected flank. Despite these losses, which included three more dead officers, the Green Howards managed to cross the German trenches, in line with the 20th Middlesex, which had also cleared their objective in the wooded spur. Both battalions were pressed into a narrow front of advance under heavy fire from the west, but struggled on, with the 20th Middlesex along the edge of the wood. The 21st Middlesex formed up behind in support to prevent any rear attack from pinching off the forward troops.

Despite being under fire from the front and both sides, a fighting patrol of the 13th. Yorkshires reached the edge of the village at 1.00 pm. Bourlon was crawling with Germans who had converted virtually every building into a pillbox and were heavily armed with many Schwarzlose machineguns. The advance party of Green Howards was seen to enter the village, the company commander fell dead, and the other men scattered out of sight.

In the wood, Welshmen had made so much progress that a

company of South Wales Borderers had also reached the eastern edge of the ruined Bourlon village. They and reinforcements from the 17th Welch proceeded to winkle out enemy machine-gunners from cellars and barns. "There was no quarter given on either side," said Jones. "After our men were cut down like corn, it was no good anybody shouting 'Nix schiessen!'"

At 4 o'clock, two determined counter-attacks by the German 175th and Grenadier Regiments threw back the surviving Welshmen from the village, and also dislodged the 19th RWF from around Bourlon's western edge. The Bantams were now exposed to fire from the village garrison small-arms and artillery in Fontaine, which still held out against repeated assaults by the 51st. Division to the right.

The 119th Brigade seemed ready for another effort against the village when Lieutenant Colonel Kennedy rode up on his horse with two companies of the 18th Welch panting along in his wake. Rallying the men as he came, Kennedy flung himself from the saddle, rushed in front of the position and waving his cane charged the enemy. "The gallant commander of the 18th Welch had only gone a dozen yards when he was shot down by the Boche."

Two more officers were each killed within minutes of taking command, then the battalion was taken over by the Adjutant, Captain F. H. Matthias. Very few officers survived long, so that platoons and even companies were led by NCOs and resourceful private soldiers. Company Sergeant Major Davies of the 18th Welch led a counter-attack so aggressively that he once even knelt down in the open to allow his shoulder to be used as a mounting for a Lewis gun, until he fell with a head-wound.

Over in the 121st Brigade sector, the 20th/21st Middlesex were hard-pressed to hold the perimeter of Bourlon village, while fending off attacks from the east. Their battalion scouts had gone into the buildings to link up with other British skirmishers, but had not been seen again. The Green Howards also were probing the rubbled streets, and managed to capture 60 prisoners. A few minutes later, the Germans sent a strong rescue party which freed the captives and killed over 20 of their escorting Yorkshiremen.

Reinforcements started to come up from the 120th Brigade to stiffen the attack and replenish the severe casualties. Clumps of small bodies in khaki lay along the line of advance, and stretcher-bearers braved sniper-fire and shells to evacuate the squirming forms of several hundred wounded men. Through this field of blood, two companies of the 12th Royal Suffolks picked their way, moving towards the trenches south of Bourlon village, which they reached in mid-afternoon.

One of their company commanders was Acting Captain Harold Leeming, whose near-miraculous survival of six months as a front line infantry officer had been rewarded by two promotions that summer. His luck held again after he dropped his revolver into deep mud then found himself staring into the barrel of a Luger aimed by an enemy officer. A group of Germans had come across on a counter-raid and blundered into the Suffolks. Leeming braced himself for the bullet, but his sergeant fired from the hip and killed the German. Lieutenant Leeming scooped up the 9mm. Parabellum to help his men dispatch the raiders, and carried it as his preferred sidearm throughout the rest of the war.

When darkness began to fall, the situation along the divisional front was confused. The Welsh Brigade was in command of most of the wood, but was under constant attack by German infantry from Bourlon village and artillery in Fontaine. The 121st Brigade had units inside the village but had lost touch with them, and all battalions were by now scattered and intermingled. At 5.15 p.m., a gloomy message was received by General Campbell at his forward headquarters in the chalkpit near Cambrai road. "The Yorks and 21st Middlesex are practically obliterated." In truth, remnants of these battalions were still fighting south of Bourlon, though they had been savagely mauled.

Edgar Robinson explained how the remaining Green Howards held on, though ammunition supplies were running low. "At dark, we went back to the starting point to carry up bombs to the front line. In my party, ten of us had to carry a heavy box of Mills bombs in each hand. On the way up, we passed the entrance to a German pillbox where two of our lads were making tea. We stacked our boxes of bombs outside, crowded round the entrance and begged a drink. I was the last in the trench."

"Suddenly, there appeared in my mind a photo we had hanging up at home of my father who had been dead fourteen years. His voice said, 'Move son, move!' It seemed to sound so real and urgent that I instantly said, 'Just a minute lads, let me pass.' As I got to the other side of the group, a German shell burst just where I had been standing, and it exploded all the Mills bombs we had stacked. The lad who had been standing in my place, also named Robinson, was blown to bits. Most of the others were killed and five badly wounded."

"I was blown about thirty feet onto the side of the trench at the corner. My gas mask was blown off, my tunic blown up around my neck and my trousers down around my ankles. Almost naked, I fell back into the trench. When I came round, it was dark and I heard groaning behind me. I picked myself up and ran for help at the first-aid dug-out. There I fell and somersaulted down the dug-out steps, calling for stretcher-bearers. Very much shaken, I landed at the feet of one. He gave me four tablets and a drink of warm tea, put me on a stretcher wrapped in a blanket, and I passed out until next morning."

When Robinson went back up the line at dawn, he found that most of the surviving 121st Brigade had been pulled back to regroup. Their place was taken by dismounted cavalry troops of the 19th Hussars. As the reserve 120th Brigade had been split up during the night—the 14th Argyll and Sutherland Highlanders were now reinforcing the Welsh in the wood—the 14th Highland Light Infantry and the 12th Suffolks were assigned to renew the attack on Bourlon village.

The 14th HLI commander, Lt.-Col. Battye, was put in charge of the operation and received verbal orders from General Campbell. The 120th Brigade was to capture Bourlon village that day, and help the Welch battalion take the rest of the wood. To do this, the HLI would attack on the right, while the 12th Suffolks went in from the left of the village. They would be supported by twelve tanks while attacking the village.

A heavy artillery bombardment pasted the village for twenty minutes, then the infantry moved forward at three o'clock in the afternoon. They were unaware that orders postponing the attack until more tanks were available had been issued by General Ponsonby. These orders could not get through in time, as shellfire had cut telephone wires and killed the runners sent forward with written countermands.

The Scots lost heavily even before reaching their jumping-off point. Just before zero-hour, a single shell dropped into the middle of No. 7 Platoon, killing or wounding all but two of them. There were more casualties when they were caught by machine-guns in an unexpected belt of wire. An observer wrote, "To tried troops, this would have been almost nothing, but to untried men like ours it was very unnerving. But the men never flinched, just plodded on."

Ahead of them, the twelve tanks lumbered into the village, lost touch with their supporting infantry, and were picked off one by one. Guns blazing, the vehicles supported each other like wounded buffalo, but only five of them managed to withdraw to their rallying point. When the infantry later fought their way in, they no longer had tanks to help them mop up. The Suffolks came under accurate artillery fire and had to pull back to trenches outside the village.

The HLI pushed three companies right through the village, discovering on the way the dead bodies of many Green Howards who had disappeared the day before. When the HLI reached the railway north-east of the village, they were pinned down by fire from all sides and cut off from the rest of their battalion. They set up headquarters in a ruined farmhouse, and herded their growing flock of German prisoners into the barn for safe-keeping. Behind them, the German garrison came up from its cellars and took over the streets of Bourlon again. The forward companies of the Scots were completely cut off. They settled down to fight or die.

During this second day of the battle, the Welsh Brigade had been withstanding repeated counter-attacks, as fresh German battalions tried to throw them out of the wood. Each time the enemy fell back, red flares would go up and a sleet of shells would descend. High-explosive, air-bursts, and poison gas deluged the Welsh, until only a few ragged clumps of splintered tree-trunks remained to hint this had recently been a dense forest.

Incessant rain and snow added to the difficulties of the troops, and to the suffering wounded of both sides who lay everywhere. Out-numbered, shell-shocked, and almost asleep on their feet, the hardy Welshmen settled in for another night of purgatory, not giving an inch of ground.

From the comfortable distance of Third Army Headquarters in Albert, the fight for Bourlon was regarded by Field Marshal Haig somewhat differently. He issued a special Order of the Day. "The capture of the important Bourlon position crowns a most successful operation and opens the way to a further exploitation of the advantages already gained."

After three years of trench warfare, machine-guns, massed artillery, and tanks, the Commander-in-Chief of the British Armies still yearned for a cavalry charge. He ordered Lieutenant General Kavanaugh to stand by for an expected breakthrough, when he was to bring up the five cavalry divisions champing at the bit at Fins. Near the horses at Fins Depot, tank repairmen sweated to patch up collandered vehicles and send them back to Bourlon where no more tanks were available for the renewed attack on Monday morning.

The 13th East Surrey were brought up early on the morning of the 25th, the only complete battalion left in the entire division. They were sent through Bourlon village to try to link up with the three beleaguered remnants of the 14th HLI holding the north-east corner of Bourlon. The East Surreys reached the Scottish battalion headquarters just in time to help repel another attack. During it, a machine-gun bullet struck the heart of Lieutenant Colonel Battye. Indomitably, he staggered back to find Lt.-Col. Warden of the East Surreys to whom he turned over his command before dying. Some grieving Highlanders buried Battye in a garden, reslung their shovels, and grimly went out to deal some retribution.

After the battle: War is over for this wounded Bantam and
the helpful German prisoner he is escorting back to a POW
cage behind British lines.

Their comrades marooned near the railway line were being slowly annihilated, though the survivors could be heard keeping up a steady fusilade against their attackers. They held out until 9:30 on the morning of the third day, until they ran out of ammunition. Only 80 HLI survived to surrender. Appalingly few Scottish Bantams at all survived Bourlon. Total casualties of the entire 14th Battalion, Highland Light Infantry, were 17 officers and 426 other ranks.

By the end of the second day, the casualties among the 119th Brigade were equally horrendous. Particularly so among the 17th Battalion, Welch Regiment, every one of whose officers were dead or wounded.

Reinforcements had been sent up the ridge by the 14th HLI and the 11th King's Own, among them Harry Stansfield. "We helped hold the high ground on the north-east edge of the wood, blasting the Germans back four separate times. The Taffies [Welsh] were so dead beat, some actually fell asleep between attacks. I remember hearing one snoring away loudly in a shellhole, with mortar bombs banging all around him."

"Just behind our lines, German prisoners and our men tended to each other's wounded, regardless of the uniform. I could not help but contrast this with the way in which Jerries had shot every Welsh prisoner they caught and how the Welsh had also given no quarter the first day. Both sides now were sick and tired of the whole stupid business."

Though Bourlon village was twice declared free of Germans, strong parties of them were soon back again, methodically killing off scattered bands of Scots, Green Howards, and Middlesex men. Almost the entire wood was in Welsh hands at midnight on the second day. They had triumphed where others had failed, but at such a terrible cost that the 40th Division could never again be a Bantam unit. The Welsh battalions were so weakened by casualties and battle-fatigue after over 48 hours of ceaseless combat that their position was now very precarious. Orders came through that the

62nd Division would come up next day to relieve the decimated 40th Division in the sector they had wrested from the enemy with so much bloodshed.

Throughout November 26th, the 119th Brigade gradually disengaged itself from the wood and came straggling back. The number of men who could walk to Anneux Chapel was shockingly few. The South Wales Borderers reached the road first. "We were marching in step," Jones noted firmly. Their casualties were ten officers and 123 men killed and missing presumed dead, 12 officers and 243 men wounded. The battalion was awarded two DSOs, six MCs, six DCMs and eleven MMs.

The two Glamorgan Bantam battalions of the Welch Regiment had suffered even more hideous casualties. The 17th Welch was awarded eight MCs, four DCMs, and fifteen MMs, but had lost 18 officers and 301 other ranks dead. Consequently, the battalion was that day declared to have "ceased to exist." The few survivors numbered only enough to be later formed into No. 9 Entrenching Company.

The 18th Welch sustained 273 casualties, and was awarded one DSO, one MC, two DCMs and fourteen MMs. The 19th Royal Welsh Fusiliers paid a costly butcher's bill too; 125 dead, and 247 wounded.

When the 121st Brigade was relieved from Bourlon village, the Green Howards fought their way back past the German right flank and regrouped at the Sugar Factory. Twenty-five officers and 450 men of the battalion went into Bourlon on the morning of November 23rd. Three days later, less than one hundred men and eight officers came back.

Edgar Robinson had survived once more, to recall, "Only sixty-five of us were left to march out with one senior officer, Colonel Baker. We must have looked a shocking sight to the fresh troops we passed going in, tired, dirty, and bloodspattered, with our Colonel ahead of us shouting, 'Make way for my poor lads!' There were tears in his eyes."

So it went on—12th Suffolks, 150 casualties; 11th King's Own, 94 casualties. In just over two days of fighting, the division altogether lost 172 officers and 4017 NCOs and men. They had been awarded dozens of awards for bravery, captured over 700 prisoners, and taken the previously-impregnable heights of Bourlon. Field Marshal Haig sent a message that he "personally wished all ranks of the 40th Division to be congratulated on their success."

Within a week, the Germans regained control of the position that had been so bloodily won, but the Bantams' sacrificial final achievement was recognized in perpetuity. Though the unit's new title became simply the 40th Division, its sign was re-designed in honour of the originals. To symbolize Bourlon Wood, two oak acorns were placed inside a white diamond shape, and behind it proudly strutted a golden Bantam rooster.

ENVOI

After the Great War finally ended on November 11, 1918, most veteran soldiers who returned to Britain did not enjoy an easy time in what politicians had promised would be "a land fit for heroes." However, despite the economic troubles of the post-war years, many ex-Bantams entered trades or the professions, and a few became popular entertainers, such as the popular comedian Arthur Askey. Billy Butlin re-settled in England, where he earned great wealth as a holiday-camps entrepreneur, and was so generously philanthrophic to charities he became Sir Billy Butlin MBE. Ex-newspaper delivery boy Lt. "Titch" Cook gained a permanent army commission, went on to serve with the Burma Rifles between the wars, then disappeared in the jungle while fighting the Japanese invasion in January, 1942. Medical orderly Philip Townsend transferred to the Royal Air Force and flew as an aircrew officer in both World Wars.

L/Sgt. Will Stones had been dead 84 years when he became a focus of the revisionist protest campaign to posthumously pardon him and all soldiers who had been executed for cowardice during the Great War. Two successive British governments explained they could not change the facts of history, but the kindly folk of Crook, Durham, inscribed Stones' name on their town war memorial, anyway. Late in life, modest retired schoolteacher Edgar Robinson became something of a media personality in his home town of Marske, Yorks., He enjoyed well-warranted fame in his twilight years, as a result of first publication of this book and its adaptation as a documentary programme by the British Broadcasting Corporation.

There were a few other pleasant outcomes, too. New awareness led to the Regimental Colours of the 15th & 16th (Bantam)

Battalions, Cheshire Regiment, being found in St. Mary's Church, Birkenhead, then refurbished and presented for safe-keeping by the Williamson Museum, Birkenhead, Cheshire, on August 1, 1980. On November 10, 1985, I was a guest at the re-dedication ceremony of the 216th Overseas (Bantams) Battalion flag at Timothy Eaton Memorial Church, Toronto, where it now hangs proudly framed in a place of honour. A year later, June, 1986, I was invited by the Royal British Legion to attend when the King's Colours of the 18th Service Battalion (Bantams), The Welch Regiment, were re-dedicated in All Saints Church, Porthcawl, Wales.

Forty-seven year old Joe Daniel came home unscathed to Victoria, BC, for a joyous reunion with his wife and three children; healthy enough to quickly sire three more after the war and live until the venerable age of 89. A noticeable number of Bantams emigrated to the United States, where they prospered for the most part. The Argentine Welshman, Jack Jones, settled in Miami, Florida, and became a well-off importer of South American goods. At least two veterans headed for California; Donald Gray settling contentedly in Hemet, while William Parkes headed for the Napa Valley.

Bill Parkes became well known as a star soccer-player who helped the San Francisco Barbarians team win the state championship in 1923. When he got into a fist-fight over sports, local newspapers called him "The Battling Bantam." He was employed as a patients' supervisor for a state hospital, married the widow of a notorious train-bandit, and lived happily for many long years. In 2000, he was one of the select few to be appointed a member of the Legion d' Honneur, awarded by France to elderly survivors of the Western Front. Then, on October 7, 2002, William Parkes died in Napa, at the age of 106, probably the very last Bantam to march off parade.

Judging by their life stories, many other ex-Bantams found that employment opportunities were always somehow scarcer for under-height men. After war service, they were once more in a prejudiced society inclined to judge them by their stature only, and less moved by their offering to work for a living than the army had been to let them volunteer to fight. Within a few years, their unique battalions faded from public knowledge, curiously unmentioned in most regimental histories. One notable exception being the 143rd. BC Bantams, which is perpetuated by the Canadian Scottish Regiment in Victoria, Canada. But for the most part, Bantams were ignored, perhaps a too uncomfortable reminder of the lengths to which officialdom had once been willing to go to feed a war of attrition.

Despite all this, not one of the surviving Bantams I contacted voiced resentment of being forgotten or regret for having served. Ex-Lancashire Fusilier Frank Heath summed up the feeling of his still-jaunty old comrades, "I was very much afraid, wounded and ill several times, but I was lucky and survived, and I would not have missed it for all the gold in Fort Knox."

Their best epitaph was written by Robert Campbell Irvine of Scotland. He served as a Highland Light Infantry Bantam for three years and one hundred and seventy-four days, and then was discharged after suffering two severe wounds. When he applied for a job with the Glasgow Tramways, he was turned down because he was "too small." Politically active in causes for ex-servicemen's rights, he himself remained unemployed most of his life, while managing to raise five children. When the 81-year-old Irvine died penniless in Erskine Hospital, he left a number of unpublished poems he had written. One goes like this:

> Two minutes silence for the dead.
> I thought of the fields when the fields were red.
> Red, not with poppies, but with blood,
> The blood of men, the image of God.
>
> Two minutes silence for the dead.
> Stood in the crowd and bowed my head.
> Not in reverence, but in shame,
> At the insult in memory of their name.

Two minutes silence for the dead.
Last Post is sounding, eyes are red.
But Reveille is sounding for me instead
Of Last Post in memory of the dead.

Those words still have an appropriate echo today, and would have read well on a Bantams' war-memorial—but none was ever built. Maybe this book will have to do instead.

Toronto, Ontario., May 31, 1980.
Victoria, British Columbia, October 20, 2003.

—END—

ACKNOWLEDGEMENTS

The book could not have been written without the generous assistance of many individuals who provided information and photographs, and the scores of publications which helped to put me in contact with them. I started my researches in 1977; only just in time to reach a rapidly-dwindling number of Great War veterans. While researching them, I repeatedly heard the sad news that yet another had reached the end of his trail. However, I was lucky enough to gather the reminiscences of 340 old soldiers first-hand, and obtain material about numerous others.

The surviving Bantams and their relatives who shared their memories with me were very elderly. Skeptics may ask, how reliable are such recollections after so long a time, expressed decades afterwards? In fact, I found without exception that the many individual accounts which I gathered from personal interviews and numerous letters corroborated each other to a remarkable degree. They were further well authenticated by the official records, battalion war diaries, newspapers, and other contemporary accounts I studied. My researches were guilded by two masterly accounts: *The History Of The 35th. Division In The Great War*, by Lieut.-Col. H.M. Davson, and *History Of The 40th. Division*, by Lieut-Col. F.E. Whitton.

I was continually impressed by the natural facility which men and women of their generation had with language. It was often conveyed in quite beautiful copperplate handwriting, that said much for the basic quality of school-teaching at the turn of the 19th/20th Century. I particularly enjoyed the Great War veterans' irrepressible sense of humour, even while sometimes telling of horrendous events. My only problem was with their modesty; an ingrained understatement which frequently made it difficult to obtain colourful details of their combat experiences.

Among the many people who helped to make this book possible, I would like to thank:

Millicent Ayrton, Hoylake, Cheshire, for permission to quote from Lt.-Col. H. Johnston's diary; W. Adams, Panania, N.S.W.; J. J. Atkins, Tranmere, Birkenhead; Mrs. Frances Worrall, Sidney, B.C. for access to the wartime diary of her father, Pte. Joseph Daniel; Mrs. M. Asselbrough, Sunderland; John S. Archer, Leeds, Yorks; Mrs. Ivy Allinson-Bailey, Toronto; C. Allinson, Starbuck, Manitoba; my brother, William G. Allinson, Southport, Lancs; Mrs. Rose Ash, Hartlepool; Tim Ashley, Maghull, Liverpool; Miss Vi Bretherton, Heswall, Wirral; J. Booth, Hyde, Cheshire; Hugh Brown, Philadelphia, Pa.; E. Butler, Birmingham; Ann Briggs, Kirkcaldy, Fife; Mr. J. Baptie, Scarborough, Ontario; George Batty, Royal Chelsea Hospital; Bill Bryant, Glossop, Derby; Mrs. Barbara Baker, Wirral; Mrs. B. Briggs, Thetford, Norfolk; Mrs. Catherine Barker, Whitley Bay; Sir William Butlin, St. John, Channel Islands; Mrs. Edith Bradbury, Dover, Kent; Rear-Admiral F.B.P. Brayne-Nichols; Alexander Batchelor, Toronto, Ontario; WO 2 Patrick Cracknell, Wessex Regiment; George Cunningham, Glasgow; Peter Campbell, Sidney, B.C.; Mrs. Frankela Corries, West Derby; Melton Campbell, Bath, Somerset; Miss Gladys Bree, Arlesly, Beds; Edmund Conroy, South Dartmouth, Mass.; Miss Lydia Crook, Woodchurch, Wirral; Horst Priess, Nordeney, Germany; Mrs. Bessie Cockburn, Birkenhead; Mrs. Sheila Carter, Stroud, Ontario; P. Cassidy, Glasgow; Tom Culshaw, Liverpool; Graham Carr, Vancouver, B.C.; Mrs Margaret Davidson, Greasby, Merseyside; Mrs. H. Dick, Belfast; Tommy Dickson, Hayes, Middx; G. K. Embley, Darlington, Durham; Mrs. J. Eldridge, Stockton-on-Tees; Joseph W. Ewing, Centre of Military History, Washington, D.C.; Mrs. Joan Foster, Victoria, B.C.; David Fox, New Hamburg, Ontario; Roland Fitzpatrick, Shipley, Yorks; R. F. Freeman-Wallace, Bristol;George Fisher, Preston, Lancs; Mrs. Gwynneth Foster, Chessington, Surrey; Gilbert Farrington, Manchester; Mrs. Ruby Goodall, Leven, Fife; Andrew Gilmour, Gifford, East Lothian; Miss

Roseann Galloway, Leeds, Yorks; W. Griffiths, Criccieth, Wales; Mrs. Mary Garrity, Greenock; Donald Gray, Hemet, California; Miss Catherine Grey, Berwick-on-Tweed; Mrs. Ivy Godden, Nedlands, Western Australia; Mrs. Annie Hudson, Sunderland; Jack House, Glasgow Evening Times; H. M. Hurst, Belfast; William Hurley, Lawrence, N.Y.; Frank Heath, Huddersfield; Mrs. Mary Hardacre, Preston, Lancs; J. J. Hutchinson, Rock Ferry; Miss Noele Heymann, Chichester; Edward Hillison, Portsmouth; Miss Elizabeth Humble, Sunderland; C. W. Hayes, Pugwash, Nova Scotia; F. Harris, Liverpool; Mrs. Shirley Hinns, Northrop Hall, Clwyd; A. J. Heaton, Richmond Hill, Ontario; Alex Hood, Bailey's Bay, Bermuda; David Hammond, New York City; Robert Irvine, Glasgow, for permission to quote his father's poem, "Two Minute's Silence"; H. R. Ingham, Littleborough, Lancs; Mrs. Mary Jones, Shotton, Wales; Ken Jackson, Kitchener, Ontario; Miss Edna May, Sidney, B.C.; Morgan Jones, Bryn Asaph, Wales; David Jenkins, Cardiff; John Jones, Warrington; David Karstadt, London; David Preece, Llandudno, Wales; Mrs. Adelaide Kemmel, Toronto, Ontario; Edwin Lofthouse, York; James Lewis, Edinburgh; John A. Lawson, Ingatestone, Essex; George Lim, Hong Kong; Mrs. Dorothy Leeming, Woodstock, N.B.; Bill Leyland, Toronto, Ontario, who sang the Canadian Bantams' song for me; Mrs. S. Laybourn, Hatfield, Herts; Victor Lill, Lyndhurst, Hants; Sidney Marven, Halstead, Essex; Arthur Morris, Gately, Hants; Lewis Morgan, Cardiff; George Marr, Wanganui, N.Z.; Joseph Mainwaring, New York City; Mrs Elizabeth Marchbank, Heswell; V. Merrick, Hartlepool, Cleveland; W.G. Mitchell, Newcastle-upon-Tyne; Mrs. Ethel Lavin, Ngongotha, N.Z.; G. Millington, Birmingham; Mrs. V. Moore, Harrogate, Yorks; Roderick Mitchell, Durham City; Ronald Marsden, Bournemouth; Len Marks, London; Brigadier H. D. McGregor, Lingfield, Surrey; George P. McLeod, Glasgow; Mrs. Frances McArthur, Winsford, Cheshire; A.W. McGill, Basildon, Essex; Mrs. E. McLarey, Birkenhead; Roland Mackie, Narrabun, N.S.W.; Mrs. I. McLaren, Dundee; Alan R. MacKenzie, Durban, South Africa; Albert Noble, Lowestoft, Suffolk; Klaus Dreiber, Salzburg, Austria; Mrs. Lily

Owens, Heswall, Cheshire; Richard Pierson, Westmount, Quebec; Bob Parker, West Islip, N.Y.; Mrs. P. Pressburger, Munich, Germany; Thomas Pemberton, Wirral; George Pearson, Houghton-le-Spring; George Palmer, King's Heath; Jack Paget, Amering, Sussex; Arthur Priestley, Toronto, Ontario; Mr. E. Pursell, St. Helens, Lancs; Jeffery Pritchard, Toronto, Ontario; Winnie Parker, Manchester; W. S. Pickford, Congleton, Cheshire; James Pringle, Bury-St.Edmunds; E. Quickenden, Wanborough, Swindon; Mr. & Mrs. Allan E. Raw, Benoni, South Africa for permission to quote from Mr. A. Bigland's book, "The Call of Empire", 1926; William Ryan, Dublin; Reg Rimmer, Chester; D.F. Robinson, Bromsgrove; A.G. Robson, Hexam, Northumberland. Mrs. Iris Riches, Southend-on-Sea; James Robertson, St. Catherines, Ontario; Arthur Swift, Huddersfield, Yorks; Peter Sullivan, Barrie, Ontario G.A.D. Smith, Tetbury, Glos; J. Nelson Spencer, Bebington, Wirral; John Smith, Tranmere; R.E. Swift, Bebington; Harry Stansfield, Ottawa, Ontario, who gallantly shared his memories with me during his last days; H.R. Statham, Guildford, Surrey; Alfred Spindlow, Yiewsley, Middx; Edward Scales, Sunderland; Sidney Sears, Vancouver, B.C.; Colonel John Forbes, The Green Howards Museum, Richmond, Yorks; L. Owen and Mrs. J.L. Sears, Prince Consort's Library; Bryn Owen, Museum of The Welch Regiment, Cardiff; John J. Slonaker,Director, U.S. Army Military History Institute; Captain D.N. Anderson, The Royal Highland Fusiliers; J. Pavey and R.H. Forey, Army Historical Branch, Ministry of Defence; J. S. Lucas, Ms Jane Carmichael, D. B. Nash, Imperial War Museum; Stephen D. Shannon, Durham Light Infantry Museum; K.M. White, Staff College, Camberley; Edward Grimshaw, Bristol Central Library; Major G.G. Egerton, South Wales Borderers; Major R.F. Tomlinson, The Prince of Wales Own Yorks Regiment; Hywel Rees, National Museum of Wales; W.A. Thorburn, Keeper, Scottish United Services Museum; The Director General, Commonwealth War Graves Commission; my friend Adjutant G. M. Rachaine, Division Logistique, French Army, Paris; Brian Clark, Military History Society of Ireland; H. J. Woodend, Royal Small Arms Factory, Enfield Lock; Major P.A. Mauldon,

The Queens Lancashire Regiment, Preston; Major G. E. Dodd,
The Sherwood Foresters Museum; Michael J. Moore, Appalachian
State University, N.C.; Lt.-Col.A. A. Blacoe, The Cheshire
Regiment; Brian Barnes, Director of Leisure Services, Wirral; G.
Langley, Avon County Library, Bristol; South African National
Museum of Military History, Johannesburg; Ron Chesterman,
Cheshire Records Offices; Frances Gundry, Provincial Archives,
Victoria, B.C.; William Doig, Glasgow Herald; Miss S. M.
Challenor, Chester Library; Lt.-Col.G. B. Eastwood, Royal Military
Academy, Woolwich; Brigadier D. B. Riddell-Webster, The
Cameronians; N. Thomas, City of Bristol Museum; Major R.H.S.
Woodward, The Gloucester Regiment; Mrs Edith Tyson, Lancaster
City Museum; M.G.H. Wright, Royal Military Academy,
Sandhurst; David A. Smith, Public Archives Canada; Col. A. V.
Tennuci, RAMC Historical Museum; Andrew Cook, British Records
Association; Colonel T. D. Lloyd-Jones, Cadet Training Centre,
Camberley; M. R. Barker, Lancashire Fusiliers Museum, Bury;
Major T. P. Shaw, The Royal Regiment of Fusiliers; Major B.W.R.
Baker, The King's Regiment; Col. B.A. Fargus, The Royal Scots;
James Benzies, Rotary Club of Portobello, Edinburgh; Miss Judith
Phillips, City of Bristol Archives; Major G. E. Dodd, The Sherwood
Foresters Museum; Major E. L. Kirby, The Royal Welch Fusiliers
Museum; Hal Gibbin, Orders & Medals Research Society; Mrs.
Patricia Moore, Glamorgan Archivist; Royal British Legion; Royal
Canadian Legion; American Legion; South African Legion; U.S.
Veterans of Foreign Wars; Australian Returned Soldiers League
;Veterans of World War I; J. F. Thomson, Dick Institute,
Kilmarnock; M. A. Smith, Central Library, Manchester; B. Millan,
Diplomatist Associates; L. F. Murray, Canadian War Museum; Peter
Newark, Historical Picture Service; Ian Mackenzie, British
Association of Retired Persons; K.I. Taylor, Australian Defence Force
Journal; Major D.I. Mack, The Royal Highland Fusiliers; David
Pearson, Military History Department, Toronto Central Reference
Library; John L. Summers, Holliston, Mass.; I. Sydenham, Aberdare,
Glamorgan; Mrs. Kathleen Scroggie, Winnipeg, Manitoba; Lt.-
Col.H.W. Sporrell, Aberporth, Cardigan; Nobby Streeter,

Beaumaris, Anglesey; E. E. Taylor, Stamford, Lincs; Peter Townsend, Knaresborough, Yorks; Edward Tottenham, Kirkcaldy, Fife; Parry Thomas, Llanfoist, Gwent; Mrs Alice Turner, Bradford, Yorks; John Taylor, Winnipeg, Man.; Algernon Villiers, Sunningdale, Berks; Ramon Villaporte, Buenos Aires; J.M. Whilde, Wellingborough, Northants; Jock Wilson, Perth, W.A.; George Wiggins, Edinburgh; Carlos Williams, Jujuiy, Argentina; Eric Willey, Greenock; Johnny Wright, Liverpool; F.R. Waley, Sevenoaks, Kent; Neil Williams, Liverpool Echo; T. Ward, Cape Town, S.A.; Lt.-Col.Sam Warwick, Durham; H. Willoughby, Grimsby, Yorks; Cyril Wright, New York City; Grace Walker, Blackpool, Lancs; Robert Wild, Paignton, Devon; Col. Minter J. Wilson, Washington, D.C.; Noel Wainwright, Brixham, Devon; Billy Watson, Newcastle-on-Tyne; Lt.-Col.Jamie W. Walton, Fort Leavenworth, Kansas; and George Mann, my literary agent.

A particular note of thanks must go to two redoubtable old veterans: Edgar Robinson, Marske, Yorkshire, for generous permission to quote excerpts from his unpublished journal, "A Teenager In The Great War", and to Jack Enrique Jones, of Miami, Florida, for extracts from his personal reminiscences.

The manuscript of the first edition could not have been finished without the patient typing skills of Pierina Minna, Leilah Pohl, and Elizabeth Rowan.

Most of all, I owe special gratitude to my dear wife, Beverley, and my sons for their affectionate understanding while I spent so many pre-occupied months away in the trenches.

BANTAM BATTALIONS

35th. (Bantam] Division

15th Battalion Cheshire Regt.—"Bigland's Birkenhead Bantams"
16th Battn., Cheshire Regt
19th Durham Light Infantry (2nd County Battalion)
14th Gloucestershire Regt (West of England Bantams)
13th Bttn., Alexandra, Princess of Wales's Own (Yorkshire Regiment),
The Green Howards
11th Bttn., King's Own Yorkshire Light Infantry (part bantam)
13th Cameronians (disbanded)
17th Royal Scots—"Rosebery Battalion"
14th Highland Light Infantry
18th Highland Light Infantry (4th Glasgow Battalion)

40th. (Bantam) Division

11th King's Own (Royal Lancaster Regt)
17th Lancashire Fusiliers
18th Lancashire Fusiliers
20th Lancashire Fusiliers (4th Salford Pals)
23rd Manchester Regt (8th City of Manchester Battalion)
20th Middlesex Regt (part bantam)
21st Middlesex Regt (part bantam)
22nd Middlesex Regt (part bantam)
12th Suffolk Regt (East Anglian Battalion)
17th Prince of Wales Own West Yorkshire Regt (2nd Leeds Battalion)
19th The Royal Welsh Fusiliers

17th The Welch Regt (1st Glamorgan) "Rhondda Bantams"

18th The Welch Regt (2nd Glamorgan Battalion)

12th South Wales Borderers (3rd Gwent Battalion)

15th Sherwood Foresters (Nottinghamshire and Derbyshire Regiment)

18th Sherwood Foresters (Nottinghamshire and Derbyshire Regiment)

12th Prince of Wales's Volunteers (South Lancashire Regt)

Canada

216 Overseas (Bantam) Battalion—"Toronto Bantams"

143 Overseas Battalion—"B.C. Bantams"

INDEX